Telephone Construction And Methods And Cost

TELEPHONE
CONSTRUCTION

METHODS AND COST

BY

CLARENCE MAYER

Formerly Cost Statistician and Facilities Engineer, Chicago Telephone Co.

APPENDIX *A*

Cost of Materials and Labor in Constructing
Telephone Line.

BY

J. C. SLIPPY

Consulting Telephone Engineer

APPENDIX *B*

Miscellaneous Cost Data on Pole Line and Underground Conduit Construction.

(Compiled by the Editors of Engineering Contracting)

CHICAGO AND NEW YORK
THE MYRON C CLARK PUBLISHING CO.
1908

GENERAL

PREFACE.

With the ever increasing knowledge of the value and essentiality of construction costs, the need of actual cost records and a practical and flexible system for their collection is generally recognized This is especially true of telephone construction Here, more than in almost any other class of construction, the need of cost records is felt, because there are generally two or more ways of accomplishing the same end.

The purpose of this book is to supply this need In its pages is explained the most approved method of doing telephone work, giving costs of such work in all its details, and presenting a simple, comprehensive and practical system for collecting, analyzing and recording telephone costs Forms for recording costs of every division of work are given, and the methods of computing, proportioning and prorating costs of all kinds are explained. I know of no work which treats of any considerable part of the field covered by this book Nearly all the matter is believed to be entirely new.

Beginning with a presentation of the advantages of cost records to telephone companies and to contractors for telephone work, I have endeavored to describe in successive chapters, the methods of construction for pole-line, aerial and underground cable, cable splicing, removing old line and renewal, underground conduit, and miscellaneous structures. Costs are given for every part of the work; the costs being averaged from actual cost records kept on many hundreds of jobs by specially trained men using a uniform system and working under my supervision.

The costs on conduit work are averaged from actual costs kept on over 250,000 feet of underground main conduit and lat-

iii

203815

erals and on over 550 vaults The costs on other classes of
work are based on similarly extensive records Detailed costs of
installing one of the largest multiple duct conduits ever built,
comprising 824,862 duct feet of conduit and 318 vaults, are given
in Chapter VI.

Special attention has been paid to the classification and item-
izing of the costs so that they may be used by telephone companies and contractors for telephone work in the preparation and
the checking of estimates.

In the chapter on pole-line construction, the cost tables not
only give costs separately for each size and style of cross arm,
wire, anchor and for each size of pole set in each kind of soil,
but, in addition, the tables give costs of each detail of construction work, such as—in the case of poles—cost of teaming, cost
of framing, cost of excavating, cost of setting and cost of supervision The cost tables given in Chapter V give separately, costs
for each number of duct, each kind of soil and each method of
constructing main conduit and laterals, and for each size and
method of constructing vaults , and, in addition, the tables give
costs of each detail of work, such as teaming, excavating, mixing
concrete, laying tile, filling in, and supervision.   Costs of almost
every kind of splice are given in Chapter III   This classification and analysis is carried throughout every division of telephone construction.

The costs are actual construction costs—not contract prices—
and have been used for making hundreds of estimates.   As the
rates of wages, construction, and methods and system of collecting and computing the costs are given for each division of telephone construction, the costs may be easily revised for use by
telephone companies and contractors for telephone work, even
where rates of wages or construction methods differ from those
shown in these pages

In Chapter VIII is explained the method of using the costs in
making estimates, taking an actual job of large size and working
out the estimate in detail, with clear explanations of all consid-
erations to be kept in mind

I gratefully acknowledge my indebtedness to Mr. Herbert
J. Dietmeyer, who read the manuscript of Chapter III, and made

many good suggestions, and to others, to whom I am indebted for photographs.

CLARENCE MAYER

Chicago, Ill., July 30, 1908.

THE APPENDICES.

The appendices supplement the first part of the book That by Mr Slippy, the well known telephone cost expert, gives costs of both labor and materials for telephone construction They were collected by Mr. Slippy, acting as cost expert, from the actual records of various telephone companies In Appendix B the publishers have assembled articles on methods and cost of pole-line and underground conduit work from various sources As giving methods and costs of individual jobs these data will be found distinctly helpful.

THE PUBLISHERS

TABLE OF CONTENTS.

vii

LIST OF TABLES.

Telephone Construction Methods and Cost.

INTRODUCTION

A system of cost keeping and a careful record of construction costs are almost indispensable in telephone construction. It is possible by the proper use of such a record of costs to estimate the cost of all future proposed work with great exactness. The advantages of this are manifold. The officers of the company, first of all, have certain knowledge of the expenditure to be provided for Second, appropriations for new work, while made with a fair margin for uncertainties, are never excessive; this holds the cost down, for it is the teaching of experience, that when more money is allowed than is necessary for the work there is a tendency to spend more than is necessary Again, in considering new ideas of construction, the adoption of new specifications or tools, or the advisability of building aerial or underground line, a decision based on correct cost data will not only eliminate many expensive experiments, but, other things being equal, meets the infallible test of expediency It would be simple to multiply proofs of the advantages to the telephone company or to the constructor for telephone construction of possessing carefully analyzed cost data, but it seems needless to do so.

This volume treats in a practical way of methods of cost keeping in telephone work, and gives records of the actual labor costs of such work on hundreds of jobs under all ordinary urban and rural conditions of telephone work Costs of materials are not given, for the reason that these materials are standard commodities whose quantities are given in specifications and whose prices are obtainable from the manufacturers and dealers upon request For convenience, the labor costs of telephone work will be divided under the following heads · (1) Cost of Line Work; (2) Cost of Cable Work; (3) Cost of Cable Splicing, (4) Cost of Reconstruction and of Removing Materials; (5) Cost of Underground Work, and (6) Special Cost Data These actual records of cost will consist of both detail and average costs based on work done by numerous foremen, under various conditions and in both city and country The system and the forms used in collecting and recording these costs are described in detail for each class of work.

CHAPTER I.

METHODS AND COST OF POLE LINE CON-
STRUCTION

CONSTRUCTION DETAILS.

Line construction as here considered comprises aerial line construction only. The items composing aerial lines are: Poles, cross-arms, anchors, stubs and anchor guys, push pole braces, and wire stringing

Poles.—The kinds of poles recorded are Poles for street and alley line, poles for farm line, poles for toll line, self-sus-

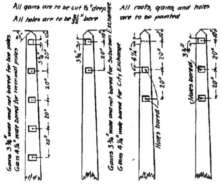

Fig 1 —Method of Cutting Roofs and Gains in Standard Poles

taining poles with ground brace, and self-sustaining poles set in concrete. The size and spacing of the poles for these several kinds of lines with co-ordinate data are given in Table I Figure 1 shows the method of cutting roofs and gains in standard poles. Table II shows the depths to which poles of various lengths are set in earth and in rock. The method of setting self-sustaining poles with ground brace is shown by Fig. 2.

I

TABLE I—Showing Standard Poles for Various Kinds of Line Construction

Kind of Line.	Toll 40 to 50 wires	Street—(Note) 20 wires	Alley 20 wires	Farm		
Ultimate capacity of line	1-50 pr 19 ga cable on a ⅜ in messenger	1-100 pr 22 ga or 2-50 pr 22 ga or 1-50 pr 19 ga cables on ⅜ inch messenger	1-50 pr 22 ga cables on a No 4 messenger	18 wires	6 wires.	2 wires.
Height of poles.	30 ft to 40 ft	30 ft to 45 ft	30 ft to 45 ft	25 ft to 30 ft.	20 ft	20 ft.
Diameter at top	7 in to 8 in	6 in to 7 in	6 in to 7 in	5 in to 6 in	5 in.	4 in.
Distance between poles	130 ft	90 ft to 120 ft	125 ft	150 ft.	150 ft.	150 ft.
No. of Cross Arms.	1 to 5	1 to 2	1 or 2 alley arms 1 buck arm	3	1 arm	2 brackets

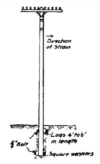

Fig 2—Self-sustaining Pole with Ground Brace

TABLE II—Showing Depths to Which Poles of Various Lengths are Set in Earth and Rock

Length of Pole.	Depth in Ground	Depth in Rock
20 ft	4 ft	3 ft
25 ft	4½ ft	3 ft
30 ft	5½ ft.	3½ ft
35 ft	6 ft	4 ft
40 ft	6 ft	4 ft
45 ft	6½ ft	4½ ft
50 ft	7 ft.	4½ ft

TABLE III—Showing Dimensions of Anchor Logs Required for Different Depths

Depth of Excavation	Dimensions of Anchor Log Length	Diameter
6 ft	5 ft	10 ins
6 ft	5 ft	16 ins
5 ft	8 ft	16 ins
4 ft	6 ft	23 ins
4 ft	8 ft	14 ins.
4 ft	10 ft	12 ins.

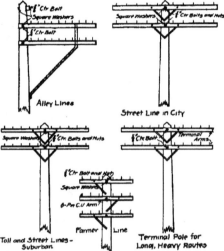

Fig 3 —Standard Cross-Arm Construction for Different Kinds of Lines

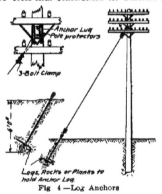

Fig 4 —Log Anchors

Cross-Arms.—Cross-arms are recorded as six-pin, ten-pin, ten-pin alley and six-pin terminal arms Fig 3 shows the standard constructions of cross arms for different kinds of lines.

Anchors, Stubs and Anchor Guys.—The kinds of anchors
and stubs recorded are: Stombaugh anchors, Miller anchors,
rock anchors, log anchors, anchored stubs, self-sustaining
stubs with ground braces, and self-sustaining stubs
set in concrete. Anchor guys, lugs, and pole protec-

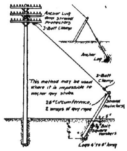

Fig 5 —Self-Sustaining Stub with Ground Braces

tors are included with the anchor and stub. Log anchors
and stubs set in different kinds of soil are recorded separately

The specified construction requires that anchor guys shall
be attached as shown by Figs. 4, 5 and 6 All excavation for
anchor logs is required to be 6 ft. when practicable. If it is

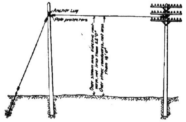

Fig 6 —Anchored Stub

impracticable to obtain this depth on account of the nature of
the soil, the excavation is required to be not less than 4 ft.
deep. The size of the anchor log is required to be proportioned to the strain taken by it and also to correspond to

the depth of the excavation according to Table III. The log is required to be firmly anchored by covering it with planks, logs or rocks, as shown by Fig. 4. Each guy stub is required to be set in the ground to a depth of at least 6 ft. and to be anchored, underbraced or set in concrete as shown by Figs. 5 and 6

Push Pole Braces.—Push pole braces are constructed as shown by Fig 7 The butt is required to be set 3½ ft in the ground and to be supported on plank, large stone or solid ledge

Wire Stringing.—The following kinds of line-work are recorded under wire stringing No 12 galvanized steel for farm line, No. 12 galvanized steel for toll circuits, 104 bare copper for toll circuits, .104 bare copper for street and alley

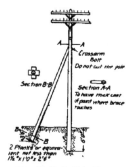

Fig 7 —Push Pole Brace

lines, line orders for city and village lines, line orders for farm line, and running drops Tieing-in and equipping is included in wire stringing. Running drops is included in line orders and also recorded separately The methods followed in stringing wire and tieing-in are specified as follows: The wires shall be run out from reels. They shall be attached to a running board, or boards, to the end or ends of which shall be attached a running rope or wire. Where there are only two wires to be run, the running board may be dispensed with Where a running board is used the reels of wire shall be placed at one end of the section When a pole is reached, the wires shall be carried up the pole and placed inside the pins of the proper arm. In the case of stringing wires from reels on a wagon, the running board may be dispensed with and the wires carried direct from reel wagon up the pole and placed inside the pins on the proper arm, as the poles are reached Wires shall be tied to insulators in the manner shown in Fig 8

COLLECTING AND REPORTING COST DATA.

Method of Collecting.—The data are collected by a time-keeper, inspector or cost man by keeping notes on the ground in special memorandum books Loose leaf memorandum

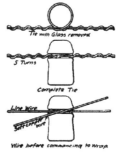

Fig 8 —Manner of Tying Wire to Insulators

books are best adapted for taking costs, and pages properly ruled should be kept in hand for each kind of construction. A sample page from this style of memorandum book is shown by Fig. 9. The ruling and headings in the memorandum book for any kind of construction correspond exactly to those of the report blank for that kind of construction, the forms of report blanks for line construction are shown by Forms 1 to 11. Figure 9 shows a page of the memorandum book filled in as it would be in the field It will be seen that when a man changes from one division of pole line construction to another, or when a change is made from one kind of construction to another, the time of change is noted opposite the name of the man or men making the change and under the

Date 4/1/07
Location
Size 35'
Kind of Soil Hard Clay   POLE LINE
No Set 6

Proportional Cost of Team
" " " Lost Time
" " " Supervision and Expense

Names	Rate p. hr	Teaming and Labor in Haul'g		Framing and Stepping		Digging and Locating		Setting		Total	
		Time	C'st	Time	C'st	Time	C'st	Time	C'st	Ti'e	C'st
Foreman	30					9 to 9 30 / 1/2 hr	25			1/2	25
Smith	34			9 30 to 10 / 10 15 to 10 40 / 55 M	31	8 30 to 9 30 / 10 to 10 15 / 1 1/4 hrs	43	10 40 to 11 / x0 M	33	2 1/4	1 07
Jones	40					8 30 to 10 15 / 1 3/4 hrs	70	10 15 to 11 / 3/4 hrs	30	2 1/4	1 00
Black	28			9 30 to 10 / 1/2 hr	14	8 30 to 9 30 / 10 to 10 15 / 1 1/4 hrs	36	10 15 to 11 / 3/4 hrs	21	2 1/4	70
Wilson	28					8 30 to 10 15 / 1 3/4 hrs	49	10 15 to 11 / 3/4 hrs	21	2 1/4	70
Adams	25	8 30 to 9 30 / 1 hr	25			9 30 to 10 15 / 3/4 hrs	19	10 15 to 11 / 3/4 hrs	19	2 1/4	63
Johnson	25	8 30 to 9 30 / 1 hr	25			9 30 to 10 15 / 3/4 hrs	19	10 15 to 11 / 3/4 hrs	19	2 1/4	63
Team	50	8 30 to 9 30 / 1 hr	50							1	50
Totals		31	1 00	1 5/12	45	8	2 90	4 1/12		16 1/4	5 43

Fig 9 —Sample Page from Memorandum Book

proper heading or headings   These data are figured either
on completion of the day's work or of the job   On account
of the small size of line gangs, which rarely exceeds 15 men,
an exact account of the work of each man is kept, five
minutes being used as the unit of time

Method of Reporting.—Reports are made on the blank
forms indicated as Forms 1 to 11, on the completion of the
job   Both the total cost of the work and the average cost per
pole, cross-arm, etc , are shown for each job   The attempt
is made in this cost system not only to divide line construction into different divisions so that in estimating it will be

possible to figure the cost of so many poles, cross-arms or miles of wire, but also to sub-divide each division so that the data may serve as a check on excessive cost and as a guide when considering different methods of accomplishing the same work The sub-divisions of each kind of construction are the natural divisions as indicated by the form for setting poles, (Form 1). Here it will be noted that "framing" (roofing, boring and gaining) and "stepping" are not separated, this is because the transition from one to the other is almost impossible to note, making any division of the two a purely arbitrary one. In the report forms each day's work is entered on one line; the total and average costs being shown at the bottom of the form

Referring to the blank forms illustrated Form 1 is that for setting street or alley poles, exactly the same form is used for farm line and toll line poles and self sustaining poles with ground braces Form 2 is used for recording the setting of self-sustaining poles in concrete In explanation of these forms it may be stated that, in "framing" is included roofing, gaining and boring and in "setting" is included filling and tamping Under "supervision and expense" is entered, (1) cost of the foreman, timekeepers and such other members of the gang as supervise and keep account of work but as do no manual labor, or such part of this time as no labor is done other than of a supervisory character, and (2) charges for car fare and incidentals Inspectors, special cost men, and office expenses are not included in the cost data, the idea being to secure rather the cost of setting a pole in a certain kind of soil or of erecting a cross-arm than the cost of a particular job which would be of little value in estimating.

The purposes of Forms 3 to 11 are stated in each case. In explanation of Form 4 it may be noted that cutting logs and attaching anchor rods are included in setting anchors When this form is used for Stombaugh anchors, the column "Digging or Drilling" is left blank, screwing the anchor into the soil being included as "Setting Anchor." Attaching anchor lugs and pole protectors is included in "Placing Guys" In Form 5 "Placing Guy" includes the guy from the stub to the pole but not the guy to the anchor.

Form 1
Data Secured by
SETTING STREET OR ALLEY POLES

30'
35' -
40'
45' and Higher

Location   Date   190
Foreman

Order No

No of Poles	Teaming and Labor in Hauling	Framing and Stepping	Digging and Locating	Setting	Sup and Exp	Total Cost	Kind of Soil	No of Hours Worked	Remarks

Form 2
Data Secured by
SETTING SELF-SUSTAINING POLES
(In Concrete)

30'
35'
40'
45' and Higher

Location   Date   190
Foreman

Order No

No. of Poles	Teaming and Labor in Hauling	Framing and Stepping	Digging and Locating	Mixing Concrete	Setting and Placing Concrete	Sup and Exp	Total Cost	Kind of Soil	No of hrs Wrk	Remarks

Form 3
Data Secured by
ERECTING CROSS-ARMS

6 Pin
10 Pin
10 Pin, Alley
Terminal

Location   Date   190
Foreman

Order No

No of Cross-arms	Teaming and Labor in Hauling	Putting on arms	Sup and Exp	Total Cost	No of Hours Worked	No of Poles	Remarks

Form 4
Data Secured by
ANCHOR GUYS AND ANCHORS

Stombaugh
Miller
Log
Rock

Location   Date   190
Foreman

Order No

No of Anchors	Teaming and Labor in Hauling	Digging or Drilling	Setting Anchor	Placing Guys	Sup and Exp	Total Cost	Kind of Soil	No of Hours Worked	Remarks

Form 5
Data Secured by
GUYING AND SETTING STUBS

15'
20'   Order No
25'   Location   Date   190
30'   Foreman

No of Stubs	Teaming and Labor in Hauling	Digging	Setting Stubs	Placing Guy	Sup and Exp	Total Cost	Kind of Soil	No of Hours Worked	Remarks

Form 6
Data Secured by
GUYING AND SETTING SELF-SUSTAINING STUBS
(With Ground Brace)

15'
20'   Order No
25'   Location   Date   190
30'   Foreman

No of Stubs	Teaming and Labor in Hauling	Digging	Setting Stubs	Placing Guy	Sup and Exp	Total Cost	Kind of Soil	No of Hours Worked	Remarks

Form 7
Data Secured by
GUYING AND SETTING SELF-SUSTAINING STUBS
(In Concrete)

15'
20'   Order No
25'   Location   Date   190
30'   Foreman

No of Stubs	Teaming and Labor in Hauling	Digging	Mixing Concrete	Setting and Placing Concrete	Placing Guy	Sup and Exp	Total Cost	Kind Soil	No of Hrs W'r k	Remarks

Form 8
Data Secured by
SETTING PUSH POLE BRACES

20'
25'   Order No
30'   Location   Date   190
35' and Higher   Foreman

No of Braces	Teaming and Labor in Hauling	Framing	Digging and Locating	Setting	Sup and Exp	Total Cost	Kind of Soil	No of Hours Worked	Remarks

		Form 9 Data Secured by WIRE STRINGING					
No 12 Galv Steel 080 Bare Copper 104 Bare Copper	Location Foreman			Order No Date 190			
Mi of Wire strung	Teaming and Labor in Hauling	Stringing and Equip	Super and Exp	Total Cost	No hrs Worked	Remarks	

		Form 10 Data Secured by LINE ORDERS					
Farm City or Village	Location Foreman			Order No Date 190			
No of Line Orders	Teaming and Labor in Hauling	Stringing and Equip	Sup and Exp	Total Cost	No hrs Worked	Mi of Wire Strung	Remarks

		Form 11 Data Secured by RUNNING DROPS					
City or Village Line Farm L ne	Exchange Foreman			Order No Date 190			
No of Drops	Length of Wire used for Drop	Teaming and Labor in Hauling	Stringing and Equipping	Sup and Exp	Total Cost	No hrs Worked	Remarks

METHOD OF FIGURING LINE CONSTRUCTION COST.

If in a day's work of a line gang, only one size of poles in one kind of soil were set—no cross-arms being erected or wire strung—the method of figuring would require little explanation The entire expense of the team, foreman or lost time, would be charged to the particular kind of work done, the lost time being prorated and added to the different sub-divisions, as "Framing," "Digging and Locating" and "Setting,"

—(lost time never being charged to "Teaming and Labor in Hauling.") and the men's time would be charged under the columns corresponding with their work. This, however, is rarely the case. A day's work of a line gang usually covers different divisions of construction, often in various kinds of soil. It is therefore necessary to explain the method of proportioning the teaming, lost time, and supervision and expense. We will assume the day's work of a line gang, composed of 6 men, 1 foreman at $4 and 1 team at $4, as shown by the memorandum data book (see Fig. 9) to have been as follows:

Fig. 10.—View Showing Method of   Fig. 11.—View Showing Method of
      Raising Pole.   Straightening Pole.

	No. of Hours Worked.	Cost.
Setting 35-ft. poles in hard clay:		
By men	15	$ 4.73
By foreman	½	.25
By team	1	.50
Erecting 10-pin cross-arms, by men.......	12	3.60
Stringing .104 copper wire, by men.......	18	5.17
Supervision and expense on the work in general, by foreman...................	7½	3.75
Teaming on the work in general, by team.	7	3.50
Loss time on the work in general, by men..	3	.90
Totals	64	$22.40

In this schedule by "Supervision and Expense on the Work in General," is meant such part of the foreman's, assistant foreman's or timekeeper's time not spent in doing manual labor, but used in supervising the work, keeping accounts, etc. It is obviously not possible when part of the gang is stringing wire and part erecting cross-arms to say what minute the foreman is supervising the wire stringing and what minute he is supervising the erection of cross-arms.

"Teaming on the work in general" means that part of the time of the team which is used to haul the men and tools to and from the jobs. If when going to and from jobs, besides hauling the men and tools, some cross-arms or wire, etc., are also hauled, there being no extra time used in hauling the cross-arms or wire, the time should not be charged, entirely to cross-arms, but should be charged proportionately on the work in general.

Fig. 12.—View Showing Method of Using Iron Barrel in Digging Pole Holes in Soft Ground.

A line gang loses time getting from its station to a job or from one job to another. Such time is charged to "General or Lost Time," and is proportioned over the different kinds of construction work carried on during the day. At times the work is in such shape that the entire gang cannot be utilized. In such cases the men not working are charged against the work being done at the time, i. e., if waiting on men framing, their time should be charged to framing, etc. An example will illustrate the procedure followed:

Method of Proportioning Lost Time.—Assuming that the lost time on the work in general was:

Grade.	Rate per hr.	Hrs. lost.	Cost.
1 lineman	$.34	½	$.17
1 lineman	.40	½	.17
2 combination men	.28 ea.	½ ea.	.28
2 groundmen	.25 ea.	½ ea.	.25
Totals		3	$.90

and the number of hours actually worked by the men (excluding the foreman) was $6 \times 8 - 3$ (lost time) we have 45 hours. Dividing the cost of lost time ($0.90) by the number of hours actually worked by the men (45), will give the cost of lost time per "man hour" as $0.02, which multiplied by the hours actually worked by the men, on each kind or di-

Fig. 13.—Removing Iron Barrel with Bars.

vision of construction, i. e., 15 (number of hours setting poles) multiplied by $0.02 (cost of lost time per man hour) equals $0.30. Continuing this operation, we have for "Cross-Arms" $0.24, for "Stringing Wire" $0.36.

Now assuming the data on setting 35-ft. poles in hard clay to have been as shown in Fig. 9, the cost of the different subdivisions is as follows:

Framing and stepping $0.45
Digging and locating 2.60
Setting 1.43

     Total $4.48

Dividing the cost of lost time ($0.30) by the cost of the different sub-division ($4.48), we have 0.0669+, which multiplied by the cost of each sub-division gives the following:

Subdivisions.	Cost.	Proportional Cost of Lost Time.	Total.
Framing and stepping	$0.45	$0.03	$0.48
Digging and locating	2.60	0.17	2.77
Setting	1.43	0.10	1.53
Totals	$4.48	$0.30	$4.78

Fig. 14.—Removing Iron Barrel with Block and Tackle.

"Labor in Hauling" being the time consumed in going to a store yard, sorting out the proper size poles, cross-arms, wire, etc., loading them on the wagon and hauling them to the job, the time lost by the gang between their station and work should not be charged to this sub-division, but to the sub-division of construction on which they are employed. If the day was spent in setting poles the lost time should be charged to "Framing and Setting," "Digging and Locating," and "Setting." It sometimes happens that the gang works on digging or setting only; in such cases the lost time should be charged to digging or setting as the case may be.

Method of Proportioning Supervision and Expense.—To find the proportion of cost of the supervision and expense to be charged to each division or kind of construction where supervising and expenses of the work in general is meant, divide the cost of the supervision and expense ($3.75) by the cost of the day's work including lost time ($14.40), but not including supervisors (foremen, etc.) or team, and multiply by the cost, including lost time of each kind or division of construction. The result will be as given in Table IV.

Method of Proportioning Teaming.—When the team is used to haul men and tools to and from work or is standing at a job, the expense being on the work in general, is proportioned in the same manner as the "Supervision and Expense."

Summary.—The data on the day's work are therefore as given by Table V.

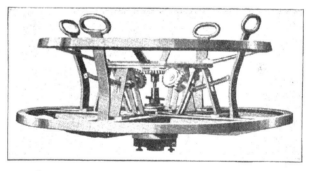

Fig. 15.—Reel for Wire Stringing.

TABLE IV.—SHOWING PROPORTIONED COST OF LOST TIME, SUPERVISION AND EXPENSE.

Divisions or Kind of Construction.	Cost not including Foreman or Team	Prop. cost of Lost Time	Total	Prop. cost of superv. and expense	Total
Setting 35 ft. poles in hard clay	$4.73	$0.30	$5.03	$1.31	$6.34
Erecting 10 pin cross-arms	3.60	0.24	3.84	1.00	4.84
Stringing .104 copper wire	5.17	0.36	5.53	1.44	6.97
Totals	$13.50	$0.90	$14.40	$3.75	$18.15

TABLE V —SHOWING PROPORTIONED COST OF LOST TIME, TEAMING, SUPERVISION AND EXPENSE

Division or Kind of Construction	Cost not including Foreman or Team	Proportional Cost of Lost Time	Total	Prop cost of Supervision and Expense	Prop cost of Team	Cost of Foreman when not on work in general	Cost of Team when not on work in general	Total Cost
Setting 35-ft poles in hard clay	$ 4 73	$0 30	$ 5 03	$1 31	$1 22	$0 25	$0 50	$8 31
Erecting 10 pin cross-arms	3 60	0 24	3 84	1 00	0 93			5 77
Stringing .104 copper wire	5 17	0 36	5 53	1 44	1 35			8 32
Totals	13 50	$0 90	$14 40	$3 75	$3 50	$0 25	$0 50	$22 40

TABLE VI —AVERAGE COST OF 30-FT STREET OR ALLEY POLES

	Teaming and Hauling Labor in	Framing and Stepping	Digging and Locating	Setting	Supervision and Expense	Average Cost Per Pole
Sand or gravel	$0 51	$0 20	$0 49	$0 25	$0 38	$1 83
Clay and sand	0 57	0 16	0 48	0 25	0 53	1 99
Sand and water	0 71	0 19	0 57	0 38	0 50	2 35
Clay	0 86	0 19	0 69	0 39	0 47	2 60
Clay and water	0 94	0 26	0 76	0 36	0 51	2 83
Hard clay	1 01	0 17	0 92	0 32	0 59	3 01
Very coarse gravel	0 99	0 18	1 23	0 60	0 62	3 62
Quicks'd and water	1 17	0 25	1 42	0 44	0 72	4 00
Rock	1 31	0 22	2 48	0 73	1 27	6 01
Rock and water	1 56	0 20	3 39	0 94	1 51	7 60
Average in all soils	0 96	0 20	1 24	0 47	0 71	3 58
Average in all soil except rock	0 85	0 20	0 82	0 37	0 62	2 78

TABLE VII —COST OF 35-FT STREET OR ALLEY POLES

	Teaming and Hauling Labor in	Framing and Stepping	Digging and Locating	Setting	Supervision and Expense	Average Cost Per Pole
Sand or gravel	$0 50	$0 26	$0 73	$0 34	$0 37	$2 20
Sand and water	0 76	0 27	0 83	0 36	0 57	2 79
Clay	1 09	0 24	0 92	0 54	0 45	3 24
Clay and water	1 28	0 31	0 95	0 45	0 50	3 49
Hard clay	1 31	0 30	1 07	0 53	0 63	3 84
Very coarse gravel	1 36	0 23	1 34	0 80	0 73	4 46
Hard pan	1 41	0 32	1 36	0 74	0 76	4 59
Quicks'd and water	1 18	0 33	1 69	0 67	0 64	4 51
Rock*	1 47	0 32	2 94	0 86	1 38	6 97
Rock and water	1 59	0 31	3 53	1 04	1 72	8 19
Average cost in all soils	1 19	0 29	1 54	0 63	0 78	4 43
Average cost in all soils except rock	1 11	0 28	1 12	0 55	0 58	3 64

*Note: When holes are blasted the cost of dynamite is included in "Supervision and Expense"

TABLE VIII —COST OF 40-FT STREET OR ALLEY POLES

	Teaming and Hauling Labor in	Framing and Stepping	Digging and Locating	Setting	Supervision and Expense	Average Cost Per Pole
Sand or gravel	$0 78	$0 28	$0 79	$0 47	$0 53	$2 87
Sand and water	0 92	0 27	0 90	0 57	0 59	3 25
Clay and water	1 25	0 25	0 96	0 63	0 61	3 51
Clay	1 02	0 22	1 04	0 68	0 54	3 70
Hard clay	1 38	0 28	1 12	0 71	0 68	4 17
Very coarse gravel	1 57	0 29	1 42	0 89	0 75	4 71
Quicks'd and water	1 43	0 29	1 97	0 93	0 76	5 13
Rock	1 60	0 41	2 99	0 92	1 45	7 27
Rock and water	1 82	0 27	3 72	1 12	1 74	8 67
Average cost in all soils	1 28	0 27	1 66	0 75	0 85	4 81
Average cost in all soils except rock	1 16	0 27	1 17	0 67	0 64	3 91

TABLE IX—COST OF 45-FT STREET OR ALLEY POLES

	Teaming and Labor in Hauling	Framing and Stepping	Digging and Locating	Setting	Supervision and Expense	Average Cost Per Pole
Sand or gravel	$0 95	$0 33	$1 08	$0 74	$0 70	$3 80
Sand and water	1 03	0 35	1 20	0 78	0 76	4 12
Clay and water	1 18	0 36	1 25	0 82	0 72	4 33
Clay	1 21	0 35	1 32	0 91	0 74	4 53
Hard clay	1 45	0 37	1 39	0 96	0 82	4 99
Very coarse gravel	1 47	0 34	1 60	1 03	0 87	5 31
Quicks'd and water	1 57	0 36	2 17	1 03	0.93	6 16
Rock	1 84	0 34	3 46	0 99	1 67	8.30
Average cost in all soils	1.35	0 35	1 68	0 91	0 90	5.19
Average cost in all soils except rock	1 28	0 35	1 43	0 90	0 79	4.75

TABLE X—COST OF 20-FT FARM LINE POLES

	Teaming and Labor in Hauling	Framing	Digging and Locating	Setting	Supervision and Expense	Average Cost Per Pole
Sand or gravel	$0 23	$0 07	$0 24	$0 12	$0 08	$0 74
Sand and water	0 23	0 05	0 25	0 14	0 09	0 76
Black soil	0 20	0 07	0 26	0 16	0 12	0 81
Black soil and water	0 24	0 06	0 33	0 10	0 11	0 84
Clay	0 35	0 05	0 32	0 12	0 13	0 97
Clay and water	0 33	0 06	0 35	0 12	0 15	1 01
Hard clay	0 35	0 07	0 69	0 17	0 23	1 51
Very coarse gravel	0 37	0 05	0 74	0 19	0 26	1 61
Quicks'd and water	0 41	0 04	0 73	0 16	0 38	1 72
Average cost in all soils	0 30	0 06	0 44	0 14	0 17	1 11

Note   Farm Lines are rarely built in rock   In the case of one or two poles, the spans are lengthened or shortened to avoid rock   Where the direct route is mostly rock some other route by which the rock may be avoided is taken, although requiring more poles

TABLE XI—COST OF 25-FT FARM LINE POLES

	Teaming and Labor in Hauling	Framing	Digging and Locating	Setting	Supervision and Expense	Av'ge Cost per Pole
Sand or gravel	$0 28	$0 12	$0 32	$0 16	$0 14	$1 02
Sand and water	0 32	0 11	0 34	0 14	0 16	1 07
Black soil	0 31	0 14	0 32	0 18	0 19	1 14
Blk soil and water	0 33	0 11	0 39	0 20	0 18	1 21
Clay	0 37	0 14	0 47	0 19	0 23	1 40
Clay and water	0 39	0 13	0 50	0 17	0 27	1 46
Hard clay	0 44	0 12	0 75	0 18	0 32	1 81
Very coarse gravel	0 52	0 14	0 82	0 24	0 38	2 10
Quicks'd and water	0 60	0 10	0 86	0 28	0 43	2 27
Average cost in all soils	0 40	0 12	0 53	0 19	0 26	1 50

TABLE XII—COST OF 30-FT FARM LINE POLE

	Teaming and Labor in Hauling	Framing	Digging and Locating	Setting	Supervision and Expense	Average Cost Per Pole
Sand or gravel	$0 43	$0 16	$0 37	$0 22	$0 23	$1 41
Sand and water	0 41	0 17	0 43	0 21	0 26	1 48
Black soil	0 47	0 15	0 38	0 23	0 31	1 54
Clay	0 67	0 12	0 57	0 28	0 32	1 96
Clay and water	0 59	0 13	0 68	0 32	0 43	2 15
Hard clay	0 71	0 17	0 85	0 37	0 48	2 58
Very coarse gravel	0 72		0 99	0 44	0 37	2 66
Average cost in all soils	0 57	0 15	0 61	0 30	0 34	1 97

Note   30 ft farm line poles cost less to set than city or alley poles on account of the average jobs being larger, poles are more easily located and conditions for work better on a country road than on a city street

TABLE XIII—Cost of 30-Ft Toll Line Poles

	Teaming and Labor in Hauling	Framing	Digging and Locating	Setting	Supervision and Expense	Average Cost Per Pole
Sand or gravel	$0 42	$0 19	$0 41	$0 22	$0 29	$1 53
Sand and water	0 48	0 21	0 44	0 24	0 27	1 64
Black soil	0 44	0 19	0 46	0 27	0 26	1 62
Clay	0 61	0 24	0 69	0 35	0 23	2 12
Clay and water	0 63	0 22	0 73	0 37	0 24	2 19
Hard clay	0 83	0 26	0 84	0 54	0 41	2 68
Very coarse gravel	0 91	0 19	0 98	0 38	0 44	2 90
Quicks'd and water*	1 47	0 26	1 45	0 92	0 70	4 80
Rock	1 30	0 27	2 17	0 71	1 08	5 53
Average cost in all soils	0 78	0 23	0 91	0 42	0 44	2 78
Average cost in all soils except rock	0 72	0 22	0 75	0 39	0 36	2 44

*In setting poles in quicksand in the country iron sand barrels are used, whereas in the city old lime or sugar barrels are used in place of sand barrels, and are left in the holes The cost of the old barrels which are left in the holes should be charged to supervision and expense

TABLE XIV—Cost of 35-Ft Toll Line Poles

	Teaming and Labor in Hauling	Framing	Digging and Locating	Setting	Supervision and Expense	Average Cost Per Pole
Sand or gravel	$0 49	$0 27	$0 67	$0 33	$0 32	$2 08
Sand and water	0 47	0 29	0 71	0 35	0 43	2 25
Black soil	0 62	0 26	0 74	0 38	0 40	2 40
Clay	0 58	0 30	0 80	0 51	0 36	2 55
Clay and water	0 78	0 27	0 93	0 66	0 43	3 07
Hard clay	0 92	0 28	1 01	0 54	0 52	3 27
Very coarse gravel	1 10	0 30	1 21	0 58	0 61	3 80
Quicks'd and water	1 46	0 29	1 68	0 96	0 73	5 12
Rock	1 38	0 30	2 60	0 79	1 14	6 21
Average in all soils	0 87	0 28	1 15	0 57	0 55	3 42
Average in all soils except rock	0 80	0 28	0 97	0 54	0 48	3 07

TABLE XV—Cost of 40-Ft Toll Line Poles

	Teaming and Labor in Hauling	Framing	Digging and Locating	Setting	Supervision and Expense	Average Cost Per Pole
Sand or gravel	$0 65	$0 30	$0 65	$0 49	$0 42	$2 51
Sand and water	0 70	0 34	0 73	0 50	0 46	2 73
Clay	0 83	0 32	0 84	0 54	0 47	3 00
Clay and water	0 87	0 30	0 89	0 64	0 45	3 15
Hard clay	0 94	0 36	1 06	0 60	0 61	3 57
Very coarse gravel	1 20	0 32	1 24	0 69	0 72	4 17
Quicks'd and water	1 68	0 37	1 70	1 24	1 10	6 09
Rock	1 80	0 31	3 34	0 90	1 21	7 56
Average in all soils	1 08	0 33	1 31	0 70	0 68	4 10
Average in all soils except rock	0 98	0 33	1 02	0 67	0 60	3 60

TABLE XVI—Cost of 45-Ft Toll Line Poles

	Teaming and Labor in Hauling	Framing	Digging and Locating	Setting	Supervision and Expense	Average Cost Per Pole
Sand or gravel	$0 82	$0 35	$0 90	$0 66	$0 60	$3 33
Clay	1 12	0 34	1 01	0 77	0 58	3 82
Hard clay	1 30	0 32	1 20	0 88	0 69	4 39
Quicks'd and water	1 98	0 30	3 86	1 44	1 26	8 84
Rock and water	2 60	0 34	7 49	1 19	1 82	13 44
Average cost in all soils	1 56	0 33	2 89	0 99	0 99	6 76
Average cost in all soils except rock	1 30	0 33	1 74	0 94	0 78	5 09

Note 45-ft toll lines not being frequently built, sufficient data on which averages could be based could not be had for some kinds of soil

TABLE XVII—COST OF SELF-SUSTAINING POLES WITH GROUND BRACES

	Teaming and Hauling	Framing and Stepping	Digging and Locating	Setting	Supervision and Expense	Average Cost Per Pole
Clay poles 30 ft	$0 79	$0 47	$1 30	$0 44	$0 53	$3 53
Hard clay, poles 30 ft	1 07	0 51	1 53	0 46	0 65	4 22
Average in all soils, poles 30 ft	0 93	0 49	1 42	0 45	0 59	3 83
Clay, poles 35 ft	0 84	0 48	1 24	0 54	0 64	3 74
Hard clay, poles 35 ft	1 19	0 50	1 57	0 58	0.71	4 55
Average in all soils, poles 35 ft	1 02	0 49	1 40	0 56	0 68	4 15
Clay, poles 40 ft	1 12	0 54	1 56	0 79	0 72	4 73
Hard clay, poles 40 ft	1 54	0 52	1 77	0 76	0 80	5 39
Average in all soils, poles 40 ft	1 33	0 53	1 67	0 77	0 76	5 06

TABLE XVIII—COST OF 30-FT SELF-SUSTAINING POLES SET IN CONCRETE

	Teaming and Hauling	Framing and Stepping	Digging and Locating	Mixing Concrete	Setting and Placing Concrete	Supervision and Expense	Average Cost Per Pole
Sand or gravel	$1 10	$0 27	$0 82	$0 35	$0 75	$1 02	$4 31
Sand and water	1 07	0 31	0 97	0 33	0 89	0 98	4 55
Clay	1 26	0 22	1 17	0 36	0 87	1 11	4 99
Quicksand and water	1 40	0 24	1 45	0 57	1 08	1 20	5 94
Average cost in all soils	1 21	0 26	1 10	0 40	0 90	1 08	4 95

TABLE XIX—COST OF 35-FT SELF-SUSTAINING POLES SET IN CONCRETE

	Teaming and Hauling	Framing and Stepping	Digging and Locating	Mixing Concrete	Setting and Placing Concrete	Supervision and Expense	Average Cost Per Pole
Sand or gravel	$1 04	$0 30	$0 86	$0 38	$0 79	$1 07	$4 44
Sand and water	1 13	0 29	1 01	0 41	1 01	1 10	4 95
Clay	1 22	0 31	1 13	0 44	1 03	1 01	5 14
Quicksand and water	1 48	0 34	1 52	0 62	1 22	1 28	6 46
Average cost in all soils	1 22	0 31	1 13	0 46	1 01	1 12	5 25

TABLE XX—COST OF CROSS-ARMS

	Teaming and Labor in Hauling	Putting on Arms	Supervision and Expense	Av Cost Per C Arm
Six-pin	$0 024	$0 074	$0 022	$0 12
Ten-pin	0 05	0 13	0 04	0 22
Ten-pin alley	0 07	0 20	0 07	0 34
Terminal	0 06	0 15	0 05	0 26

TABLE XXI—COST OF ANCHORS INCLUDING ANCHOR GUYS

Item—	Stombaugh	Miller	Rock
Teaming and labor in hauling	$0 11	$0 33	$0 34
Boring		0 73	
Drilling			0 90
Setting anchor	0 20	0 13	0 19
Placing guy	0 23*	0 31†	0 44†
Supervision and expense	0 12	0 34	0 17
Average cost per anchor including guy	0 66	1 84	2 14

*No 4 galvanized steel wire used for guys, this anchor used for farm line   † ⅜-in strand used for guys

TABLE XXII—Cost of Log Anchors Including Anchor Guys

	Teaming and Labor in Hauling	Digging	Setting Anchor	Placing Guy	Supervision and Expense	Average Cost per Anchor, inc Guy
Sand or gravel	$0 37	$0 81	$0 31	$0 37	$0 33	$2 19
Sand and water*	0 56	1 71	0 91	0 20	1 57	4 95
Black soil	0 43	0 76	0 35	0 44	0 30	2 28
Clay	0 63	1 40	0 60	0 49	0 63	3 75
Clay and water	0 60	1 70	1 00	0 60	0 73	4 63
Hard clay	0 59	1 75	0 85	0 63	0 59	4 41
Hard pan	0 81	2 04	0 84	0 43	0 67	4 79
Very coarse gravel	0 96	2 10	0 97	0 55	0 93	5 51
Quicks'd and water	0 87	2 39	1 19	0 65	1 10	6 20
Av cost in all soils	0 65	1 63	0 78	0 48	0 76	4 30

*Note—Hole often caves in if not sheeted

TABLE XXIII—Cost of Guying and Setting Stubs

	Teaming and Labor in Hauling	Digging	Setting Stubs	Placing Guys	Supervision and Expense	Average Cost per Stub, inc Guy
15 Ft Stubs—						
Sand or gravel	$0 37	$0 74	$0 26	$0 32	$0 36	$2 05
Clay	0 53	0 85	0 24	0 36	0 50	2 51
Clay and water	0 49	0 93	0 36	0 41	0 48	2 67
Hard clay	0 67	0 96	0 37	0 48	0 53	3 01
Av cost in all soils	0 51	0 88	0 31	0 39	0 47	2 56
20 Ft Stubs—						
Sand or gravel	0 41	0 73	0 32	0 31	0 35	2 12
Clay	0 49	0 96	0 34	0 35	0 48	2 62
Clay and water	0 54	1 04	0 44	0 42	0 43	2 87
Hard clay	0 65	1 07	0 42	0 39	0 59	3 10
Very coarse gravel	0 72	1 16	0 44	0 41	0 62	3 35
Av cost in all soils	0 56	0 99	0 39	0 38	0 49	2 81
25 Ft Stubs—						
Sand or gravel	0 69	0 79	0 47	0 41	0 52	2 88
Clay	0 76	0 86	0 54	0 39	0 64	3 19
Clay and water	0 74	1 01	0 59	0 46	0 66	3 46
Hard clay	0 89	1 10	0 53	0 42	0 61	3 55
Av cost in all soils	0 77	0 94	0 53	0 42	0 61	3 27

TABLE XXIV—Cost of Guying and Setting Self-Sustaining Stubs in Concrete

	Teaming and Labor in Hauling	Digging	Mixing Concrete	Setting Stubs and Placing Concrete	Placing Guys	Supervision and Expense	Av'ge Cost per Stub inc Guy
15 ft Stubs—							
Sand or gravel	$0 88	$0 97	$0 38	$0 60	$0 37	$0 83	$4 01
Sand and water	0 83	1 16	0 37	0 66	0 41	0 86	4 29
Black soil	0 77	0 97	0 41	0 59	0 38	0 74	3 86
Black soil and water	0 99	1 00	0 36	0 64	0 39	0 91	4 29
Quicksand and water	1 08	1 41	0 43	0 93	0 43	0 98	5 26
Average cost in all soils	0 91	1 10	0 39	0 65	0 40	0 86	4 34
20 ft Stubs—							
Sand or gravel	0 86	1 02	0 45	0 68	0 41	0 89	4 31
Sand and water	0 92	1 11	0 46	0 73	0 43	0 90	4 55
Black soil	0 83	0 98	0 40	0 76	0 37	0 86	4 20
Quicksand and water	0 97	1 46	0 36	1 07	0 36	0 94	5 16
Average in all soils	0 90	1 11	0 42	0 81	0 39	0 90	4 56
25 ft Stubs—							
Sand or gravel	1 02	0 98	0 52	0 76	0 44	0 88	4 60
Sand and water	1 08	1 06	0 46	0 84	0 37	0 96	4 77
Quicksand and water	1 22	1 50	0 41	1 12	0 43	0 99	5 67
Average in all soils	1 11	1 18	0 46	0 91	0 41	0 94	5 01

TABLE XXV—COST OF GUYING AND SETTING SELF-SUSTAINING STUBS WITH GROUND BRACES

	Teaming and Labor in Hauling	Digging	Setting Stubs	Placing Guy	Supervision and Expense	Average Cost per Stub inc Guy
15 ft —						
Clay	$0 77	$0 94	$0 42	$0 39	$0 74	$3 26
Hard clay	0 86	1 18	0 40	0 35	0 83	3 62
Av cost in all soils	0 82	1 06	0 41	0 37	0 78	3 44
20 ft —						
Clay	0 84	0 92	0 46	0 38	0 82	3 42
Hard clay	1 02	1 12	0 49	0 43	0 87	3 93
Av cost in all soils	0 93	1 02	0 48	0 40	0 85	3 68
25 ft —						
Clay	1 01	0 98	0 57	0 41	0 79	3 76
Hard clay	1 04	1 16	0 64	0 46	1 07	4 37
Av cost in all soils	1 03	1 07	0 60	0 44	0 93	4 07

TABLE XXVI—COST OF PUSH POLE BRACES

	Teaming and Labor in Hauling	Framing	Digging	Setting	Supervision and Expense	Average Cost per Brace
20 ft —						
Sand or gravel	$0 27	$0 18	$0 22	$0 28	$0 23	$1 18
Sand and water	0 34	0 17	0 28	0 24	0 30	1 33
Black soil	0 30	0 27	0 26	0 29	0 26	1 38
Clay and water	0 43	0 19	0 31	0 26	0 37	1 56
Av cost in all soils	0 33	0 20	0 27	0 27	0 29	1 36
25 ft —						
Sand or gravel	0 28	0 26	0 29	0 25	0 26	1 34
Sand and water	0 41	0 21	0 34	0 31	0 38	1 65
Black soil	0 27	0 14	0 32	0 24	0 23	1 20
Clay	0 53	0 17	0 38	0 27	0 49	1 84
Av cost in all soils	0 37	0 20	0 33	0 27	0 34	1 51

TABLE XXVII—COST OF WIRE STRINGING

	Teaming and Labor in Hauling	Stringing and Equipping	Supervision and Expense	Average Cost per Mile
No 12 galv steel for farm lines	$0 89	$3 04	$0 90	$4 83
No 12 galv steel for toll circuits	0 99	3 25	0 72	4 96
104 bare copper for toll circuits	1 18	3 65	0 80	5 63
080 bare copper for street and alley lines	1 22	3 18	0 66	5 06

Note—The cost of trimming trees is not included in wire stringing This cost varies so greatly that averages are of no value The reel shown in Fig 14 was used to string most of the wire on which these costs are based On account of being equipped with a friction brake, adjustable to any size coil, and designed for handling either one or two coils, this style reel was found to facilitate wire stringing and reduce its cost

TABLE XXVIII—COST OF LINE ORDERS

	Teaming and Labor in Hauling	Stringing and Equipping	Supervision and Expense	Average Cost per Line Order
City or village lines	$0 49	$1 60	$0 43	$2 52
Farm lines	0 35	1 38	0 36	2 09

Note—Line orders include only the cost of stringing and equipping the line wire and drop to the house, necessary for a telephone installation, the inside wiring and installation of telephone set being done by "installers As the principal cost of line orders is in the equipping, they are averaged by number of line orders instead of miles as in stringing wire It makes little difference in cost whether two, three or four spans of wire are strung The average line order in cities and villages requires four to five spans of circuit and for farm lines seven to eight spans In cities and villages to complete the average line order very little work other than stringing wire and setting one or two poles and cross arms is necessary The jobs being small, the time lost between jobs makes the cost higher than on farm lines where it usually requires one or two days work for each line order

TABLE XXIX —COST OF DROPS

	Teaming and Labor in Hauling	Stringing and Equipping	Supervision and Expense.	Average Cost per Drop
City and village lines. .	$0 15	$0 54	$0 07	$0 76
Farm lines	0 10	0 47	0 10	0 67

Note—When for a line order the stringing of a drop is all that is necessary, it is put under "Drops" instead of "Line Orders."

CONSTRUCTION COST DATA.

The data given in Tables VI to XXIX are average costs based on over 10,000 poles, cross-arms, anchors, etc , erected on over 500 jobs in both city and country, and in all seasons of the year In general, winter work is found to average in cost with spring work. In winter the frost makes digging and setting more expensive and the cold increases the cost of stringing wire, erecting cross-arms and work requiring men to be on the poles. These drawbacks are balanced in the spring by bad roads, muddy tools and slippery footing Summer and fall work costs about 10 per cent. less than winter and spring work.

Wages.—The rates of wages paid and on which the costs in Tables VI to XXXVII are based are as follows:

Station gangs

Foremen, per month	$90.00 to	$100.00
Timekeeper, per 8-hour day	2.25 to	2 50
Linemen, per 8-hour day	2 95 to	3 25
Combination men, per 8-hour day..........	2 25 to	2 50
Groundmen, per 8-hour day	2 00 to	2 15
Teams, per 8-hour day......	4.00 to	4 50

Floating gangs ·

Foremen, per month and board. .	65.00 to	75 00
Timekeeper, per 8-hour day and board. ..	1.25 to	1 40
Linemen, per 8-hour day and board.....	1 80 to	2 00
Combination men, per 8-hour day and board	1.25 to	1 40
Groundmen, per 8-hour day and board.	1.00	
Teams, per 8-hour day and board.	3.00 to	4 00

From 50 to 75 cts per day are allowed for board of team and $1 per day, including Sundays, is allowed for board of each man. In the cost data given, the rate for men in floating gangs is found by dividing the board per month, $30 or $31, by the number of working days, 26 or 27, and adding the amount to their rate per day   Mistakes in construction such as digging a hole in the wrong location are not included in these averages

Classifications of Soils.—Combinations of soil being almost endless, the divisions assumed are necessarily, to some extent, arbitrary   Loam is included with clay   When quicksand is dry and does not run it is classed as sand   Very coarse gravel includes clay and cobbles   If the soil is one-half hard clay and one-half clay and water, it is classed as hard clay; if one-half hard clay and one-half clay, it is classed as clay and water   The "average cost in all soils" and the "average cost of all soils except rock" are figured as if each pole was set in a different kind of soil, whereas in most districts clay predominates, except in the spring of the year, when the greatest percentage of the digging is in clay and water   In estimating work, the average costs in those soils predominating in a district should be used.

CHAPTER II

METHODS AND COST OF CABLE CONSTRUCTION

While cable requires more careful handling than wire, still the percentage of linemen or other skilled labor necessary is small, as a foreman at one end of the job and an assistant, or lineman, at the other end, can readily supervise and direct the work of the men The average cost of labor per hour is therefore 3 cts to 5 cts. less than for line work The average supervision, however, is higher on account of cable work being done mostly in large districts where foremen are better paid than in small districts This also applies to foremen who install toll cable, they being experienced and highly paid—men used for difficult jobs or work requiring very careful handling

Although the specification set forth the manner in which cable is to be handled, still there is a greater chance for foremen to display judgment in cable work than in line work, especially in the laying out of work Line work can generally be dropped for the day at almost any time, whereas, a cable reel once opened the cable must be erected or pulled in the same day on account of its liability to injury

Cable being the main arteries of a telephone plant in cities and towns, no expense is spared to install it in the most efficient and permanent manner The costs given are based on high grade work, foremen being held responsible in any case where the work is not standard

CONSTRUCTION DETAILS

Sizes of Cable.—The cable referred to in these labor costs is loose core, paper insulated, lead sheathed cable The diameter, thickness of sheath, and weight are as follows:

25

22 B & S Gage

No of Pairs	Outside Diameter, inches	Thickness of Sheath.	Weight, lbs , per 100 ft
10	$\frac{3}{4}$	$\frac{1}{12}$	$59\frac{1}{2}$
15	$\frac{7}{8}$	$\frac{1}{12}$	70
25	$\frac{15}{16}$	$\frac{1}{12}$	93
50	$1\frac{1}{8}$	$\frac{1}{12}$	132
100	$1\frac{1}{4}$	$\frac{3}{32}$	$212\frac{1}{2}$
200	$1\frac{3}{4}$	$\frac{1}{8}$	400
400	$2\frac{5}{16}$	$\frac{1}{8}$	606
600	$2\frac{3}{4}$	$\frac{1}{8}$	802

19 B & S Gage

No of Pairs	Outside Diameter, inches	Thickness of Sheath.	Weight, lbs , per 100 ft
25	1	$\frac{1}{12}$	142
50	$1\frac{3}{8}$	$\frac{5}{52}$	228
100	$1\frac{15}{16}$	$\frac{1}{8}$	444
200	$2\frac{3}{16}$	$\frac{1}{8}$	581
300	$2\frac{5}{8}$	$\frac{1}{8}$	751

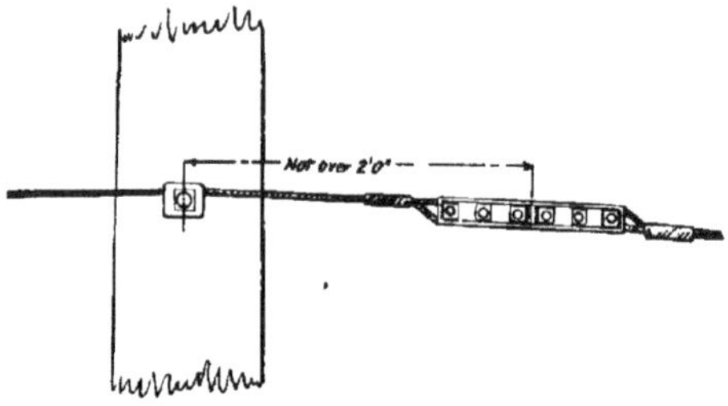

Fig 16—Method of Splicing Messenger Strand

Erecting Messenger.—Messenger is. (1) No 4 Steel Wire, (2) ⅜-in Strand, and (3) ½-in. Strand, constructed according to the following specifications ·

A No 4 steel wire messenger shall be used to sustain 25 pr. 22 ga. aerial or lighter cables The messenger shall be secured to the pole with a No 4 messenger support and a 7-in. lag screw, tightly but carefully screwed up so as not to strip the threads in the wood of the pole

A ⅜-in. strand shall be used for the suspension of 25 pr 19 ga and 50 pr. 22 ga aerial cables, and for 100 pr 22 ga and 50 pr 19 ga aerial cables in spans not longer than 145 ft The strand shall be attached to the pole by means of a ⅜-in strand support and one 7-in and one 4-in lag screws

The ½-in strand shall be used to sustain all aerial cables heavier than 50 pr. 19 ga or 100 pr. 22 ga , and for 50 pr. 19 ga and 100 pr 22 ga in spans longer than 145 ft   The strand shall be attached to the pole by means of a ½-in strand support and two 6-in lag screws   The method of splicing strand is shown by Fig 16.

Aerial Cable.—Aerial cable is of the following kinds : 10 pr , 22 ga ; 15 pr., 22 ga , 25 pr , 22 ga. and 19 ga ; 50 pr., 22 ga. and 19 ga ; 100 pr., 22 ga. and 19 ga., 200 pr., 22 ga. and 19 ga. The specifications for aerial cable work are as follows:

Aerial cable may be erected by the use of capstan, by winch, by horsepower, or by hand. The speed should not exceed 50 ft per minute, and the armor of the cable should be inspected carefully for imperfections as it is unreeled

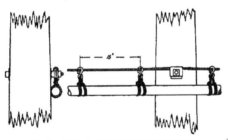

Fig 17 —Method of Fastening Cable to Pole

In setting up, cable should always be taken from the top of the reel   The reel should be set up as nearly in line with the lead wire as possible. For four spans or less, no lead wire will be required   It is not advisable to pull lengths of cable in excess of 1,000 ft.

After the reel is set up and the cable ready to be pulled, the lagging shall be removed from the cable reel and the cable rope shall be fastened to the end of the cable In fastening the rope to the cable either a clevis, wrapping of wire or marlin should be used, depending upon the pull, size of cable, etc. The cable rope must be provided with a swivel hook or ring. The winch, capstan, or whatever device is used for pulling the cable, shall be placed at the farther end of the run and suitably braced   The end of the cable rope shall be carried to the drum and wrapped about it

The cable is attached to messenger wire by means of standard cable clips. The clips shall be attached to the cable by passing the double loop of marlin around the cable and drawing the cable up through the loop   The clip shall be attached to cable as it is unreeled and shall be spaced 15 ins apart for 200 pr., 22 ga. and 100 pr , 19 ga cable, and be spaced 20 ins. apart for all smaller cables. The method of fastening the cable to the pole is shown in Fig 17.

Where cable is liable to injury from chafing trees or poles, buildings, etc , wooden cleats shall be placed around the cable at such points as shown in Fig 18   If it is necessary to prevent slipping of cleats, rubber tape may be wrapped around the ends of the cleats and cable

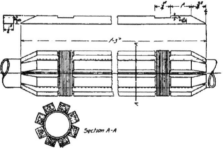

Fig 18 —Guard to Protect Cable from Chafing

Equipping Cable or Terminal Poles —The equipment used on cable or terminal poles is as follows   50 pr. protected terminal boxes (with ground rods) , 25 pr. protected terminal boxes (with ground rods) , 25 pr. unprotected terminal boxes; 15 pr. unprotected terminal boxes, and pole seats   The specifications for this work are as follows

Protected terminals shall be used where open wire lines which are one mile or over in length take cable and where cable is in close proximity to electric light or power wires   On alley lines the terminal boxes shall be attached as shown in Fig 19   On center arm lines the terminal boxes shall be attached to the pole below the bottom arm so as to clear the lowest wires   Cable poles equipped with 25 or 50 pr cable boxes shall have pole seats which shall be attached as shown in Fig 20   Ground rods for protected boxes shall be a plain iron rod ½-in x 5-ft , with 3 ft of No 12 N. B S. soft copper wire soldered to one end   Ground rods shall be driven into the earth alongside of the pole so that the top shall be on a level with the ground   A No 5 copper wire shall be attached to the No 12 N B S wire and secured to the pole by means of staples driven every 2 ft.

Wiring Cable or Terminal Poles.—This division covers the cost of bridling line or open wires to cable boxes   The specifications are as follows.

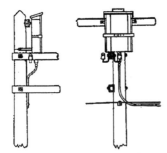

Fig 19 —Method of Attaching Terminal Boxes on Alley Lines.

No 18 twisted pair rubber covered bridle or jumper wire shall be used in connecting line wires to cable boxes   The bridle wires shall be attached to the pole between the cable box and the cross-arms in a neat bunch, and shall be run along the under side of the cross-arms through wooden cleats

Rodding Underground Cable.—The duct in which cable is to be placed shall first be rodded   To the end rod shall be attached a length of No. 12 steel wire, which shall be used to pull into the duct the steel rope, used in pulling the cable

Main Underground Cable.—Underground cable is of the following kinds 50 pr , 22 ga and 19 ga , 100 pr., 22 ga and 19 ga , 200 pr , 22 ga and 19 ga , 300 pr , 22 ga and 19 ga , 400 pr , 22 ga . 600 pr , 22 ga , 150 pr , 16 ga . toll cable, and

120 pr., ½-14 ga and ½-16 ga. toll cable   The specifications for underground cable work are as follows:

The cable may be pulled by capstan, by winch, by horse power or by hand, at a speed not to exceed 50 ft per minute In setting up, the reel should be as nearly in line with the duct as possible and ahead of the vault rather than back of it, so that the cable will feed from the top of the reel. To the end of the No 12 steel wire which is pulled in when rodding the duct, shall be fastened a steel rope which in turn shall be

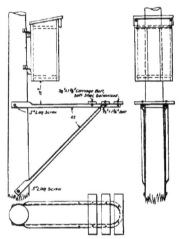

Fig 20 —Method of Attaching Pole Seats

fastened to the cable by means of a cable clamp, wire hitch or other approved method. Skids and sheaves shall be set up as nearly as possible in a straight line from the mouth of the duct   The cable should be fed in at a uniform speed and the armor carefully inspected. Where the cable is 2 ins. or more in diameter, the ducts should be swabbed with soapstone, mica or graphite, except in the case of short straight runs Cable in passing through vaults shall be divided so that cable entering the vault on either side of the center of the vault shall be carried around that side of the vault to the duct where it leaves vaults again, as shown in Fig 21

Lateral Underground Cable.—Lateral underground cable is of the following kinds 25 pr , 22 ga and 19 ga ; 50 pr , 22 ga and 19 ga ; 100 pr., 22 ga and 19 ga , and 200 pr., 22 ga and 19 ga. The specifications for this work are as follows

Lateral cable shall be set up and pulled in the same manner as main cable. Where the cable is 1 in or over in diameter, the duct should be swabbed with soapstone, mica or graphite, except in the case of short, straight laterals, 100 ft or less.

Forms for Reporting Costs.—The manner in which the costs are reported is shown by Forms 12 to 18 inclusive. The method of collecting the data and figuring cable work costs is similar to the method used for line construction, which has been explained.

Fig 21 —Diagram Showing Method of Passing Cable Through Vaults

CABLE WORK COSTS.

With the exception of underground toll cable, the following cost data, Tables XXX to XXXVII, are based on work done in cities and towns   The data were collected and figured on the same principle as "Line Construction Costs," data on over 500,000 ft of cable and messenger being used in drawing the averages.

Fig. 22.—Unloading Reel of Cable   Fig. 23.—Feeding Cable Into Vault.
from Wagon.

Fig. 24.—Pulling Cable.   Fig. 25.—Placing Cable Box on Pole.

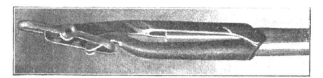

Fig. 26.—Cable Grip.

Form 12
Data Secured by
ERECTING MESSENGER

No 4 Steel Wire
⅜" Strand
½" Strand

Location   Order No
Foreman   Date   190

No Ft Erected	Teaming and Labor in Hauling	Erecting	Super and Expense	Total Cost	No hrs Worked	Remarks

NOTE —The cost of erecting messenger, besides being reported separately, is included in the cost of erecting aerial cable On the forms used for reporting the cost of erecting aerial cable, the teaming and labor in hauling and supervision and expense of erecting messenger are included respectively in the cost of teaming and labor in hauling, and supervision and expense of erecting cable The cost of erecting messenger is reported in the special column headed ' Erecting Messenger

Form 13
Data Secured by
AERIAL CABLE

10 pr 22 Ga
15 " 22 "
25 " 19 or 22 Ga
50 " 19 " 22 "
100 " 19 " 22 "
200 " 19 " 22 "

Location   Order No
Foreman   Date   190

No Ft of Cable	Teaming and Labor in Hauling	Erecting Messenger	Erecting Cable	Total Cost	No hrs Worked	Super and Exp	Remarks

Form 14
Data Secured by,
EQUIPPING CABLE POLES

Size of Box
Protected
Unprotected

Location   Order No
Foreman   Date   190

No of Poles Equ p'd	Teaming and Labor in Hauling	Attaching Cable Box and Gr'nd Rod	Attaching Pole Seat	Super and Exp	Total Cost	No of Hours Worked	Remarks

NOTE —No seat being attached to poles equipped with 15 pr boxes the corresopnding column is left blank When unprotected boxes are attached "Ground Rod" is erased

Form 15
Data Secured by
WIRING CABLE POLES

Location   Order No
Foreman   Date   190

No of Pairs Cut in	Teaming and Labor in Hauling	Wiring	Super and Expense	Total Cost	No. of Hours Worked	Remarks

			Form 16				
			Data Secured by				
			RODDING				
City		Location				Order No	
Country		Foreman.		Date			190
No of Duct Feet Rodded	Teaming and Labor in Hauling	Rodding	Super and Expense	Total Cost	No of Hours Worked	Remarks	

NOTE·—On account of the great difference between the cost of rodding conduit built through the country, and conduit built in cities the data are kept separate The reasons for this difference in cost are that very few vaults in the country districts have drainage or sewer connections as in cities, this makes it necessary to pump out almost every vault before rodding The distance from the station to the work being much greater in the country than in city work, also increases the cost The cost of rodding besides being reported separately is included in the cost of installing underground cable, teaming, and supervision and expense of rodding being included in the form for reporting "Underground Cable" in the columns headed respectively "Teaming and Labor in Hauling," and "Supervision and Expense" Rodding is reported in the special column headed "Rodding."

50 Pr 19 or 22 Ga			From 17				
100 " 19 " 22 "			Data Secured by				
200 " 19 " 22 "			UNDERGROUND CABLE (MAIN)				
300 " 19 " 22 "							
400 " 19 " 22 "						Order No	
600 " 19 " 22 "			Location		Date		190
150 " 16 Ga							
120 " ½-14 Ga and ½-16 Ga		Foreman					

No Ft pulled in	Teaming and Labor in Hauling	Rodding	Pulling	Total Cost	Super and Exp	No of Hours Worked	Remarks

		Form 18					
		Data Secured by					
		UNDERGROUND CABLE (LATERAL)					
25 Pr 19 or 22 Ga						Order No	
50 " 19 " 22 "							
100 " 19 " 22 "		Location		Date			190
200 " 19 " 22 "		Foreman					

No of Laterals	No Ft Pulled in	Teaming and Labor in Hauling	Pulling	Super and Exp	Total Cost	No of Hours Worked	Remarks

NOTE —The average cost of lateral cable is figured per foot and per lateral, the cost per lateral being found useful in estimating where the exact length of laterals is not known No rodding is necessary for laterals as they are wired when building

TABLE XXX—COST OF ERECTING MESSENGER.

	Teaming and Labor in Hauling	Erecting	Supervision and Expense	Average Cost per Foot
No 4 steel wire	$0 0015	$0 0050	$0 0015	$0 0080
⅜-in strand	0 0011	0 0052	0 0010	0 0073
½-in. strand	0 0013	0 0057	0 0012	0.0082

Note—No 4 steel wire costs more to erect, comparatively, than strand on account of the former being used to suspend small cable which is frequently installed where interference from trees is bad Erecting messenger or cable through trees increases the expense considerably

TABLE XXXI—Cost of Aerial Cable Per Foot

	Teaming and Labor in Hauling	Erecting Strand	Erecting Cable	Supervision and Expense	Average Cost per Foot
10 Pr—22 Ga *	$0 0053	$0 0049	$0 0099	$0 0065	$0 0271
15 Pr—22 Ga *	0 0046	0 0048	0 0135	0 0045	0 0274
25 Pr—22 Ga	0 0044	0 0051	0 0130	0 0042	0 0267
25 Pr—19 Ga	0 0065	0 0047	0 0108	0 0050	0 0270
50 Pr—22 Ga	0 0044	0 0054	0 0128	0 0039	0 0265
50 Pr—19 Ga	0 0054	0 0057	0 0114	0 0034	0 0259
100 Pr—22 Ga	0 0052	0 0058	0 0116	0 0035	0 0261
100 Pr—19 Ga	0 0057	0 0064	0 0126	0 0034	0 0281
200 Pr—22 Ga	0 0053	0 0062	0 0128	0 0037	0 0280

*See note on "Erecting Messenger" Not sufficient data on 200 Pr 19 Ga to draw an average

TABLE XXXII—Cost of Equipping Protected Cable Poles

	Teaming and Labor in Hauling	Attaching Cable Box and Ground Rod	Attaching Pole Seat	Supervision and Expense	Average Cost per Pole
25 Pr Box	..$0 26	$0 59	$0 32	$0 26	$1 43
50 Pr Box	0 32	0 66	0 33	0 30	1 61

TABLE XXXIII—Cost of Equipping Unprotected Cable Poles

	Teaming and Labor in Hauling	Attaching Cable Box	Supervision and Expense	Average Cost per Pole
15 Pr Box	$0 17	$0 44	$0 15	$0 76
25 Pr Box	0 20	0 46	0 18	0 84

TABLE XXXIV—Cost of Wiring Cable Poles

Teaming and Labor in Hauling	Wiring	Supervision and Expense	Average Cost per Pair
$0 027	$0 121	$0 019	$0 167

TABLE XXXV—Cost of Rodding

	Teaming and Labor in Hauling	Rodding	Supervision and Expense	Average Cost per Foot
City	$0 0010	$0 0036	$0 0016	$0 0062
Country	0 0018	0 0061	0 0019	0 0098

TABLE XXXVI—Cost of Underground Cable (Main)

	Teaming and Labor in Hauling	Rodding	Pulling	Supervision and Expense	Average Cost per Foot
50 Pr—19 Ga	$0 0048	$0 0034	$0 0061	$0 0017	$0 0161
100 Pr—22 Ga	0 0042	0 0037	0.0065	0 0018	0 0162
100 Pr—19 Ga	0 0054	0 0039	0 0062	0 0019	0 0172
200 Pr—22 Ga	0 0057	0 0036	0 0067	0 0015	0 0175
200 Pr—19 Ga	0 0061	0 0031	0 0071	0 0021	0 0184
300 Pr—22 Ga	0 0066	0 0036	0 0097	0 0018	0 0217
?00 Pr—19 Ga	0 0073	0 0030	0 0093	0 0024	0 0220
150 Pr—16 Ga Toll Cable	0 0101	0 0058	0 0147	0 0043	0 0349
120 Pr—½-14 Ga and ½-16 Ga Toll Cable	0 0122	0 0068	0 0138	0 0048	0 0396

Note The weight of a reel of 120 Pr—½-14 Ga and ½-16 Ga averages between 3¾ and 5 tons The cable grip shown in Fig 26 was used on some jobs in pulling in the cable It reduces the cost, as it may be connected and removed instantly, whereas a wire hitch takes some time to attach and remove It also is superior to a wire hitch because it does not injure the cable and will not pull off

TABLE XXXVII—Cost of Underground Cable (Lateral)

	Teaming and Labor in Hauling per Foot	Pulling per Foot	Supervision and Expense per Foot	Average Cost per Foot	Average Length of Laterals in Feet	Average Cost per Lateral
25 Pr—22 Ga	$0 0044	$0 0112	$0 0029	$0 0185	117	$2 17
50 Pr—22 Ga	0 0063	0 0198	0 0042	0 0303	132	4 01
50 Pr—19 Ga	0 0071	0 0226	0 0062	0 0359	123	4 42
100 Pr—22 Ga	0 0068	0 0220	0 0059	0 0347	126	4 36
100 Pr—19 Ga	0 0111	0 0316	0 0064	0 0491	115	5 64
200 Pr—22 Ga	0 0109	0 0310	0 0061	0 0480	112	5 39
200 Pr—19 Ga	0 0138	0 0354	0 0076	0 0568	117	6 62

Note 25 Pr—22 Ga costs much less to install than other cable, as it is always pulled in by hand, and its small diameter and light weight make it easily handled

CHAPTER III.

METHOD AND COST OF CABLE SPLICING.

Of all outside construction the most delicate work is cable splicing, and it requires the most skilled and careful labor The careless removal of the insulation from conductors has been known to cause crosses which cost hundreds of dollars to locate and clear. A splice when not properly made is always a source of "trouble cases" which are difficult to locate and expensive to clear; but even the cost of locating and clearing is small in comparison with the loss of revenue and the annoyance to subscribers caused by the interruption of service, especially when a main cable is in trouble Above all things, good splicing requires conscientious work, and on the personnel of the men depends the quality of the splice Cheap splicing is not generally good splicing, therefore in estimating the cost of splicing, no attempt should be made to force quick work, which is nearly always expensive in the end.

The organization of splicer gangs is somewhat different from line gangs, the gangs being composed of a head splicer, one or two splicers, and an equal number of helpers. Each gang is assigned to a district and is stationed in the principal town in the district When necessary a gang is increased by drawing from other gangs, and all men receive board when working outside of the town in which they are stationed The head splicer usually splices or tests out when the gang is small, little supervision being necessary

A great deal of overtime is worked because of most splices which cause interruption of the service being made at night and also on account of splices being often worked on until finished This sometimes makes a splicer s wages per one-half month between $60 and $100 dollars

CLASSIFICATION AND DEFINITIONS.

Systematizing the costs of cable splicing is more difficult than in any other branch of telephone construction, first, be-

36

cause of the general confusion in the names of the different
splices, and second, because of the endless combinations in
splicing In order to avoid confusion, a leg of a cable box
will be referred to as a cable and two sections of a cable not
already spliced will be called two cables, thus if two sections
of a 100-pr cable are to be spliced they will be referred to as
two 100-pr cables For the purposes of this chapter the splicing of conductors will be used to indicate the kind of splice,
and splices will be referred to as follows.

Straight Splices.—(1) When all the conductors of two
cables are spliced together, each joint of conductors being
composed of two wires, (2) when the conductors of one
cable are spliced into a cable containing a larger number of
conductors, part of which are left "dead," each joint of conductors being composed of two wires; and (3) where either
part or all of the conductors of two or more cables are spliced
into part or all of the conductors of another cable, each joint
of conductors being composed of two wires and the conductors not spliced being left "dead "

Bridge Splices.—(1) When all the conductors of three or
more cables are spliced together, each joint of conductors being composed of the same number of wires, (2) when all
the conductors of a cable are spliced into a cable composed of
one-half, one-quarter, etc , the number of conductors, each
joint of conductors being composed of like number of wires

Straight-Bridge Splices.—When some of the conductors of
a cable are spliced, as described under "Straight Splice" and
some as described under "Bridge Splice "

There are endless combinations in splicing, as for example,
into a 100-pr cable may be spliced a 10, 15, 25, 50 or
100-pr cable, etc , or a 10, 15, 25 and 50-pr cable, etc. Also
the splice may be straight, bridge, straight-bridge or change
of count, it may be tagged or not tagged In estimating it is
not necessary to have data on every possible splice If data
showing the average cost of common and usual splices is accessible a very close estimate of any splice may be made.

CONSTRUCTION DETAILS

Materials.—The materials principally used in cable splicing are. (1) Paper sleeves for covering the joints in each con-

ductor   The sleeves may or may not be boiled in paraffin before received, but if they are damp, they should be boiled in hot paraffin before using, (2) good commercial paraffin or beeswax for drying the splice, (3) strips of muslin about 2 to 3 ins wide for wrapping the core of the cable and binding ends of a cable after the splice; (4) lead sleeves which shall be pure lead, ⅛-in in thickness

The sizes of sleeve to be used for different size cables are as follows:

For 2 Cables in a Straight Line

No. of prs.	19 Gage Inside Diam. Inches.	Length Inches	22 Gage Inside Diam. Inches	Length. Inches.
15	1	16	1	16
25	1½	16	1½	16
50	2	18	2	18
100	3	18	2½	18
200	3½	20	3	20
300	4½	22	3½	20
400	.		3½	22
600		.	4	26

For 2 Cables Forming a "Y."

No. of prs.	Inside Diam. Inches.	Length Inches	Inside Diam. Inches	Length. Inches.
10	1	16	1	16
25	1½	16	1½	16
50	2½	18	2½	16
100	3½	20	3½	20
200	4½	22	4	20
300	4½	22	4½	22
400		.	4½	22
600	.		4½	26

For splicing intermediate sizes a sleeve for next larger size of cable is used   For splicing cables larger than are given above, sleeves should be used of a length equal to about eight times the outside diameter of the cable and with an inside diameter of about 50 per cent greater than the outside diameter of the cable.

Split sleeves are used in the following cases: (1) Where cables form a double "Y"; (2) where on account of the position or bends in the cables it is impossible to slip a sleeve back and run it up in place again over the splice when it is completed; (3) where in splicing a branch cable into a working cable, only the conductors to be spliced are cut, the other conductors remaining in service and the old sleeve not being used again on making the new splice

Instructions for Making Splices.—If it is possible splices should be finished and soldered up the day they are begun If the weather be dry, the splice may be left open over night, provided it is protected from moisture by having a rubber blanket or other suitable moisture-proof substance wrapped around it However, work on a splice in a moist place should be continued until completed. It is recommended that the splice be boiled out after splicing every 50 pairs, when moisture is likely to get into the splices. When a cable is cut it should be thoroughly dried and its ends sealed tight with solder Just as much care should be taken with a temporary job as a permanent one.

If moisture has entered the end of a cable or if it is even suspected that it has, a short piece of the cable should be cut off and dipped into hot paraffin. If moisture is present it will be detected by a frying noise. The damp part of the cable should be cut away gradually if it can be spared, and each piece tested for moisture If the length of the cable will not allow the damp portion to be cut away, the exposed damp portion shall be boiled out and then a portion of the lead sheath of the cable cut and slipped over it and the new exposed part boiled out. This process, known as slipping, shall be continued until all moisture is expelled. Care must be taken not to tear the insulation in slipping the sheath and all joints shall be closed by the regular wiped joint. When it is found that there is no more moisture present, the cable should be spliced.

Whenever a cable is cut for any purpose and it is necessary to leave the cable end, it should be thoroughly dried and sealed with half and half solder, or the end turned down and securely taped Care should be taken to see that the joint is made just as secure and air tight as if it is to be permanent The following splices namely straight, bridge and straight-bridge are made exactly the same way in both aerial and underground work The same is true for "changing count" and for "cuts "

Straight Splices.—The following operations, in this order, shall be performed in splicing two cables in a straight line

(1) A light indentation shall be made in the sheath of each cable with a clipping knife to mark the point at which the sheath is to be removed This shall be made at a distance from the end of each cable equal to the length of the lead sleeve to be used A portion of the sheath of each cable for about four inches beyond this mark shall be scraped bright and rubbed with tallow or something equally as good to keep the cables clean during splicing The sleeve for a distance of about 4 ins from each end shall be scraped bright and treated in the same manner The tallow acts as a flux in making the joints.

(2) The lead sheath of each cable shall be cut on the marks above described to a sufficient depth to break readily on bending, and the ends removed Care must be used in removing the sheath not to injure the insulation.

(3) The core shall be bound tightly with narrow strips of muslin at the end of the cable sheaths, packing the muslin under the sheath as much as possible so as to prevent the sheath from cutting the insulation on the conductors

(4) As soon as possible after removing the lead sheath from the cable, the cable should be boiled out with hot paraffin until all the moisture is removed The muslin binding should be boiled also Paraffin remaining in the core will form a seal to keep all moisture out during the splicing The temperature of the paraffin shall not be hot enough to scorch or injure the insulation on the wires. In boiling out cables great care must be exercised that the paraffin is not too hot. Paraffin when too hot, not only injures the insulation of the cable conductors, but is dangerous to life If paraffin be heated so hot that white fumes arise it should be allowed to cool before being used The paraffin should never be so hot as to injure rubber insulated wire when immersed in it for one minute. In drying or boiling out a cable with paraffin, always begin at the cable sheath and work towards the center of the splice or end of conductors, so as not to force moisture under the lead sheath The paraffin should be poured on

with a ladle, a pan or the pot being used to catch the paraffin draining off

(5) Next the lead sleeve shall be slipped over one of the cables and pushed back out of the way

(6) If several lengths of a cable are to be spliced at successive places, or in making the first splice on any cable, no testing or tagging is necessary. The splice shall be made without regard to the conductor assignment of the pairs, the red wires being spliced to the red wires and the white wires to the white wires   Pairs in corresponding layers should

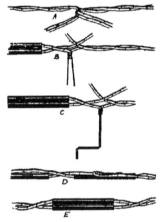

Fig 27 —Sequence of Operations in Making Straight Splices

be spliced together   In all other cases it is necessary to splice according to conductor assignment, and a battery shall be put on one pair of conductors and this be picked up by the splicer at the other end   This pair shall be used as a talking pair and then the other pairs in the cable shall be selected in a similar manner and tagged

When branch splices are made on a working cable, care must be taken not to unnecessarily disarrange the lay of conductors   Particular care must be taken not to nick the wire and not to cut the insulation any more than is necessary   If the insulation be cut it is liable to unwind from the wire, causing crosses in the splice

When a splicer is hunting pairs in a working cable of a central battery exchange, he must connect a condenser in series with his knife and head telephone. This is to prevent him from causing the switchboard lamps of working lines which he touches to flash, thus giving signals to the operator. In all tagged splices the extra pair shall be so tagged when a splice is completed that it may be readily accessible in clearing trouble

(7) The cables shall be lined up straight and securely fastened, the distance between the ends being about three inches less than the length of the lead sleeve.

(8) 'After the cables are lined up in position, the conductors shall be bent out of the way at the sheath and then spliced in the following manner:

(9) Starting at the center or lower back side of the cables, a pair of wires from each cable is brought together with a partial twist, as shown in Fig 27A, thus marking by the bend in the pair the point at which the joint is to be made   Remove the insulation from both wires beyond the twist, care being taken not to scrape the conductors.   Slip on a paper sleeve over each wire of one pair of conductors and push back out of the way to make room for the joint

The wires shall be connected by the ordinary twist joint. The like wires from the two pairs to be spliced shall be brought together at the point marked in the bend, and given two or three twists as shown in Fig. 27B   The two wires are now to be bent as shown and twisted together as if turning a crank.   The ends of the wires shall be cut off so as not to leave the twisted wires shorter than 1 in.   The twist shall be bent down along the insulated wire and the paper sleeve slipped over the joint as shown on Fig 27D.   The completed joint is shown also.

Care should be taken in picking out pairs to be spliced to take the center pairs first and to arrange the outer pairs about them neatly   The wire joints shall be distributed along the length of the splice in order to keep the splice uniform in size and shape

(10) When all the wire joints have been made the splice shall be boiled out again with hot paraffin until all moisture has disappeared. The paraffin should be applied as described before, working towards the center of splice.

(11) The splice (while hot) shall be wrapped with strips of muslin 2 or 3 ins. wide and compressed so as to be admitted into the lead sleeve. The splice must not be compressed so tightly as to cause crosses in it. It will not be necessary to boil the splice out again unless moisture has gotten in during the wrapping with muslin. The muslin must not be boiled in paraffin before wrapping.

(12) The lead sleeve shall be slipped into place before the splice is cool. The ends of the lead sleeve, which should overlap the ends of lead sheath on cables about 1½ ins., shall be beaten down to conform with the cable sheath and a wiped joint carefully made at each end. In making wiped

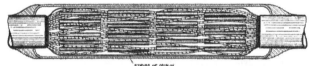

Fig. 28.—Completed Cable Splice.

joints, strips of gummed paper shall be used to limit the joints. All wiped joints should be carefully inspected, using a mirror, when necessary, to detect any imperfections in the seal. Figure 28 shows a completed cable splice.

The method of making a joint in cable splices where the size of the conductor is 16 gage or greater, shall be the same as for the ordinary splice described above, except that in the process of twisting the conductors together, one wire shall be taken in each hand and each wire given five turns around the other.

The method of making a straight splice when three cables form a "Y," is generally the same as for splicing cables in a straight line. The ends of the cables are prepared in the same manner by removing the lead sheath from each cable a distance equal to the length of the lead sleeve to be used. The two cables forming a straight line are secured with the ends of the sheaths a distance apart equal to about 3 ins. less than the length of the sleeve Then the third cable shall be lashed to one of the other cables (depending upon the direction in which the third cable is to be run) with ends of sheaths even, and directly opposite to that on the single cable

The method of making a straight splice when four cables form a double "Y" is generally the same as described above The ends of the cable are prepared in the same manner and the cables lashed together as described in the method of splicing three cables forming a "Y." The cables running in the same direction are lashed together with ends of their lead sheaths opposite each other Spit sleeves shall be used on such splice The seam of the spit sleeve must be carefully soldered, and the ends of the sleeve beaten down to conform to the sheath of the cables and soldered with a wiped joint at both ends After finishing wiping the ends, the seam should be touched up again to make certain that it is tight.

Bridge Splices.—The method of making a bridge splice is the same as for a straight splice except that the wire joints are made by twisting together like wires of three or more pairs of conductors.

Straight-Bridge Splices.—Straight-bridge splices are made in the same way as straight splices except that some wire joints are made by twisting together like wires of three or more pairs of conductors as in making a bridge splice, and some wire joints are made by twisting together like wires of two pairs of conductors as described in straight splicing.

Changing Count.—When in the redistribution of cable it becomes necessary to change the assignment of conductors of a branch cable to other conductors of a main cable it is known as changing count. This splice is generally a tag splice except when the conductors of the branch cable are to be spliced into pairs left "dead"

The joint shall be blown by melting the wiped joint at each end of the lead sleeve and the sleeve cut away or slipped back if in condition to be reused Then a pair of conductors shall be disconnected and joined to a pair of conductors on the new count, this process being continued until the change of count is complete. The general method of making the splice is otherwise the same as for a straight splice, a bridge-splice or a straight-bridge splice, depending on the number of wires composing each joint of conductors.

When the change of count on a branch cable is made into a working cable of which part of the conductors are not to be cut, a split sleeve must be used if the old sleeve is not in condition to be reused.

t is sometimes necessary to lengthen the conductors in order to make the wires of sufficient length for resplicing This is done in the following manner

A pair of conductors in the main cables is cut To one end of each conductor shall be spliced a short piece of bare wire of the same size as the cable conductors This wire should be twisted about the insulation of the wire two or three times to prevent its pulling back on the conductors The second end of the main conductor, the free end of the bare wire and a like conductor of a pair in the branch cable shall be twisted together, in the same manner already described and covered with a paper sleeve, which shall be long enough to cover both ends of the bare wire.

Aerial Cuts.—When a branch cable is cut off of one cable and spliced into another, it is known as a cut In disconnect ing the cable the joint shall·be blown in the same manner as described for changing count. The conductors shall be disconnected by cutting or pulling apart and the joint sealed up as usual The branch cable splice is then made into the new cable, the method of splicing being the same as for a straight, a bridge, or a straight-bridge splice. depending on the number of wires composing each joint of conductors

Splicing Toll Cable Into Cable Terminating in a Loading Coil or Pot.—The cost data on splicing toll cable into cable terminating in a loading pot are based on splicing 120-pair, 14 gage or 120-pair, 16 gage into a 120-pair, 18 gage cable terminating in a loading pot—60 pair being taken from each of two 120-pair one-half 14 gage and one-half 16 gage toll cables, and splicing the balance (60 pairs from each toll cable) straight through. The 14 gage part of the toll cable is spliced into a cable terminating in a loading pot about every 7,000 ft , and the 16 gage part, about every 9,000 feet

Each cable must first be tested for crosses, grounds and insulation as is the case in splicing all toll cable In splicing toll cable into cable terminating in a loading pot the method will be as follows:

The sheaths of cables are to be removed in the same manner as described for three cable forming a Y, except that one of the toll cables shall have its sheath removed for a distance equal to about twice the length of the sleeve to be used. The cable terminating in the loading pot shall be placed on top of the toll cable which has had its sheath removed for a distance equal to double that of the other toll cable, and shall be lashed together with ends of sheaths even with each other   The single toll cable shall be secured in a position directly opposite to the other two cables with ends of sheaths a distance apart equal to about 3 ins less than the length of sleeve. The conductors shall then be spliced in the same manner as for any straight splice except in the following particulars The conductors of the toll cable which is lashed to the cable terminating in the loading pot shall be looped up so as to bring them in position for splicing into the cable which terminates in the loading pot

In the process of twisting the conductors together one wire shall be taken in each hand and each wire given five turns around the other

Where only part of each toll cable is to be spliced into cable terminating in a loading pot and the balance spliced straight through, the method of making the splice is the same as described above except in the following particulars: The toll cable which is lashed to the cable terminating in the loading pot shall have the conductors which are to be spliced straight through, cut off at a distance from the end of the sheath equal to the length of the sleeve to be used and the balance of the conductors shall be looped up as described before.   The conductors of each toll cable which are to be spliced straight through, shall be joined together at the bottom of the splice in the manner described for straight splicing.

Potheads for Terminating Aerial Cables.—Aerial cables terminate in a standard pothead on protected terminal boxes. The pothead being attached to the terminal boxes when re-

ceived from the manufacturer very few of these splices are
made by splicing gangs. Although no data on the cost of
these splices are on hand, they are explained on account of being work which cable splicers are sometimes required to per-
form.

In making aerial potheads only No. 22 gage okonite, twisted
pair wires shall be spliced to paper insulated lead covered
cables. The twisted wires are to have an insulation of 7/64
in. thick and one of each pair of wires to have a light cover
to be used as a tracer. The colors of the okonite wire and
wires of cable to be spliced to match, and the splice staggered
over a distance. The joints of conductors are to be covered

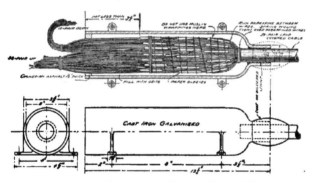

Fig. 29.—A 50-Pr. Pothead for Protected Terminal Box.

by paper sleeves. When the splice is finished, it is boiled out
with hot paraffin, beginning at the lead sheath ends and
working towards the center of the splice, in order to expel the
moisture. Then the splice shall be bound with hot muslin
just previously having been boiled out in hot paraffin, the
muslin strip to be about ¾-in. wide. After the splice is
tightly wrapped with the muslin strip, it is bound up with
waxed linen twine and the pothead castings pulled over same.
Care must be taken to see that none of the muslin or twine
stick above the line shown on drawing of pothead, Fig. 29,
and that no fibrous material is in the upper layer of the compound. The pothead and cable are joined by a cast or sol-

dered joint. This must be absolutely tight and carefully inspected.

After arranging the splice in the pothead casting and arranging the okonite wires at the top of the casting so as not
to be in contact with each other, the pothead casting shall be
filled with ozite compound, or its equivalent, to within ½ in
of its top As the compound settles more shall be added to
keep it to height mentioned The pothead casting should be
warmed to a temperature of 200° F before filling same and
while the ozite compound is settling should be kept at a temperature of about 140° F. The ozite compound must be a
perfect insulator, and must not shrink on cooling, or crack
at a temperature of 10° below zero The ozite compound, or
its equivalent, must not flow under its own weight at a temperature lower than 60° F , and it must be a perfect fluid at
220° F. The pothead is then filled to the top with cimmerian
asphalt, or its equivalent, which seals the ozite, and prevents
it from flowing in hot weather. This compound must be flexible at a temperature of zero deg Fahrenheit and melting
point of 200° F.

When the upper ends of the okonite wires are to be connected to brass studs in the terminal boxes, both studs and
ends of wire must have been previously tinned by using acid
or salt flux, which has been neutralized with wood alcohol
The wires can be soldered to terminal stud with plain or resin
flux solder.

**Potheads for Connecting Main Cable to Distributing Rack
Cables.**—Potheads for connecting main cable to distributing
rack cables are always made by a splicing gang It is never
a tag splice, but is tested to find extra pairs The distributing
rack cable shall be silk and cotton insulated. lead covered,
either 20-pr or 40-pr cable The method of making a pothead shall be as follows

The main cable shall be prepared for splicing in the same .
manner as for a straight splice, with the exception of the boiling out process. In boiling the cable out, a mixture of about
one-half paraffin and one-half beeswax shall be used The
ends of the silk and cotton distributing rack cables shall be
boiled out with the same mixture. When this mixture is used,

the paper insulation is not so likely to crack, and it will not be necessary to carry two pots for boiling and during splicing—the paraffin for the paper insulated cable and the beeswax for the distributing rack cable. The ends of all the cables to be spliced will be prepared in the same manner.

A lead sleeve of the proper size shall be slipped over the main cable and the distributing rack cables passed through the small wood disc. This disc is shown in Fig. 30, and is drilled in each case, to correspond with the number of distributing rack cables to be spliced. The holes to be just large enough to admit the cables and the disc to fit snugly inside

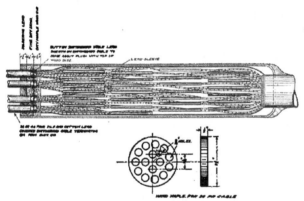

Fig. 30.—Method of Splicing Underground and Distributing Rack Cable.

the lead sleeve. The cables are then lined up as straight as possible and the splicing done the same as for a straight cable splice. The wood disc which had been previously run up on the distributing rack cables shall now be slipped down just so that the lead sheath on the distributing rack cables shall come flush with the bottom of the disc and the lead sleeve is then run up so as to bring the top of the disc about 1 in. below the top of the lead sleeve. The lead sleeve is then wiped to the main cable as usual.

Upon the top of the wood disc shall be placed a layer of fine dry sand one-half of an inch thick. Upon the top of this layer of sand shall be placed a layer of wiping solder in the proportions of 1 part tin to 2 parts lead, flush with the top of the lead sleeve Care should be taken to see that the layer of lead is soldered perfectly tight about the lead sheath of each cable and the lead sleeve covering the splice When this is done in a neat and mechanical manner the pothead will be finished

Connecting Cables to Distributing Rack.—From the pothead the distributing rack cables are carried either in a rack or runway or vertically upward to the distributing rack, the method depending upon the relative position of the pothead rack below and the distributing rack above. The pothead is always made after the cables are distributed on the rack.

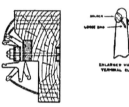

Fig 31—Method of Soldering Switchboard Cable Conductor to Terminal
Blocks on Main Distributing Frames

The rack ends of the distributing rack cables are prepared as follows: The lead sheath is removed from the ends of the cables for a distance great enough to allow the conductors to fan out properly upon the distributing block The cable ends are boiled out in beeswax until the moisture is removed in the same manner as described for boiling out process in splicing cables. At the butt of the lead sheath, waxed muslin will be crowded under the sheath as closely as possible and the butt of the cables wrapped tightly with waxed lacing twine. The twine shall extend about $\frac{1}{2}$-in back on the lead sheathing and about $\frac{1}{2}$-in. onto the core of the cables Then the core of the cable shall be fanned out upon the distributing block and the wire neatly laced in place with waxed lacing twine

After the cable has been prepared for fanning out the conductors shall be passed through holes in the terminal block in line with the clips to which they are to be soldered. The wires shall be pulled tight enough to take out any slack and cut off so as to project about a ¼ in. beyond the end of the clip to which it is to be soldered. The insulation shall then be cut back about ⅜ in., and the wire brightened by scraping. The end of the wire shall then be given one-half a turn around the clip in the neck and soldered with one drop of flux solder. The end of the wire shall not be soldered to the clip but left projecting about 1/32 in. in order to afford plier hold in case of removal. The method above described is illustrated in Fig. 31.

The distributing rack cables shall then be taken up vertically into the center of the distributing rack and as close as possible to the arm upon which it is to be laced. The cables shall be laced tightly to the horizontal arms of the distributing rack

Fig. 32.—View Showing Cable Ready for Splicing.   Fig. 33.—View Showing Completed Cable Splice.

with waxed lacing twine. When the distributing rack cables have to cross arms or part of the frame at right angles and in such a manner as to rest on them the frame shall be wrapped with at least two layers of adhesive tape wherever contact with the cable is made to prevent the grounding of the conductors should the sheath be injured. When the cables are carried above the distributing rack in a rack or runway, they will distribute down vertically into the center of the distributing rack, as close as possible to the block upon which they are to be fastened.

General Order of Making Splices.—Splicing a cable into a working cable or a cable connected with the distributing rack or the splicing together of two cables which are connected with counts, is generally a final splice and it is necessary to test and tag all the cables spliced on account of subsidiary splices being made prior to this splice It is unnecessary in splicing the leg of a terminal box or in splicing a lateral cable into a main cable to tag the first splice when the main cable has not been connected or spliced to any other cable

After the several lengths of the main cable have been spliced a leg of a terminal box or a branch cable—as the case may be—is spliced into the main cable It is generally best first to splice in the terminal box or branch cable containing the largest number of pairs, as this splice would otherwise require the most tagging The balance of the splices are then made, each splice being tested and tagged The amount of pairs tagged depends on the size of the branch cable or terminal box, and the number of pairs tested depends on the size of the cables

Form 19
Data Secured by
STRAIGHT SPLICE
(Aerial)

Diagram of Splice
Size of Cables   Location   Order No
No of Prs Spliced Foreman   Date   190

No of Splices	Team-ing	Fram-ing	Tagg-ing & Test-ing	Splic-ing	Wip-ing Joints	Sup and Exp	Total Cost	Extra Hours Worked	Total Hours Worked	Re-marks

NOTE — Framing" includes the cost of erecting the platform, cutting the sheath and preparing the cables for splicing ' Splicing" includes joining the conductors, boiling out, wrapping and getting in shape to put on lead sleeve "Wiping Joints" includes putting lead sleeve in place and wiping joints

Form 20
Data Secured by
BRIDGE SPLICE
(Aerial)

Diagram of Splice
Size of Cables   Location   Order No
No of Prs Spliced Foreman   Date   190

No of Splices	Team-ing	Fram-ing	Tagg-ing & Test-ing	Splic-ing	Wip-ing Joints	Sup and Exp	Total Cost	Extra Hours Worked	Total Hours Worked	Re-marks

NOTE —Where a splice is made on a working cable the blowing of the joint is included in "Framing" A notation should be made under ' Remarks" if the splice is made on a working cable

Form 21
Data Secured by
STRAIGHT-BRIDGE SPLICE
(Aerial)

Diagram of Splice
Size of Cables {Straight Location   Date   Order No
No of Prs Spliced {Bridged Foreman   190

No of Splices	Team-ing	Fram-ing	Tagg-ing & Test-ing	Splic-ing	Wip-ing Joints	Sup and Exp	Total Cost	Extra Hours Worked	Total Hours Worked	Re-marks

Form 22
Data Secured by
CHANGING COUNT.
(Aerial)

Diagram of Splice
Size of Cables {Straight Location   Date   Order No
No of Prs Spliced {Bridged Foreman   .   190

No of Splices	Team-ing	Fram-ing	Tagg-ing & Test-ing	Splic-ing	Wip-ing Joints	Sup and Exp	Total Cost	Extra Hours Worked	Total Hours Worked	Re-marks

NOTE — Framing" includes the cost of blowing the joint, erecting the platform and preparing cables for splicing

Form 23
Data Secured by
CUTS.
(Aerial)

Diagram of Splice
Size of Cables {Straight Location   Date   Order No
No of Prs Spliced {Bridged Foreman   190

No of Splices	Team-ing	Fram-ing	Tagg-ing & Test-ing	Splic-ing	Wip-ing Joints	Sup and Exp	Total Cost	Extra Hours Worked	Total Hours Worked	Re-marks

NOTE — 'Framing" includes blowing the joint and disconnecting wires, erecting platform and preparing cables for new splice.

Form 24
Data Secured by
STRAIGHT SPLICE
(Underground)

Diagram of Splice
Size of Cables   Location   Date   Order No
No of Prs Spliced   Foreman   190

No of Splices	Team-ing	Pump-ing	Fram-ing	Test-ing & Tagg-ing	Splic-ing	Wip-ing J'nts	Sup and Exp	Total Cost	Extra Hours Worked	Total Hours Worked	Re-marks

NOTE—Splicing of loading pot cables and toll cable are reported on this form

Form 25
Data Secured by
BRIDGE SPLICE
(Underground)

Diagram of Splice
Size of Cables   Location
No of Prs Spliced   Foreman
        Order No
        Date   190

No of Splices	Team-ing	Pump-ing	Fram-ing	Test-ing & Tagg-ing	Splic-ing	Wip-ing J'nts	Sup and Exp	Total Cost	Extra Hours Worked	Total Hours Worked	Re-marks

Form 26
Data Secured by
STRAIGHT-BRIDGE SPLICE
(Underground)

Diagram of Splice
Size of Cables {Straight   Location
No of Prs Spliced {Bridged   Foreman
        Order No
        Date   190

No of Splices	Team-ing	Pump-ing	Fram-ing	Test-ing & Tagg-ing	Splic-ing	Wip-ing J'nts	Sup and Exp	Total Cost	Extra Hours Worked	Total Hours Worked	Re-marks

Form 27
Data Secured by
CHANGING COUNT
(Underground)

Diagram of Splice
Size of Cables {Straight   Location
No of Prs Spliced {Bridged   Foreman
        Order No
        Date   190

No of Splices	Team-ing	Pump-ing	Fram-ing	Test-ing & Tagg-ing	Splic-ing	Wip-ing J'nts	Sup and Exp	Total Cost	Extra Hours Worked	Total Hours Worked	Re-marks

Form 28
Data Secured by
CUTS
(Underground)

Diagram of Splice
Size of Cables {Straight   Locat on
No of Prs Spliced {Bridged   Foreman
        Order No
        Date   190

No of Splices	Team-ing	Pump-ing	Fram-ing	Test-ing & Tagg-ing	Splic-ing	Wip-ing J'nts	Sup and Exp	Total Cost	Extra Hours Worked	Total Hours Worked	Re-marks

colspan="10"	**Form 29** Data Secured by POTHEAD

Diagram of Splice   Location   Order No
Size of Cables   Location   Date   190
No of Prs Spliced   Foreman

No of Splices	Fram-ing	Test-ing & Tagg-ing	Splic-ing	Wip-ing Joints	Sup and Exp	Total Cost	Extra Hours Worked	Total Hours Worked	Remarks

NOTE —There is no column for teaming on this form as this class of work is done in telephone exchanges and the material is hauled by the line gang

	**Form 30** Data Secured by CONNECTING CABLE TO DISTRIBUTING RACK

No Pairs Connected   Location   Order No
Size of Cable   Foreman   Date   190

Placing Cable Bet Pothead and Rack	Fram-ing	Distribut-ing Wires on Rack and Con-necting to Term Blocks	Lac-ing	Solder-ing Wires to Term Blocks	Sup and Exⁿ	Total Cost	Extra Hours Worked	Total Hours Worked	Remarks

NOTE —No column for teaming is put on this form as this class of work is done in telephone exchanges and the material is always hauled and stored on the premises by the line gang "Framing" includes stripping armour, boiling out with beeswax and preparing cable for frame "Lacing" includes lacing wires together, lacing cables to rack and to runway

FORMS FOR REPORTING COSTS.

The forms for reporting the cost of cable splicing are shown in Forms 19 to 30 Very little explanation of these forms is necessary as the divisions compare with the actual division of splicing already described. On most of these forms spaces for entering the number of pairs tested and the number of pairs tagged will be found. Except in the case of splicing into working cable, no separation is made in the cost data between the same kind and size of tagged splices whether more or less pairs are tested and tagged, as they average about the same in either case On account of it being necessary to pump out some vaults before splicing, a special column for recording the cost of pumping will be found on the forms for underground cable splices. Unlike the forms used for line construction and cable work, the forms used for cable splicing do not include "labor in hauling" with "teaming" on account of practically no labor being expended in hauling material.

Method of Figuring Cable Splicing Costs.—The method of figuring cable splicing costs is the same as described for Line Construction and Cable Work except that board is included in "Supervision and Expense." This is done on account of board being paid in addition to the regular wages only when the splicers are working away from their station. Splicers are required to return to their station each day when possible. In this case board is allowed for one meal only.

CABLE SPLICING COST DATA.

Cable splicing costs, Tables XXXVIII to LXII, are based on the following rate of wages:

	Per 8-hour day.
Head splicers	$3.40 to $3 70
Splicers	3.00 to 3.20
Helpers	1 75 to 2.00
Rigs (usually single)..	2 50 to 3 00

Time and one-half is paid for overtime. There being practically no difference between the cost of splicing 19 gage and 22 gage cables they are not separated in the following cost data. The cost of making several splices of the same kind and size have been found to vary very little. Except when the splicing is done by splicers who have worked all night, usually splices of the same kind and size will not vary more than 10 per cent.

The cost of splicing into working cable is kept separate on account of being more expensive than splicing into other cable. The difference is caused by it being necessary to test and tag all cables spliced, the care used to prevent unnecessary interruption of service and also because the splice is often worked on after regular hours for which splicers are paid time and one-half.

The cost of blowing the joint of a working cable and the cost of cutting the sheath off of cables in preparing for a splice, are about equal.

In making a change of count or a cut it is often necessary to lengthen the conductors by splicing on a piece of wire of the same gage This adds considerably to the cost of splicing conductors together.

TABLE XXXVIII—COST OF STRAIGHT SPLICES, AERIAL, NOT TAGGED

Number and Size of Cables Spliced—	Team'g	Fram'g	Splic'g	Wiping Joints	Supervision and Exp'se	Aver Cost per Splice
2-15 Pr	$0 34	$0 42	$0 35	$0 50	$0 49	$2 10
2-25 Pr	0 31	0 51	0 52	0 60	0 37	2 31
2-50 Pr .. .	0 58	0 57	0 82	0 57	0 60	3 14
2-100 Pr	0 62	0 76	1 44	0 62	1 02	4 46
2-200 Pr	0 77	0 97	3 08	0.70	1 50	7 02
1-15 Pr into 1-25 Pr, 10 Prs Left Dead	0 29	0 47	0 37	0 56	0 50	2 19
1-15 Pr into 1-50 Pr, 35 Prs Left Dead	0 34	0 44	0 39	0 52	0 53	2 22
1-25 Pr into 1-50 Pr, 25 Prs Left Dead	0 41	0 42	0 58	0 54	0 49	2 44
1-50 Pr into 1-100 Pr, 50 Prs Left Dead	0 62	0 64	0 87	0 61	0 64	3 38
1-15 Pr and 1-25 Pr into 1-50 Pr, 10 Pr Left Dead	0 55	0 63	0.85	0 64	0 58	3 25
2-15 Pr into 1-50 Pr, 20 Prs Left Dead	0 47	0 59	0 66	0 62	0 50	2 84
2-25 Pr into 1-50 Pr	0 61	0 66	0.90	0 59	0 70	3 46

Note—A straight splice is rarely made on a working cable When an extension is necessary it is usually made by pulling in a new cable and bridging it into a main cable In the above data each section of cable is referred to as one cable

TABLE XXXIX—COST OF STRAIGHT SPLICES, AERIAL, TAGGED

Number and Size of Cables spliced	Teaming.	Framing	Testing and Tagging	Splicing.	Wiping Joints	Supervision and Expense	Av'ge Cost per Splice
2-15 Pr	$0 29	$0 46	$0 44	$0 36	$0 44	$0 62	$2 61
2-25 Pr	0 36	0 44	0 58	0 49	0 46	0 64	2 97
2-50 Pr .	0 59	0 55	1 02	0 77	0 50	0.70	4 13
2-100 Pr	0 66	0 78	1 66	1 49	0 60	1 11	6 30
1-15 Pr into 1-25 Pr, 10 Prs Left Dead	0 31	0 48	0 48	0 40	0 50	0 60	2 77
1-25 Pr into 1-50 Pr, 25 Prs Left Dead	0 39	0 50	0 69	0 54	0 45	0 64	3 21
1-50 Pr into 1-100 Pr, 50 Prs Left Dead	0 60	0 60	1 08	0 82	0 60	0 73	4 43
1-15 Pr and 1-25 Pr into 1-50 Pr, 10 Prs. Left Dead	0 51	0 63	0 96	0 79	0 66	0 70	4 25
2-15 Pr into 1-50 Pr, 20 Prs Left Dead	0 49	0 58	0 79	0 62	0 65	0 59	3 72

TABLE XL—COST OF STRAIGHT SPLICES, UNDERGROUND

(Cost of splicing 60 prs from each of two 120 pr ½-14 gage and ½-16 gage toll cables into a 120 pr 18 gage cable terminating in a loading pot, and splicing the balance straight through)

Part of Cable Spliced Straight Through	Teaming	Pumping	Framing	Testing	Splicing	Wiping Joints	Supervision and Expense	Average Cost per Splice
14 Gage	$1 04	$0 62	$1 68	$1 80	$8 69	$1 82	$6 47	$22 12
16 Gage	1 01	0 64	1 64	1 86	8 88	1 79	6 52	22 34

Note—This class of work is generally done in the country The supervision of a head splicer and board for the gang make the cost of "Supervision and Expense" high

TABLE XLI—COST OF STRAIGHT SPLICES, UNDERGROUND, NOT TAGGED.

Number and Size of Cables Spliced	Team- ing	Pump- ing	Fram- ing	Splic- ing	Wiping Joints	Supervision and Expense	Av'ge Cost per Splice
2-50 Pr . . .	$0 46	$0 53	$0 49	$0 80	$0 45	$0 60	$3 33
2-100 Pr . .	0 59	0 56	0 60	1 42	0 49	0 86	4 52
2-200 Pr . .	0.59	0 58	0 87	2 86	0 57	1 38	6 85
2-300 Pr	0 61	0 55	0 91	3 67	0 61	1 59	8 04
1-25 Pr into 1-50 Pr, 25 Prs Left Dead	0 40	0 42	0 44	0 65	0 42	0.54	2 87
1-50 Pr into 1-100 Pr, 50 Prs Left Dead	0 52	0 51	0 52	0 84	0 49	0 72	3 60
1-100 Pr into 1-200 Pr, 100 Prs Left Dead	0 58	0 57	0 76	1 51	0 54	0.94	4 90

TABLE XLII—COST OF STRAIGHT SPLICES, UNDERGROUND, TAGGED

Number and Size of Cables Spliced	Team- ing	Pump- ing	Fram- ing	Testing and Tag- ging	Splic- ing	Wiping Joints	Supervision and Ex- pense	Av'ge Cost per Splice
2-50 Pr .	$0 42	$0 49	$0 51	$0 98	$0 78	$0 42	$0 64	$4 24
2-100 Pr	0 56	0 54	0 62	1 58	1 37	0 51	1 11	6 29
2-200 Pr	0 59	0 58	0 85	2 80	2 78	0 60	1 72	9 92
2-300 Pr	0 60	0 57	0 89	4 06	3 69	0 62	2 06	12 49
2-150 Pr 16 Gauge Toll Cable	0 96	0 61	0 92	1 56	2 37	0 63	3 17	10 22
2-120 Pr ½-14 and ½-15 Ga Toll Cable	0 94	0 60	0 91	1 39	1 96	0 66	2 89	9 35
1-50 Pr into 1-100 Pr, 50 Prs Left Dead	0 49	0 50	-0 54	1 07	0 84	0 59	0 71	4 74
2-50 Pr into 1-100 Pr	0 57	0 54	0 83	1 62	1 44	0 67	1 16	6 83

Note—Toll cable is always tested for crosses, grounds and insulation, but not tagged Teaming and supervision and expense are higher for toll cable than for other cable on account of the work being done in the country

TABLE XLIII—COST OF BRIDGE SPLICES, AERIAL, NOT TAGGED

Number and Size of Cables Spliced	Teaming	Framing	Splicing	Wiping Joints	Supervision and Expense	Average Cost per Splice
3-15 Pr	$0 50	$0 61	$0 52	$0 64	$0 57	$2 84
3-25 Pr	0 62	0 65	0 87	0 62	0 70	3 46
3-50 Pr	0 64	0 63	1 61	0 68	0 81	4 37

TABLE XLIV—COST OF BRIDGE SPLICES, AERIAL, TAGGED

Number and Size of Cables Spliced	Teaming	Framing	Testing and Tagging.	Splicing	Wiping Joints	Supervision and Expense	Average Cost per Splice
3-15 Pr	$0 53	$0 59	$0 74	$0 54	$0 65	$0 64	$3 69
3-25 Pr	0 59	0 66	0 98	0 84	0 68	0 76	4 51
3-50 Pr	0 66	0 69	1 71	1 58	0 71	1 06	6 41

TABLE XLV—COST OF BRIDGE SPLICES, AERIAL, ONTO WORKING CABLE

Number and Size of Cables Spliced	Teaming	Framing	Testing and Tagging	Splicing	Wiping Joints	Supervision and Expense	Average Cost per Splice
1-15 Pr Bridged onto a Splice of 2-15 Pr	$0 64	$0 66	$0 78	$0 45	$0 68	$0 64	$3 85
1-25 Pr Bridged onto a Splice of 2-25 Pr	0 68	0 69	1 04	0 63	0 66	0 72	4 42
1-50 Pr Bridged onto a Splice of 2-50 Pr	0 72	0 70	2 32	1 08	0 74	1 30	6 86
1-100 Pr Bridged onto a Splice of 2-100 Pr	0 78	0 77	3 96	2 04	0 81	1 76	10.12

TABLE XLVI —COST OF BRIDGE SPLICES, UNDERGROUND, NOT TAGGED.

Number and Size of Cables Spliced	Teaming	Pumping	Framing	Splicing	Wiping Joints	Supervision and Expense	Average Cost per Splice
3-50 Pr	$0 44	$0 50	$0 61	$1 56	$0 65	$0 78	$4 54
3-100 Pr ..	0 53	0 47	0 76	2 78	0 72	1 18	6 44
3-200 Pr .	0 58	0 53	0 91	5 37	0 89	1.74	10 02

TABLE XLVII —COST OF BRIDGE SPLICES, UNDERGROUND, TAGGED.

Number and Size of Cables Spliced	Teaming	Pumping	Framing	Testing and Tagging	Splicing	Wiping Joints	Supervision and Expense	Average Cost per Splice
3-50 Pr	$0 46	$0 48	$0 62	$1 52	$1 53	$0 66	$1 27	$6 54
3-100 Pr	0 42	0 52	0 74	2 39	2 52	0 70	1 58	8 87
3-200 Pr. . .	0 63	0 52	0 87	3 72	4 39	0 82	2 02	13 47

TABLE XLVIII —COST OF BRIDGE SPLICES, UNDERGROUND, ONTO WORKING CABLE

Number and Size of Cables Spliced	Teaming	Pumping	Framing	Testing and Tagging	Splicing	Wiping Joints	Supervision and Expense	Average Cost per Splice
1-50 Pr Bridged onto a Splice of 2-50 Pr	$0 69	$0 53	$0 68	$2 26	$0 97	$0 76	$1 27	$7 16
1-100 Pr Bridged onto a Splice of 2-100 Pr	0 75	0 49	0 73	3 79	1 82	0 82	1 83	10 23
1-200 Pr Bridged onto a Splice of 2-200 Pr	0 69	0 61	0 86	5 82	3 68	0 81	2 26	14 73

TABLE XLIX —COST OF STRAIGHT-BRIDGE SPLICES, AERIAL, NOT TAGGED

Number and size of Branch Cables Spliced into Main Cables	Number and Size of Main Cables Spliced	Teaming	Framing	Splicing	Wiping Joints	Supervision and Expense	Av'ge Cost per Splice
1-15 Pr	1-25 Pr	$0 48	$0 48	$0 49	$0 67	$0 52	$2 64
1-15 Pr	2-25 Pr	0 51	0 52	0 63	0 65	0 59	2 90
1-15 Pr	2-50 Pr	0 54	0 59	1 17	0 63	0 63	3 56
1-15 Pr	2-100 Pr	0 63	0 72	1 82	0 68	1 05	4 90
1-25 Pr	2-50 Pr	0 57	0 64	1 31	0 66	0 70	3 88
1-25 Pr	2-100 Pr	0 66	0 75	1 96	0 73	1 09	5 19
1-50 Pr	2-100 Pr	0 70	0 72	2 24	0 76	1 16	5 58

TABLE L —COST OF STRAIGHT-BRIDGE SPLICES, AERIAL, TAGGED.

No and size of Branch Cables Spliced into Main Cables	Number and Size of Main Cables Spliced	Teaming	Framing	Testing and Tagging	Splicing	Wiping Joints	Supervision and Expense	Av'ge Cost per Splice
1-15 Pr	2-25 Pr	$0 51	$0 54	$0 68	$0 66	$0 57	$0 64	$3 60
1-15 Pr	2-50 Pr	0 44	0 54	1 24	0 95	0 61	0 90	4 68
1-15 Pr	2-100 Pr	0 58	0 59	1 95	1 64	0 67	1 24	6 67
1-25 Pr	2-50 Pr	0 56	0 57	1 33	1 10	0 63	1 13	5 32
1-25 Pr.	2-100 Pr	0 54	0 64	2 07	1 78	0 75	1 32	7 10
1-50 Pr.	2-100 Pr	0 64	0 67	2 29	1 97	0 79	1 41	7 77
2-15 Pr	2-50 Pr	0 59	0 69	1 46	1 33	0 88	1 19	6 14
2-15 Pr	2-100 Pr	0 63	0 73	2 10	1 85	0 90	1 37	7 58
2-25 Pr	2-100 Pr	0 62	0 74	2 40	2 10	0 85	1 46	8 17
1-50 Pr	2-100 Pr	0 69	0 81	2 57	2 31	0 89	1 65	8 92

TABLE LI—COST OF STRAIGHT-BRIDGE SPLICES, AERIAL, ONTO WORKING CABLE

No and Size of Branch Cables Spliced into Main Cable.	Size of Main Cable	Team-ing	Fram-ing	Testing and Tag-ging	Splic-ing	Wiping Joints.	Supervision and Expense	Av'ge Cost per Splice
1-15 Pr.	25 Pr	$0 58	$0 56	$0 90	$0 44	$0 69	$0 66	$3 83
1-15 Pr.	50 Pr	0 61	0 50	1 43	0 63	0 72	0 96	4 85
1-15 Pr	100 Pr	0 67	0 62	2 30	0 74	0 70	1 19	6 22
1-25 Pr	50 Pr	0 64	0 59	1 52	0 76	0 74	1 02	5 27
1-25 Pr	100 Pr	0 68	0 62	2 69	0 86	0 79	1 26	6 90
1-50 Pr	100 Pr	0 78	0 70	3 06	1.25	0 84	1 40	8 03

TABLE LII—COST OF STRAIGHT-BRIDGE SPLICES, UNDERGROUND, NOT TAGGED.

No and Size of Branch Cables Spliced into Main Cables	Number and Size of Main Cables Spliced	Team-ing	Pump-ing	Fram-ing	Splic-ing	Wiping Joints.	Supervision and Expense	Av'ge Cost per Splice
1-25 Pr	2-50 Pr	$0 38	$0 46	$0 56	$1 24	$0 62	$0 74	$4.00
1-25 Pr	2-100 Pr.	0 52	0 51	0 70	1 83	0 71	1 06	5 33
1-25 Pr	2-200 Pr	0 46	0 47	0 78	3 32	0 78	1 48	7 29
1-50 Pr	2-100 Pr	0 54	0 54	0 71	2 10	0 72	1 14	5 75
1-50 Pr	2-200 Pr.	0 47	0 59	0 82	3 58	0 84	1 60	7 90
1-50 Pr	2-300 Pr	0 60	0 52	0 91	5 95	0 88	1 68	10 54
1-100 Pr	2-200 Pr	0 64	0 57	0 84	4 03	0 82	1 61	8 51
1-100 Pr	2-300 Pr	0 57	0 55	0 98	6 21	0 91	1 74	10 96
1-200 Pr	2-300 Pr	0,59	0 61	1 06	6 86	0 84	2 05	12 01

TABLE LIII—COST OF STRAIGHT-BRIDGE SPLICES, UNDERGROUND, TAGGED.

No and Size of Branch Cables Spliced into Main Cables.	Number and Size of Main Cables Spliced.	Team-ing	Pump-ing	Fram-ing	Testing and Tagging	Splic-ing	Wiping Joints	Supervision and Expense	Av'ge Cost per Splice
1-25 Pr	2-50 Pr	$0 41	$0 49	$0 59	$1 13	$1 03	$0 56	$1 02	$5 23
1-25 Pr	2-100 Pr	0 47	0 53	0 68	2 01	1 69	0 64	1 30	7 32
1-25 Pr	2-200 Pr	0 51	0 51	0 79	3 16	2 89	0 67	1 71	10 24
1-50 Pr	2-100 Pr	0 50	0 47	0 73	2 18	1 82	0 62	1 36	7 68
1-50 Pr	2-200 Pr	0 60	0 54	0 84	3 37	3 16	0 69	1 79	10 99
1-50 Pr	2-300 Pr	0 57	0 62	0 94	4 18	4 99	0 78	2 28	14 36
1-100 Pr	2-200 Pr	0 54	0 56	0 83	3 67	3 61	0 72	1 84	11 77
1-100 Pr	2-300 Pr	0 62	0 61	1 01	4 49	5 48	0 66	2 41	15 28
1-200 Pr	2-300 Pr	0 59	0 64	0 99	4.87	6 49	0 71	2 63	16 92
1-25 Pr, 1-50 Pr	2-100 Pr	0 53	0 59	0 82	2 39	2 16	0 83	1 50	8 82
1-25 Pr, 1-50 Pr	2-200 Pr	0 56	0 59	1 03	3 48	3 47	0 91	1 87	11 91
2-25 Pr, 2-50 Pr	2-100 Pr	0 49	0 56	0 75	2 26	1 96	0 87	1 41	8 30
2-50 Pr, 1-50 Pr	2-200 Pr	0 53	0 61	0 97	3 62	3 76	0 91	1 92	12 32
1-50 Pr, 1-100 Pr	2-200 Pr	0 61	0 66	1 14	4 04	4 54	0 89	2 20	14 03
1-50 Pr, 1-100 Pr	2-300 Pr	0 64	0 64	1 16	4 68	5 88	0 94	2 68	16 62
1-50 Pr, 2-100 Pr, 1-25 Pr	2-300 Pr	0 69	0 68	1 37	5 15	6 86	1 17	2 91	18 83
1-25 Pr, 1-50 Pr, 1-100 Pr	2-200 Pr	0.62	0.73	1.26	3.90	4 07	1 10	2 18	13 86

TABLE LIV—Cost of Straight-Bridge Splices, Underground, Onto Working Cables

No. and Size of Branch Cables Spliced into Main Cable	Size of Main Cable	Team-ing	Pump-ing	Fram-ing	Testing and Tagging	Splic-ing	Wiping Joints	Supervision and Expense	Av'ge Cost per Splice
1-25 Pr	50 Pr	$0 46	$0 52	$0 53	$1 36	$0 72	$0 64	$1 08	$5 31
1-25 Pr	100 Pr	0 51	0 47	0 57	2 74	0 80	0 63	1 29	7 01
1-25 Pr	200 Pr	0 47	0 50	0 64	3 74	0 87	0 71	1 44	8 37
1-50 Pr	100 Pr	0 44	0 53	0 55	3 06	1 18	0 61	1 39	7 76
1-50 Pr	200 Pr	0 52	0 49	0 67	4 19	1 23	0 68	1 57	9 35
1-50 Pr	300 Pr	0 54	0 61	0 69	5 30	1 31	0 79	1 80	11 04
1-100 Pr	200 Pr	0 51	0 58	0 74	4 70	2 06	0 80	1 76	11 15
1-100 Pr.	300 Pr	0 62	0 51	0 72	5 82	2 14	0 74	1 99	12 54
1-200 Pr	300 Pr	0 57	0 67	0 88	7 06	3 70	0 82	2 52	16 02
1-25 Pr } 1-50 Pr } 2-50 Pr }	200 Pr	0 54	0 62	0 89	4 33	1 84	0 96	1 63	10 81
1-25 Pr } 1-50 Pr }	200 Pr	0 63	0 53	1 01	4 17	2 16	1 01	1 91	11 42
1-50 Pr	300 Pr	0 58	0 59	0 96	5 51	1 97	0 97	2 02	12 60

Note—All the data on straight-bridge splices, both aerial and underground, is based on splicing branch cables on separate counts. It makes little difference in the cost, however, whether the branches are spliced on the same or separate counts In all the data on straight-bridge splices the two sections of the continuous cable, when not already spliced, are entered in the column, "Number and Size of Main Cables Spliced," as 2-25 Pr, 2-50 Pr, etc. When the cable is already spliced, as in the data under "Working Cables," it is referred to as 25 Pr, 50 Pr, etc.

TABLE LV—Cost of Changing Counts, Aerial, Not Tagged

No. and Size of Branch Cables	Size of Main Cable	No. of Pairs Spliced Straight.	No. of Pairs Bridged.	Team-ing	Fram-ing	Splic-ing	Wiping Joints.	Supervision and Expense	Av'ge Cost per Splice.
1-25 Pr *	100 Pr	25		$0 68	$1 18	$1 08	$0 69	$0 91	$4 54
1-50 Pr †	100 Pr		50	0 75	1 64	1 72	0 64	1 19	5 94

†These splices were made onto pairs left dead
*The main cable ended at the splice

TABLE LVI—Cost of Changing Counts, Aerial, on Working Cable, Tagged.

No. and Size of Branch Cables.	Size of Main Cable.	No. of Pairs Spliced Straight.	No. of Pairs Bridged	Team-ing	Fram-ing	Testing and Tagging	Splic-ing	Wiping Joints.	Supervision and Expense	Av'ge per Splice
1-15 Pr	50 Pr	..	15	$0 70	$0 80	$1 28	$0 93	$0 61	$1 16	$5 48
1-25 Pr	50 Pr		25	0 72	1 07	1 61	1 46	0 66	1 28	6 81
1-25 Pr	100 Pr		25	0 86	1 24	2 83	1 57	0 71	1 61	8 82
1-50 Pr	100 Pr		50	0 84	1 53	3 21	3 06	0 69	1 90	11 23

TABLE LVII—Cost of Changing Counts, Underground, Not Tagged

No. and Size of Branch Cables.	Size of Main Cable	No. of Pairs Spliced Straight	No. of Pairs Bridged.	Team-ing	Pump-ing	Fram-ing	Splic-ing	Wiping Joints.	Supervision and Expense.	Av'ge Cost per Splice.
1-25 Pr *	100 Pr	25		$0 59	$0 43	$1 11	$1 96	$0 58	$0 96	$4 70
1-25 Pr	200 Pr		25	0 53	0 52	1 22	1 28	0 67	1 07	5 29
1-50 Pr	200 Pr		50	0 67	0 49	1 62	1 91	0 69	1 30	6.58

†These splices were made onto pairs left dead
*The main cable ended at the splice

TABLE LVIII—Cost of Changing Counts, Underground, on Working Cable, Tagged

No. and Size of Branch Cables	Size of Main Cable	No. of Pairs Spliced Straight	No. of Pairs Bridged	Teaming	Pumping	Framing	Testing and Tagging	Splicing	Wiping Joints	Supervision and Expense	Average Cost Per Splice
1-25 Pr	100 Pr	25		$0 63	$0 57	$1 06	$2 74	$1 44	$0 67	$1 66	$8 77
1-25 Pr	200 Pr	25		0 74	0 62	1 18	3 79	1 53	0 64	1 79	10 39
1-50 Pr	100 Pr		50	0 83	0 71	1 34	3 11	2 99	0 71	1 85	11 55
1-50 Pr	200 Pr		50	0 72	0 68	1 43	4 12	3 18	0 69	2 08	12 90
1-100 Pr	200 Pr		100	0 84	0 61	2 56	4 88	5 21	0 73	2 57	17 40
1-100 Pr	300 Pr		100	0 79	0 52	2 70	5 74	5 53	0 70	2 91	18 89

TABLE LIX — COST OF AERIAL CUTS *

No and Size of Branch Cables	Size of Cables off of which Branches were Cut	Size of Cables into which Branches were Spliced	No of Pairs Spliced Straight	No of Pairs Bridged	Teaming	Framing	Testing and Tagging	Splicing	Wiping Joints	Supervision and Expense	Average Cost Per Splice
1-15 Pr	50 Pr	50 Pr		15	$0 67	$1 06	$1 03	$1 20	$1 01	$1 21	$6 18
1-25 Pr	50 Pr	50 Pr		25	0 76	1 38	1 66	1 94	1 02	1 46	8 22
1-25 Pr	100 Pr	100 Pr		25	0 79	1 44	2 98	1 97	1 14	1 70	10 02
1-50 Pr	100 Pr	100 Pr		50	0 87	1 73	3 17	3 77	1 20	1 98	12.72

*See note on "underground cuts."

TABLE LX — COST OF UNDERGROUND CUTS

No and Size of Branch Cables	Size of Cables off of which Branches were Cut	Size of Cables into which Branches were Spliced	No of Pairs Spliced Straight	No of Pairs Bridged	Teaming	Pumping	Framing	Testing and Tagging	Spl cing	Wiping Joints	Supervision and Expense	Average Cost Per Splice
1-25 Pr	100 Pr	100 Pr		25	$0 66	$0 51	$1 32	$2 82	$1 91	$1 01	$1 67	$9 90
1-25 Pr	200 Pr	200 Pr		25	0 70	0 54	1 37	3 90	2 04	0 94	1 83	11 32
1-50 Pr	100 Pr	100 Pr		50	0 62	0 47	1 59	3 12	3 64	1 08	1 94	12 45
1-50 Pr	200 Pr	200 Pr		50	0 72	0 62	1 71	4 03	3 72	0 96	2 02	13 78
1-100 Pr	200 Pr	200 Pr		100	0 78	0 68	2 67	4 80	5 53	1 03	2 66	18 15
1-100 Pr	300 Pr	300 Pr		100	0 61	0 56	2 93	5 84	5 76	1 01	2 79	19 50
1-200 Pr	200 Pr	200 Pr.		200	0 73	0 59	3 31	5 89	8 13	1 08	3 24	22 97
2-25 Pr	200 Pr	200 Pr		50	0 81	0 54	2 14	4 09	3 96	1 33	2 23	15 10
2-50 Pr	200 Pr	200 Pr		100	0 83	0 63	2 78	4 74	5 73	1 49	2 58	18 78

Note—Cable off of which the branches are cut is generally a working cable

TABLE LXI — COST OF POTHEADS

No and Size of Main Cable	No. and Size of Distributing Rack Cables	Framing	Testing and Tagging	Splicing	Wiping Joints	Supervision and Expense	Av'ge Cost per Pothead
100 Pr	5-20 Pr	$0 80	$0 48	$1 93	$0 86	$1 46	$5 53
200 Pr	10-20 Pr	1 28	0 61	3 76	0 99	3 00	9 64
300 Pr	15-20 Pr	2 80	0 82	4 94	1 70	3 74	14 00

TABLE LXII — COST OF CONNECTING CABLE TO DISTRIBUTING RACK

Size of Cable Connected	Placing Cable between Pothead and Rack.	Framing	Distributing Wires on Rack and Connecting to Terminal Blocks	Lacing	Soldering Wires to Terminal Blks.	Supervision and Expense	Av'ge Cost per Cable
100 Pr	$3 90	$0 72	$1 22	$2 27	$0 48	$2,30	$10 89
200 Pr	5 61	1 17	2 01	5 30	0 72	4 38	19 19
300 Pr	6 43	1 62	2 94	8 18	1 32	7 14	27 63
Average Cost of Connecting all Size Cables per Pair .	266	058	103	263	042	230	Average Cost per Pair 962

CHAPTER IV.

METHODS AND COST OF REMOVING OLD LINE
AND OF RECONSTRUCTION

Cost data on the removal of old line, or costs of removal, as this work will be termed here, are valuable for many reasons. They are of particular value, however, when considering the advisability of making changes in a telephone plant or when deciding as to the relative expediency of building a line overhead or underground which must ultimately be installed underground. This is a point that is often overlooked in considering the advisability of keeping such costs.

In estimating the cost of changing the equipment of a route from open wire to cable or from aerial to underground, the main items to be taken into consideration are · The cost of the new material plus the cost of installation, the value of the old material less cost of removal, and the value of the increase in facilities. In the case of an exchange in a town or village, the population of which is almost stationary and the prospects of new business at a minimum, very little allowance can be made for the value of any increase in facilities; therefore, if the route to be changed is still in fair condition, the question of expediency in making the change resolves down to whether the value of the material removed less the labor cost of removing will be much less than the cost of the material and labor required in making the change

Very often a new sub-division is opened in a section of the city which is building up very rapidly, or an extension of an elevated railroad or trolley line is built causing immediate and prospective demands for telephone service, which necessitate the building of a main feeding line which must now or ultimately be installed underground. The question of the most advisable way to build for the present depends upon whether the cost of building overhead plus the cost of removing material, interest on plant ,and depreciation, would

63

cause a saving in the intervening three or five years before the line must be put underground.

Removing Old Line.—Material removed is either "junked" or "recovered." When it is to be junked the work of removing is usually rough, requiring less skill than any other division of telephone work. Material to be recovered, however, requires careful and skillful handling. The method of removal requires very little explanation as in general it is the reverse of the methods used for installing which have already been explained. The work of removing material is done by the construction gangs which are used for line work.

Anchors are rarely removed as the expense of removal is more than the value of the article. Old poles and stub are always removed no matter how valueless on account of being unsightly and dangerous to traffic, and also, because it is the policy of most companies to have as few poles standing as possible.

Removing Poles.—Poles to be removed are dug up when they are to be recoverd or when conditions are such that a stub left in the ground would be unsightly or objectionable to property owners. In other cases the poles are removed by chopping so that the top of the stub is on a level with the surface of the street or roadway. The method for removing poles which are to be dug up is the reverse of the method described for erecting poles. Poles to be removed by chopping must be guyed with ropes, when possible, so that they may be lowered gradually.

Removing Cross-Arms.—The method for removing cross-arms is the reverse of the method described for erecting cross-arms.

Removing Wire.—All wires to be removed are first untied from the insulation on each cross-arm, and then test connectors are removed. The wire must be removed by winding on a take-up reel or other suitable appliance, not more than one wire being removed at a time. When copper wire is to be recovered, special care must be taken in removing to prevent kinks, bends, nicks, etc., in the wire.

Removing Messenger.—The method for removing messenger is the reverse of the method described for erecting messenger.

Removing Aerial Cable.—In removing aerial cable, the cable must be cut at each splice and securely sealed, unless the cable is to be junked. The lead wire must be attached in the same manner as in erection and the cable must be pulled toward the reel. In transferring the hooks past the poles all hooks shall be placed back upon the messenger except on the lead wire where every fourth or fifth hook is sufficient.

Removing Underground Cable.—All underground cable to be removed must be cut at each splice and have the ends of the sections sealed, before they are removed from the duct, unless the cable is to be junked. The apparatus is placed at the vault from which the cable is to be pulled. In place of the steel rope used in pulling in, a manila rope is used on account of its greater flexibility. The vault skids and sheaves are placed in the same manner as for pulling in cable, and the manila rope passed over them in the usual manner. To the end of the rope is attached a servage strap made of manilla strand about 1 in. in diameter. This strap is placed on the cable in the form of a noose which .grips the cable when pulled one way, but may be pushed along the cable in the reverse direction. The strap is then slipped around the end of the cable as close to the duct as possible, and power applied to the pulling line. After the cable has been moved a foot or two, the rope is slackened off and the noose is again pushed forward against the duct. This process is known as "luffing." The "luffing" is continued until the cable is removed from the duct. As the cable is pulled out, if it is to be recovered, it is reeled upon a reel placed back of the manhole, so as to avoid unnecessary sharp turns. If it is to be junked the cable is usually cut with an axe into 5 or 6 ft. lengths as it is being pulled out.

RECONSTRUCTION.

Under reconstruction, only moving poles, replacing cross-arms, and rewiring cable poles will be treated, as, with the exception of these operations, reconstruction work generally consists of removing old equipment and then installing new.

The data may easily be separated, and when estimating the cost of erecting and the cost of removing material, they may be more readily figured when the data on the new work and old work are separated.

Moving poles is naturally a division of reconstruction, as the poles are not hauled to or from the work as in removing or setting poles, or gained and roofed as in new work. In replacing cross-arms and rewiring cable poles the work of removing the old material and installing the new cannot be divided on account of there being no definite separation between the two parts of the work   It requires only one climbing of a pole to remove an old cross-arm and to replace it with a new one, or to remove old bridle wires and to replace them with new wires Then again, when replacing cross-arms the work of removing is not always completed until after the new cross-arm has been secured to the pole It is therefore obvious that it is not possible to compute separately the time spent in removing the old equipment and installing the new.

The methods of moving poles, replacing cross-arms and rewiring cable poles have already been described both in erecting and removing material, and the methods in general being a combination of both, require no further description

Method of Recording Costs.—The forms used for reporting the labor costs of removing material and of reconstruction are shown in Forms 31 to 39. These forms are divided in the same style as the forms used for reporting line construction and cable work costs. On account of the difference in the cost of removing wire and cable when they are junked and when they are recovered, caused by the extra skill and care required in handling material to be recovered, the words "junked and recovered," one of which is to be crossed out, are printed on the forms.

Method of Figuring the Cost of Removing Material and of Reconstruction.—The method of figuring the cost of removing material and reconstruction is the same as described for line construction and cable work. Labor expended in hauling removed material from the job to the store yard is included in teaming

Construction Cost Data.—The rates of wages on which the costs given in Tables LXIII to LXXX are based are the same as for line construction costs. No separation is made of the data on removing poles in the various kind of soil because the quantity of soil excavated is so small that there is very little difference in the cost of removing poles of the same size whether set in one kind of soil or another. The average cost of some divisions is not included in the following costs as sufficient data on which averages could be based were not available.

Form 31
Data Secured by
REMOVING STREET AND ALLEY LINE POLES

30'
35'
40'
45' and Higher   Location   Date   190
Foreman   Order No

No of Poles	Teaming and Labor in Hauling	Chopping or Digging and Removing	Super and Exp	Total Cost	No of Hours Worked	Remarks

NOTE.—The forms for recording toll line and farm line poles are the same as this except that the "size of poles" is different

---

Form 32
Data Secured by
REMOVING CROSS-ARMS

6 Pin
10 Pin
10 Pin (Alley)   Location   Date   190
Foreman   Order No

No of Cross-Arms	No of Poles	Teaming and Labor in Hauling	Removing	Super and Exp	Total Cost	No of Hours Worked	Remarks

---

Form 33.
Data Secured by
REMOVING WIRE.

No 12 Galv Steel
080 Bare Copper
104 Bare Copper   Location   Date   190
Junked or Recovered   Foreman   Order No

No Miles of Wire Removed	No of Contacts Removed	Teaming	Removing	Super and Exp	Total Cost	No of Hours Worked	Remarks

Form 34.
Data Secured by .
REMOVING MESSENGER.

No 4 Galv Steel
Strand   Location   Date   Order No
Strand   Foreman   190

No of Feet Removed	Teaming and Labor in Hauling	Removing	Super and Exp	Total Cost	No of Hours Worked	Remarks

NOTE—No separation is made in the data between messenger "junked or recovered"
as the method for removal is the same in either case

Form 35.
Data Secured by...
REMOVING AERIAL CABLE.

Size of Cable Pr Gauge   Location   Date   Order No
Junked or Recovered   Foreman   190

No of Feet Removed	Teaming and Labor in Hauling	Removing	Super and Exp	Total Cost	No of Hours Worked	Remarks

---

Form 36
Data Secured by .
REMOVING U G CABLE

Size of Cable Pr Gauge   Order No
Junked or Recovered   Location .   Date
Cut up or put on reel   Foreman   190

No of Feet Removed	Teaming and Labor in Hauling	Removing	Super and Exp	Total Cost	No of Hours Worked	Remarks

---

Form 37
Data Secured by   .
MOVING POLES

Size of Poles
Street or Alley Line   Order No
Farm Line   Location   Date
Toll Line   Foreman   190

No of Poles	Teaming and Labor in Hauling	Digging and Locating	Moving and Resetting	Super and Exp	Total Cost	Kind of Soil	No of Hours Worked	Remarks

NOTE—"Digging" includes the excavating necessary to remove and reset poles, and
it also includes back-filling the holes out of which the poles were removed

Form 38

Data Secured by

REPLACING CROSS-ARMS

6 Pin
10 Pin
10 Pin (Alley)

Location   Date   Order No   190

Foreman

No of Cross-Arms	No of Poles	Teaming and Labor in Hauling	Removing and Erecting	Super and Exp	Total Cost	No of Hours Worked	Remarks

Form 39

Data Secured by

REWIRING CABLE POLES

Location   Date   Order No   190

Foreman

No of Prs Bridle Wires cut in	No of Prs Bridle Wires cut out	Teaming	Removing & Running Bridle Wires	Super and Exp	Total Cost	No of Hours Worked	Remarks

TABLE LXIII—COST OF REMOVING STREET AND ALLEY LINE POLES

	Teaming and Labor in Hauling	Digging and Removing	Supervision and Expense	Average Cost per Pole
30 Ft	$0 22	$0 58	$0 17	$0 97
35 Ft	0 26	0 76	0 19	1 21
40 Ft	0 37	0 96	0 31	1 64
45 Ft	0 48	1 32	0 40	2 20

TABLE LXIV—COST OF REMOVING FARM LINE POLES.

20 Ft	$0 08	$0 18	$0 06	$0 32
25 Ft	0 16	0 32	0 12	0 60
30 Ft	0 24	0 54	0 16	0 94

TABLE LXV—COST OF REMOVING TOLL LINE POLES.

30 Ft	$0 26	$0 59	$0 15	$1 00
35 Ft	0 31	0 72	0 25	1 28
40 Ft	0 40	0 89	0 32	1 61

TABLE LXVI—COST OF REMOVING STREET AND ALLEY LINE POLES

	Teaming and Labor in Hauling	Chopping and Removing	Supervision and Expense	Average Cost per Pole
30 Ft	$0 13	$0 31	$0 11	$0 55
35 Ft	0 17	0 41	0 13	0 71
40 Ft	0 24	0 53	0 17	0 94

TABLE LXVII—COST OF REMOVING FARM LINE POLES.

20 Ft	$0 03	$0 09	$0 02	$0 14
25 Ft	0 07	0 16	0 06	0 29

TABLE LXVIII—COST OF REMOVING TOLL LINE POLES

	Teaming and Labor in Hauling	Chopping and Removing	Supervision and Expense	Average Cost per Pole
30 Ft	$0 15	$0 28	$0 09	$0 52
35 Ft	0 20	0 44	0 14	0 78
40 Ft	0 27	0 58	0 20	1.05

TABLE LXIX—COST OF REMOVING CROSS-ARMS

	Teaming and Labor in Hauling	Removing	Supervision and Expense	Average Cost per Cross-Arm
6-Pin	$0 015	$0 020	$0 011	$0 046
10-Pin	0 025	0 041	0 013	0 079
10-Pin Alley	0 033	0 061	0 018	0 112

TABLE LXX—COST OF REMOVING WIRE

Junked—	Teaming and Labor in Hauling	Removing	Supervision and Expense	Av Cost per Mile of Wire
No 12 Galv Steel	$0 22	$0 72	$0 16	$1 10
080 Bare Copper	0 29	1 07	0 21	1 57
104 Bare Copper	0 26	1 17	0 26	1 69
Recovered—				
No 12 Galv Steel	$0 27	$1 16	$0 20	$1 63
080 Bare Copper	0 39	1.85	0 32	2 56
.104 Bare Copper	0 44	1 92	0 34	2 73

TABLE LXXI—COST OF REMOVING MESSENGER.

	Teaming and Labor in Hauling	Removing	Supervision and Expense	Average Cost per Foot.
No 4 Galv Steel	.$0 0003	$0 0021	$0 0002	$0 0026
⅜-in Strand	0 0006	0 0029	0 0002	0 0037
½-in. Strand	0 0007	0 0032	0 0003	0 0042

TABLE LXXII.—COST OF REMOVING AERIAL CABLE (JUNKED).

	Teaming and Labor in Hauling	Removing	Supervision and Expense	Average Cost per Foot.
15 Pr —22 Ga	$0 0026	$0 0072	$0 0018	$0 0116
25 Pr —22 Ga	0 0029	0 0069	0 0022	0 0120
50 Pr —22 Ga	0 0025	0 0072	0 0024	0 0121
50 Pr —19 Ga.	0 0030	0 0076	0 0027	0 0133
100 Pr —22 Ga	0 0032	0 0079	0 0027	0 0138
100 Pr —19 Ga	0.0034	0 0083	0 0030	0 0147

Note—Removing aerial cable does not include cost of removing strand

TABLE LXXIII—COST OF REMOVING AERIAL CABLE (RECOVERED)

	Teaming and Labor in Hauling	Removing	Supervision and Expense	Average Cost per Foot
15 Pr —22 Ga	$0 0028	$0 0084	$0 0024	$0 0136
25 Pr —22 Ga	0 0031	0 0080	0 0026	0 0137
50 Pr —22 Ga	0 0029	0 0086	0 0027	0 0142
50 Pr —19 Ga	0 0033	0 0089	0 0032	0 0154
100 Pr —22 Ga	0 0032	0 0085	0 0030	0 0147
100 Pr —19 Ga	0 0038	0 0091	0 0035	0 0164

TABLE LXXIV—COST OF REMOVING UNDERGROUND CABLE (JUNKED)

	Teaming and Labor in Hauling	Removing	Supervision and Expense	Average Cost per Foot
50 Pr —22 Ga	$0 0038	$0 0072	$0 0019	$0 0129
50 Pr —19 Ga	0 0043	0 0079	0 0021	0 0143
100 Pr —22 Ga	0 0041	0 0075	0 0017	0 0133
100 Pr —19 Ga	0 0054	0 0083	0 0024	0 0161
200 Pr —22 Ga	0 0056	0 0086	0 0019	0 0161
200 Pr —19 Ga.	0 0061	0 0094	0 0026	0 0181
300 Pr —22 Ga	0 0073	0 0108	0 0029	0 0210

TABLE LXXV—COST OF REMOVING UNDERGROUND CABLE (RECOVERED)

	Teaming and Labor in Hauling	Removing	Supervision and Expense	Average Cost per Foot
25 Pr—22 Ga	$0 0034	$0 0073	$0 0018	$0 0125
50 Pr—22 Ga	0 0041	0 0079	0 0017	0 0137
50 Pr—19 Ga	0 0044	0 0084	0 0022	0 0150
100 Pr—22 Ga	0 0050	0 0086	0 0023	0 0159
100 Pr—19 Ga	0 0053	0 0093	0 0026	0 0172
200 Pr—22 Ga	0 0058	0 0089	0 0022	0 0169
200 Pr—19 Ga	0 0064	0 0099	0 0028	0 0191
300 Pr—22 Ga	0 0077	0 0115	0 0033	0 0225

TABLE LXXVI—COST OF MOVING STREET AND ALLEY POLES

30-FT POLES

	Teaming and Labor in Hauling	Digging and Locating	Moving and Resetting	Supervision and Expense	Average Cost per Pole
Sand or Gravel	$0 42	$0 99	$0 43	$0 48	$2 32
Black Soil	0 57	0 96	0 42	0 54	2 49
Sand and Water	0 82	1 11	0 54	0 52	2 99
Clay	0 80	0 96	0 59	0 61	2 96
Clay and Water	0 86	1 23	0 51	0 50	3 10
Hard Clay	0 92	1 64	0 57	0 65	3 78
Coarse Gravel	0 96	1 95	0 87	0 60	4 38
Quicksand and Water	1 02	2 16	0 67	0 75	4 60
Average Cost in all Soils	0 80	1 38	0 57	0 58	3 33

35-FT POLES

Sand or Gravel	0 44	1 12	0 59	0 54	2 69
Black Soil	0 61	1 08	0 51	0 53	2 73
Sand and Water	0 81	1 27	0 62	0 59	3 29
Clay	0 87	1 16	0 70	0 58	3 31
Clay and Water	0 91	1 32	0 67	0 64	3 54
Hard Clay	0 97	1 72	0 74	0 70	4 13
Coarse Gravel	1 04	2 03	0 89	0 73	4 69
Quicksand and Water	1 11	2 39	0 79	0 79	5 08
Average in all Soils	0 84	1 51	0 69	0 64	3 68

40-FT POLES

Sand or Gravel	0 69	1 30	0 87	0 63	3 49
Clay	0 88	1 42	0 98	0 70	3 98
Clay and Water	0 94	1 51	1 03	0 69	4.17
Hard Clay	0 92	1 76	1 17	0 77	4 62
Quicksand and Water	1 29	2 11	1 99	0 89	6 28
Average Cost in all Soils	0 94	1 62	1 21	0 74	4 51

45-FT POLES

Sand or Gravel	0 78	1 87	1 09	0 76	4 50
Clay	0 93	2 01	1 11	0 84	4 89

TABLE LXXVII—COST OF MOVING FARM LINE POLES

20-FT POLES

Sand or Gravel	$0 18	$0 49	$0 29	$0 17	$1 13
Black Soil	0 16	0 46	0 27	0 19	1 08
Sand and Water	0 20	0 58	0 31	0 14	1 23
Clay	0 17	0 60	0 38	0 21	1 36
Clay and Water	0 24	0 67	0 34	0 16	1 41
Hard Clay	0 27	0 76	0 41	0 24	1 68
Coarse Gravel	0 25	0 87	0 47	0 26	1 85
Average Cost in all Soils	0 21	0 63	0 35	0 20	1 39

25-FT POLES

Sand or Gravel	0 24	0 67	0 34	0 21	1 46
Black Soil	0 21	0 64	0 36	0 19	1 40
Sand and Water	0 27	0 76	0 40	0 26	1 69
Clay	0 19	0 85	0 45	0 27	1 76
Clay and Water	0 22	0 93	0 42	0 25	1 82
Hard Clay	0 31	1 17	0 44	0 31	2 23
Coarse gravel	0 31	1 24	0 51	0 37	2 43
Quicksand and Water	0 34	1 51	0 53	0 43	2 81
Average Cost in all Soils	0 26	0 97	0 43	0 29	1 95

TABLE LXXVIII—Cost of Moving Toll Line Poles

30-FT POLES

	Teaming and Labor in Hauling	Digging and Locating	Moving and Resetting	Supervision and Expense	Average Cost per Pole
Sand or Gravel . .	$0 39	$0 96	$0 45	$0 42	$2 22
Black Soil .	0 48	0 98	0 47	0 44	2 37
Sand and Water .	0 66	1 07	0 51	0 46	2 70
Clay	0 72	0 98	0 54	0 53	2 77
Clay and Water .	0 81	1 17	0 60	0 58	3 16
Hard Clay	0 84	1 56	0 58	0 54	3 52
Coarse Gravel .	0 89	1 83	0 74	0 62	4 08
Quicksand and Water	0 98	2 07	0 68	0 67	4 40
Average Cost in all Soils ..	0 77	1 33	0 57	0 53	3 15

35-FT POLES

Sand or Gravel	0 45	1 08	0 52	0 49	2 54
Sand and Water. .	0 43	1 19	0 59	0 52	2 73
Clay	0 57	1 23	0 57	0 61	2 98
Clay and Water .	0 66	1 27	0 63	0 54	3 15
Hard Clay	0 74	1 53	0 64	0 61	3 57
Quicksand and Water	0 98	2 47	0 83	0 70	4 98
Average Cost in all Soils	0 64	1 47	0 64	0 58	3 33

40-FT POLES

Sand or Gravel	0 71	1 34	0 81	0 66	3 52
Clay	0 69	1 39	0 95	0 72	3 75
Hard Clay . .	0 88	1 67	1 09	0 69	4 33
Average Cost in all Soils	0 76	1 47	0 95	0 69	3 87

TABLE LXXIX—Cost of Replacing Cross-Arms

	Teaming and Labor in Hauling	Removing and Erecting	Supervision and Expense	Average Cost per Cross-Arm
6-Pin	$0 06	$0 29	$0 04	$0 39
10-Pin	0 08	0 36	0 06	0 50
10-Pin Alley. .	0 09	0 42	0 07	0 58

TABLE LXXX—Cost of Rewiring Cable Poles

Teaming	Removing and Running Bridle Wires	Supervision and Expense	Average Cost per Pair
035	190	.025	.250

CHAPTER V.

METHODS AND COST OF CONSTRUCTING UNDER-GROUND CONDUIT.

The value of cost data on conduit construction is so obvious to everyone owning, building or using conduit that no extended proof of the matter seems necessary. Some discussion of cost keeping methods and of the advantages and disadvantages of various cost keeping procedures is desirable however.

Hints on Cost Keeping Methods.—In devising a system for obtaining costs of conduit construction special care should be taken to avoid numerous, arbitrary, or indefinite divisions While it is desirable to have each division of construction subdivided as much as possible, so that the costs may be analyzed and may be useful in figuring on new methods and inventions which apply to only part of the work, still any attempt to make complicated and arbitrary divisions increases the liability of error, and if the subdivisions are too numerous, cost men will find it almost impossible to secure accurate data With the large gangs, which are used in constructing conduit, any system requiring the taking of costs every few minutes must result in failure, as cost men will find their task almost impossible of accomplishment and they will soon become disgusted—no matter how conscientious they may be. In the winter season it becomes almost a physical impossibility for a man securing data on out-door work to take time and to write every two or three minutes.

Many companies have what is known as a work report cost system In this system the foreman reports at the end of each day the work accomplished and the time spent on each part of the work The worthlessness of this system will be readily perceived if we consider that data cannot be correctly reported without notes being taken during the day, and that it is improbable that any foreman will be able to take correct

73

notes on costs and to properly supervise the work   The task may be accomplished in some ideal case, as when only one division of construction is worked on during the day—which rarely happens.

There are also costs obtained by timing for a few minutes the excavating or the laying of tile or the mixing of concrete, etc., and drawing conclusions from these data. Such a system is so obviously inaccurate that it is hard to conceive how any-one would dare to use the costs, yet many contractors and telephone companies base their estimates on data secured in this manner. The cost of mixing concrete for example, if mixed by hand, must include the cost of moving the mixing boards and other apparatus, and if mixed by machine, must include the cost of moving the mixer, etc   Besides, if water is carted to the work, this cost must also be included   There is in any kind of construction, time expended in preparing for

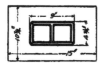

Fig. 34—McRoy Tile, 2-Duct Conduit, Class "A" Construction.

work, which is as much a part of the cost as any of the time spent in actual work, and this time cannot be secured by keep-ing account of the work for a few minutes or even a few hours.

In view of the essential nature of conduit construction costs and of their recognized value, it is surprising that so few attempts have been made to obtain costs based on a system which is feasible   Usually data on a conduit job are obtained in such a manner that they are of little use in estimating the cost of other jobs where the multiple of duct, the soil-or the other conditions differ   Where several sections of a conduit composed of different multiples are built, no separation of the various sections is made in gathering the data, or where a separation is made of each different run of duct, no separation is made of the sections built in clay, hard clay, sand, etc.

Then again the data to be feasible should also have the cost of each section separated when the pavement or location varies

Location is a matter of special importance in estimating. It appears from a cursory investigation much cheaper to build in a wide roadway than in a narrow alley, as in the case of the former, the material may be more advantageously placed, causing a minimum expense for rehandling. Also the excavated earth may be placed so as to cause the least interference in laying tile, placing concrete, etc., and so as to be most convenient for the teams used in carting away the surplus When, however, it is considered that in most cases a trench in an alley may be resurfaced in almost any style, while a street, even if unpaved, must generally be left in a condition as good as or better than the original, we see that the cost of

 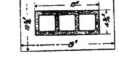

Fig. 35 —McRoy Tile, 2-Duct Conduit, Class "A" Construction   Fig 36 —McRoy Tile, 3-Duct Conduit, Class "A" Construction

building in an alley—other things being equal—may be the cheaper, as it often is The relative position of the conduit and street curb will also cause variation in cost. It is cheaper to build next to the curb on asphalted streets than 2 or 3 ft away on account of the liability of injury to the asphalt between the trench and the curb by the caving in of the side of the trench. Dangerous conditions for working, and rehandling of material incident to its being inconveniently placed will increase the cost of building a conduit in a street used by a trolley, especially if the street is narrow. Building a conduit in a street where the grade has not been established is often more expensive than building in paved streets as it is sometimes necessary to excavate the trench 2 or 3 ft deeper than usual in order to provide for future changes in the street level.

The question of what material shall be used in constructing a conduit or the question of the expediency of adopting a new device or new method requires a knowledge of the durability, the tensile strength, the cost of material, and also the cost of installation. Without this last item of information experiments entailing a great loss of money cannot be avoided. Almost every company owning conduits has built sections using material which proved so espensive to install as to increase the cost of conduit, although the reason for adopting this material was to reduce the cost of construction   For example, a method of installing vitrified clay tile known as class "B" construction, which is explained in another part of this chapter, has been and still is a standard method of construction   As this method falls far below what is known as class "A" construction in durability, in protection from injury

Fig 37 —McRoy Tile, 4-Duct Conduit,   Fig 38 —McRoy Tile, 5-Duct Conduit,
    Class "A" Construction.   Class "A" Construction

by foreign excavations and in stability of alignment, the only apparent object in building class "B" conduits would be their cheapness   Without the assistance of cost data one may readily conceive how class "B" construction might be considered much cheaper than class "A," but if data on the cost of constructing both classes are available, it is hard to conceive how any company for the small increase in the cost of installing class "A" would be so short-sighted as to install class "B "   It is clear that a lack of proper cost data has been responsible for the standardizing of the class "B" method of construction, as this is the only explanation which accounts for the mistake of its adoption.

Organization of Working Force.—Conduit work is done by unskilled day labor. The organization of a gang is composed of a foreman, one or more assistant foremen depending on the size of the gang, a timekeeper, watchman, waterboys and laborers Usually the gang if large is subdivided in the same order as the work, with an assistant foreman in charge of each division. This system has many advantages. The concrete mixers soon learn the proper proportions of material to use and the required consistency of the concrete, and also in the other divisions of the work each man soon becomes proficient in his task; it increases economy in the handling of labor, avoiding the loss of time incident to continual shifting of men; it aids assistant foremen in soon becoming acquainted with their men, whereby they are able to eliminate men who will not do their work; it puts the foreman in a position to be able to hold his assistants responsible for the work accom-

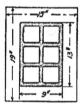 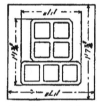

Fig. 39 —McRoy Tile. 6-Duct Conduit,   Fig 40 —McRoy Tile, 7-Duct Conduit,
Class "A" Construction   Class "A" Construction

plished, and it facilitates the work in general, reduces the cost and improves the construction.

Generally two or three men having had experience or showing adaptability are selected for the work of laying tile, which is the most important part of conduit construction. These men are very often paid a trifle more than the balance of the laborers in order to induce conscientious work

A foreman of conduit construction, while requiring less skill and technical knowledge than a foreman of either line or cable construction, has more opportunity to exhibit his proficiency and ability as a foreman. By capable handling of men and good judgment in laying out work, a good foreman may complete work 20 per cent cheaper than a man having equal technical knowledge of construction but lacking ability as a foreman. A cost man on a job has a tendency to increase the volume of work accomplished. Rivalry is established between the several foremen which spurs them to do their best. It may be asserted as a general rule that a cost man on a job, irrespective of the value of the data secured, is rather a saving than an expense

CONSTRUCTION DETAILS.

In the construction of the conduit on which the following data are based the tile used for main conduit was either McRoy vitrified clay tile or creosoted pump log The latter

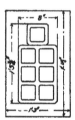

Fig 41 —McRoy Tile, 7-Duct Conduit, Class "A" Construction

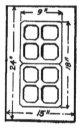

Fig 42 —McRoy Tile, 8-Duct Conduit, Class "A" Construction

was installed in comparatively few instances. Its use was generally confined to straight lateral built in separate trench to a building or in the yards and plant of a large works, and where used the soil was very wet, or subsequent excavations were expected, or the conduit was subject to constant shocks. Some or all of these conditions were generally encountered when installing conduit in the yards, under buildings or on the site of prospective buildings in large plants where heavy machinery is used, such as in a steel plant.

The McRoy tile used was 1, 2, 3, 4 or 6-duct Formerly tile of larger cross section was used but their use has been abolished by most companies on account of their weight, which is approximately 8½ lbs per duct foot, increasing the cost of laying and handling tile, and also on account of the large percentage of breakage incident to the handling of fragile material of great weight.

One-duct McRoy tile was used only where conditions required a conduit cross section to be built up of a 2-duct and a 1-duct instead of a 3-duct, or of a 6-duct and a 1-duct instead of a 4-duct and a 3-duct or a 5-duct and a 2-duct. In no case was McRoy tile installed where the conduit cross section was one duct. Where main conduit is built one duct is rarely installed, as the prospects are that where a main conduit is required, eventually a greater multiple may be used, and the cost of installing 2-duct is so little more than that of installing 1-duct that it is poor policy to install the latter. The excavation, teaming, laying tile, filling in and repaving cost the same for 1-duct as 2-duct. The only difference in the cost of in-

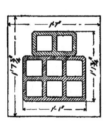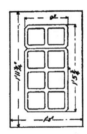

Fig 43 —McRoy Tile, 8-Duct Conduit,   Fig 44 —McRoy Tile, 8-Duct Conduit,
Class "A" Construction   Class "A" Construction

stalling a 1-duct tile and a 2-duct tile being in the cost of the tile (.04 + 2% per duct foot) and a small amount for concrete material and mixing concrete.

Except where 1-duct tile was required in building up a cross section of a specified multiple, the 1-duct conduits built were laterals constructed exclusively of 3-in. sewer tile or creosoted pump log. The latter was rarely used. For the benefit of those not familiar with this class of conduit a brief description of laterals may be pertinent.

Lateral conduit, sometimes called subsidiary conduit, is so named from the direction in which it runs to the main conduit. Laterals are built in order to carry subsidiary cable underground to a building or a pole. A lateral always ends in a vault of the main conduit where the cable it carries is spliced

into the main cable. Where the vault is built at street intersections the lateral is installed in a separate trench if it runs
to a pole situated on a street running in an opposite direction
to the street on which the main conduit is built, or if the pole
is situated at the intersection of a cross street and an alley
running parallel to the street on which the main conduit is installed. If the lateral is to be built to a pole or building along
the line of the main conduit it is included in the main trench
to a point in front of the ·pole or building and then takes a
separate trench. Where a pole is situated in an alley running
parallel to the street on which the main conduit is built, and it

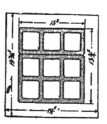

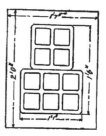

Fig. 45 —McRoy Tile, 9-Duct Conduit,   Fig. 46 —McRoy Tile, 10-Duct Con-
    Class "A" Construction   duit, Class "A" Construction

is set midway between two streets, as is the case where only
one pole is used for block distribution, a lateral built to this
pole is generally included in the main trench to a point opposite the pole and then run in a separate trench along the lot
line, if possible, to the alley.

Sewer tile is used in lateral construction because it serves
the purpose better than either McRoy tile or pump log and
because it is cheapest to install. Whereas the McRoy tile requires a foundation in order to keep its alignment—dowel pins
not entirely serving this purpose—and both pump log and
McRoy tile require a trench that has a level bottom and is
wide enough to permit foot room; sewer tile requires no concrete foundation, as the bell joints when cemented hold the
alignment sufficiently well for lateral construction, it may be
laid in a trench that is excavated in a V-shape, thereby saving

time in excavating. The bottom of the trench may be very uneven as the bell ends of sewer tile bridge the parts between joints, and the only requirements in laying are that the end of one tile shall fit into the bell end of another This may readily be done by scraping away any excess earth with a stick of wood. On account of the usual small diameter of lateral cable the lateral conduit may be installed without special regard to alignment, except when the lateral is very long, whereas if McRoy tile is laid without care being used in alignment the armor of the cable would probably be cut or caught on the ends of the ducts when pulling in the cable.

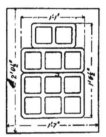 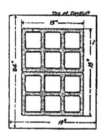

Fig 47—McRoy Tile, 11-Duct Conduit, Class "A" Construction   Fig 48—McRoy Tile, 12-Duct Conduit, Class "A" Construction

As it is required that lateral shall have a curve of 90° at the point where it leaves the main conduit trench and also at the pole where the tile lateral ends, and as 90° sewer tile bends are made whereas McRoy tile and pump log are only made in straight length they do not fill all the requirements of lateral construction

The difference between the cost of McRoy tile and sewer tile is small—generally depending on the freight to point of installation. Where small quantities are required sewer tile is usually cheaper. Pump log is more expensive than either McRoy tile or sewer tile

In the construction of main conduit the superiority of McRoy tile as against sewer tile is generally conceded. It forms a more flexible conduit, being readily increased in mul-

tiple; when laid in concrete—as is advisable in building conduit having a large cross section—it requires less concrete than sewer tile; it forms a smoother duct for the, passage of large cable; it is not readily thrown out of alignment in the work of laying tile or by foreign excavations on account of its weight and flat surfaces, and it makes, in general, more permanent construction, and it is cheaper to install unless the multiple is small.

The formation of a conduit cross section is an important matter, as it makes considerable difference in cost whether an 8-duct run is composed of two 4-duct or a 6-duct and a 2-duct and whether the ducts are laid side by side or one on

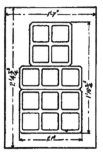
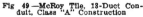
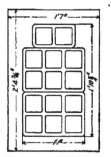

Fig 49 —McRoy Tile, 18-Duct Con-   Fig 50 —McRoy Tile, 14-Duct Con-
    duit, Class "A" Construction   duit, Class "A" Construction

top of the other. The 4 and 6-ducts are made in 3-ft lengths, the 2 and 3-ducts in 2-ft. lengths The 4 and 2-ducts require one dowel pin and the 6-duct two dowel pins.

In comparing the cost of 8-duct conduits where one is composed of a 6-duct and a 2-duct and the other is composed of two 4-ducts, it will be seen that on account of the length of a 2-duct more burlap will be required in closing the joints of a 6 and 2 formation and more dowel pins are also required on account of the use of a 6-duct On account of its weight (about 151 lbs) the percentage of breakage in handling 6-duct is larger than that of 4-duct, and it requires three men in laying 6-duct (one man being used to pass the tile down to the two men laying) where two men are all that is necessary for 4-duct on account of its lighter weight (about ⅓ less).

A 4-duct may be laid on any one of its four sides, while either a 6-duct or a 2-duct must be laid on one of their two narrow sides or two wide sides, depending upon the specified formation of the conduit.

As frequently tile is not level on all sides, it will be seen that the chances are a level side may be found when laying a 4-duct, where in the case of either a 6-duct or a 2-duct a level side may not be found. This makes a difference in the cost of laying tile, because it is sometimes necessary to throw out a 6-duct or a 2-duct, or scrape off the concrete foundation in order to allow for the hump in tile.

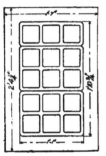

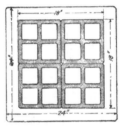

Fig. 51.—McRoy Tile, 15-Duct Con-   Fig. 52.—McRoy Tile, 16-Duct Con-
    duit, Class "A" Construction.   duit, Class "A" Construction.

Comparing the methods of laying tile, it will be found that a 6-duct laid "flat" (on one of its wide sides) with a 2-duct on top, as shown in Fig. 43, requires the excavation of more cubic yards of earth and the use of more concrete than two 4-ducts laid side by side or one on top of the other as shown in Fig. 42; or a 6-duct laid on "edge" (on one of its narrow sides) with a 2-duct on top, laid "flat" as shown in Fig. 44; or a 6-duct laid "flat" with a 2-duct laid on "edge" against it. The 6-duct and 2-duct being evidently designed for laying "flat," when laid on "edge" are readily thrown out of alignment during the progress of construction, especially when placing the concrete around them.

Taking all these points into consideration it is clear that two 4-ducts are laid with greater facility, form a more stable construction and cost less for material and labor than a 6-duct and a 2-duct formation, and in deciding whether to lay two 4-ducts side by side or one on top of the other, the preference should be given to the former, because work is easier in a wide trench; and, as a rule, it is cheaper to dig wide than deep even if the street is paved—repairing contractors charge for a yard although the trench may be 15 ins. wide.

Materials.—The materials used in constructing the conduits on which the costs given are based are as follows:

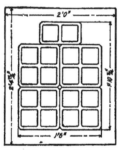 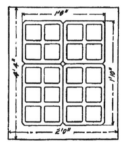

Fig 53.—McRoy Tile, 18-Duct Con-   Fig 54.—McRoy Tile, 20-Duct Con-
    duit, Class "A" Construction   duit, Class "A" Construction.

(1) McRoy tile, used in building main conduits. It is made of vitrified clay, in 1, 2, 3 and 6-duct sizes. The 1, 2 and 3-duct are 2 ft long and the 4 and 6-duct 3 ft. long.

(2) Sewer tile, used in building underground laterals. The inside diameter is 3 ins., the shell ½ in., and the length 2 ft. (See Fig 79.)

(3) Creosoted pump log, used in building conduit where the soil is very wet and frequent excavations liable. It is made of yellow or Norway pine, creosoted. The section is 4½ ins square, with a 3-in bore. Each log is provided with mortise and tenon. Its length is 2 ft. to 8 ft.

(4) American Portland cement, crushed limestone, washed gravel and torpedo sand, used in making concrete.

(5) Standard sewer brick, used in building manholes.

(6) Vault frame and cover, used as the name implies.

(7) Dowel pins, used to preserve alignment of McRoy tile

(8) Creosoted plank, used in class "B" conduit construction and in lateral construction to protect from injury in subsequent excavations The sizes are 1½ ins. x 9 ins and 1½ ins. x 4½ ins , various lengths

(9) Burlap, used in covering joint of McRoy tile; strips 6 ins. wide.

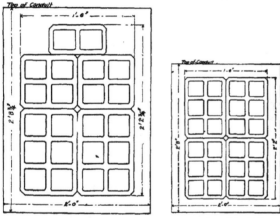

Fig 55 —McRoy Tile, 22-Duct Con-   Fig 56 —McRoy Tile 24-Duct Con-
    duit, Class "A" Construction   duit, Class "A" Construction

(10) St. Louis "Y," used in connecting lateral to iron lateral pipe at the base of a pole when the lateral drains toward the pole. Fig 80

DIVISIONS OF UNDERGROUND CONDUIT CONSTRUCTION.

McRoy Tile Conduit.—The trench for conduit shall be excavated to such a depth as will leave between the top of the concrete or protecting plank over the conduit and the grade of the street a distance of not less than 24 ins Where conduit is laid in parkways a distance of not less than 18 ins.

shall be maintained. Where obstructions are encountered **and** it is desirable to construct the conduit above the obstructions, the conduit may be so laid, provided that the top of the enclosing concrete shall not be less than 12 ins. from the surface of the street if such street is permanently paved on a concrete foundation, and not less than 18 ins. from the grade of unimproved streets. In case the surface of an unimproved street is below grade the conduit shall be so laid that the top of the enclosing concrete shall be 4 ins below the surface of the street. A sufficient quantity of dirt shall be placed over the conduit to form a covering of not less than 18 ins.

Fig 57 — McRoy Tile, 2-Duct Conduit,   Fig 58 — McRoy Tile, 3-Duct Conduit,
    Class "B" Construction   Class "B" Construction

The width of the trench shall be such as to permit convenient laying of the conduit and to allow between the duct and the side of the trench a distance of not less than 3 ins. The desirable formations and size of trenches for McRoy tile are shown in Figs. 34 to 61, inclusive

Before installing conduit the trench shall be opened to its full depth for a distance of 200 ft. in advance of the conduit being laid. The sides of the trench shall be cut clean and be vertical from the bottom to a point level with the concrete on the top of the duct formation. From this point to the surface of the ground the sides of the trench may slope, if the soil is of such a nature as to make this method less expensive than shoring. Otherwise, where necessary, the sides of the trench shall be shored to prevent caving

Where it is necessary to include service pipes in the concrete protection of a conduit, such pipes shall be surrounded by a split pipe of iron having a diameter of not less than

2½ ins. This method shall be followed in order to avoid damage to the surrounding concrete through removal or replacement of the service pipes

The bottom of the trench shall be well tamped and leveled. The trench shall be graded as follows The summit shall be midway between the vaults and shall be of a depth as will allow 24 ins between the top of the protecting plank or concrete and the grade of the street. The slope toward each vault shall be not less than 30 ins. from the grade of the street. Where it is impracticable to grade both ways from the summit, the grade may be continuous from one vault to the next. If practicable, the summit for two consecutive lengths shall be at the same vault and then at alternate vaults, so that the duct in a vault will enter at the same level

Fig 59 —McRoy Tile, 4-Duct Conduit,   Fig 60 —McRoy Tile, 6-Duct Conduit,
      Class "B" Construction   Class "B" Construction

Conduit should be laid in a straight line. Where it is necessary to avoid obstructions or to conform to the changes in line of the street or alley, conduit may be laid so as to vary from a straight line, but under no circumstances shall the conduit be laid so as to form too sharp an angle or an S.

The method of installing class "A" construction, shown in Figs. 34 to 56, inclusive, shall be as follows:

The trench shall first be prepared with a foundation of 3 ins of concrete, leveled and tamped. Upon this the tile shall be laid. Insert the necessary dowel pins and place the next tile in line, centering the tile by means of the dowel pins. Cover the top and sides of each joint with a strip of burlap 6 ins wide to prevent the entrance of concrete into the duct

The successive length of tile shall then be laid in similar manner. When two or more sections are laid side by side all

joints shall be staggered. In joining 2, 3 or 6-duct sections at
least one dowel pin shall be used, or if the duct is designed for
more than one, two shall be used   When the tile is laid it is
enclosed at the sides and top with a wall of concrete 3 ins
thick and well tamped.

If the conduit has a large cross section it will be built up in
tiers. When the first tier is laid and lined up the sides of the
trench shall be filled in with well tamped concrete to a thickness of 3 ins. and to a height flush with the top of the tile.
The upper tiers shall then be laid successively, one upon the
other, in a manner similar to the first tier   The complete section shall be covered with 3 ins of well-tamped concrete, after
which the trench shall be refilled   In dumping concrete into
the trench and in laying tile care should be taken not to knock

Fig 61.—McRoy Tile, 8-Duct Conduit, Class "B" Construction

off earth into the trench   Any dirt falling onto the work
shall be carefully removed before proceeding with the construction.

In refilling the trench the better part of the material excavated shall be used. It must be well tamped into place and
the trench covered with a crown of 3 or 4 ins. If the street
is paved, all surplus must be gathered up and carried away,
and the displaced paving material shall be replaced tem-
porarily. After conduit runs are completed all ducts shall be
closed with wooden plugs (Figs. 64 and 65).

Concrete may be mixed by hand or by machine. If mixed
by hand it shall be done on a timber platform to prevent waste
of water and material, except where the following pavements
are encountered: (1) asphalt; (2) brick; (3) macadam; (4)
creosoted wood block   When mixing concrete on any of these

pavements the street shall be swept clean for a place sufficient to allow for mixing the concrete. The stone or gravel shall first be placed in a layer about 4 ins. thick, sand or screenings added and spread out evenly, and the cement added and evenly distributed. The dry mixture shall be turned over by shovels at least three times so that it is thoroughly mixed. Sufficient water shall be used so that when placed in a wheelbarrow the concrete shall be very moist and in a semi-fluid condition. All concrete shall be free from dirt or any foreign material Concrete shall be used within 2 hours of the time it is mixed.

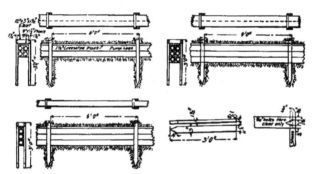

Fig 62 —Method of Laying Pump Log

The proportions of materials to be used in mixing concrete for conduit construction shall be as follows: If crushed stone concrete is used, 1 part of American Portland cement, 4 parts ¼-in. screenings and 8 parts No 3 (¾-in) stone. If gravel concrete is used, 1 part American Portland cement, 4 parts sand and 8 parts gravel, 1 bag of cement shall be considered 1 cu ft

The method of installing class "B" construction, shown by Figs 57 to 61, inclusive, shall be the same as described for class "A," except in the following particulars:

The tile shall be laid on a 4-in bed of concrete Upon the top of the tile there shall be placed 2 ins. of earth, which shall be free from large stone Upon this layer of earth a 1½-in.

creosoted plank shall be laid of the same width as the conduit formation. The tile joints shall be closed by means of strips of burlap which shall be placed around the tile so as to cover the top and sides. The burlap shall be saturated with a thin neat cement mortar, and shall be plastered on the sides and top with ½ in. of cement mortar mixed in the proportion of 1-2. The burlap shall be 6 ins wide and of sufficient length to overlap the width of the tile.

Pump Log Conduit.—The trench for pump log shall be excavated in the same manner as described for McRoy tile conduit construction   Pump log shall be laid directly upon the bottom of the trench. Where two or more ducts are used they

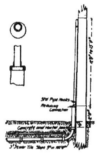

Fig 63 —Method of Extending Lateral Up Pole

shall be laid so as to break joints   When the pump log is laid and well settled in position, a creosoted plank 1½ ins. thick and of the width of the conduit shall be laid on top of the ducts. There shall then be driven, one on either side, 3 in. x 1½ in. x 3 ft creosoted stakes. The stakes shall be sharpened to a point and driven at intervals of 6 ft. with a 3-in. face parallel to the line of the conduit. The tops of the stakes shall be fastened together by a cleat, of the same size as the stakes, cut to length and drilled for two 3½-in. wire nails. The trench shall then be refilled. The method of laying pump log is shown by Fig. 62.

Sewer Tile Lateral Conduit.—Laterals when laid in the main trench, or in a separate trench, shall be single duct, 3-in.

sewer tile. Connections between lateral laid in the main trench and lateral laid in a separate trench shall be made with standard bends of sewer tile. Where lateral is laid in the main conduit trench it shall be located at the top of the conduit formation and shall be included in the enclosing concrete.

Where lateral is laid in separate trench the trench shall be wide enough to permit convenient laying and of sufficient depth to make the completed lateral with its protecting plank at least 18 ins. below the grade of the street. Joints of lateral shall be well protected with cement mortar or concrete. Over the lateral, when laid in separate trench, shall be placed about 3 ins of earth, which shall be free from large stones. This earth shall be well tamped, and on top of this shall be placed a creosoted plank, 1½ ins x 9 ins , to prevent injury in sub-

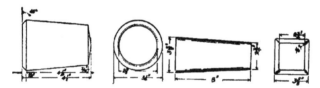

Fig 64 —Round Conduit Plug   Fig 65 —Square Conduit Plug

sequent excavations. Where lateral is extended up a pole with a curve and an iron pipe the manner of making such extension shall be that shown in Fig 63 All lateral shall be laid with the bell end of the tile pointing away from the vault

Where joints are made between tile and iron pipe the joint shall be wrapped with burlap to prevent the concrete from getting into the interior of the pipe.

Lateral shall slope toward the vault This slope, where lateral is laid in a separate trench, shall be, when practicable, not less than 9 ins in 100 ft In case it is impracticable to grade toward the vault, the lateral may slope in the opposite direction In this case, if the lateral is to be extended up a pole, a St Louis "Y" shall be used at the base of the pole in place of a curve. The St Louis "Y" shall be placed with one of its curved parts upward with end against the pole, and the other curved part shall be placed downward after first having excavated a hole of sufficient depth to allow for drainage. The bottom of this hole shall be concreted.

All laterals shall be rodded, fish wires of No. 12 galvanized steel wire installed and ends closed with wooden plugs (shown in Fig. 64), at the time of installation.

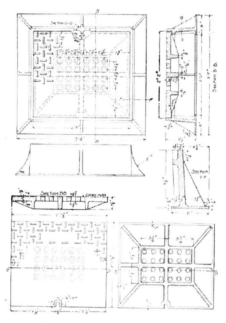

Fig. 66.—Cast Iron Cover for Vault.

Vault or Manhole Construction.—The location of a vault shall be barricaded and excavation then made to such a depth as to bring the bottom of the concrete top 17½ ins. below street grade. If the vault is built in advance of street improvements, the necessary information as to grade shall be obtained from the city engineer. The excavation for brick

vaults shall be sufficiently wide and long enough to leave a
space of 6 ins around the outside of the wall of the manhole
when finished

In stiff clay, the excavation may be made of the outside
dimensions of the vault The standard manhole or vault shall
be of either brick with a concrete bottom, concrete top and
cast iron frame and cover, or of concrete throughout, with cast
iron frame and cover   In size it shall be approximately of the
inner dimensions specified on the plan of the work   For

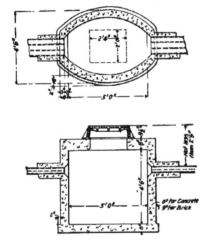

Fig 67 —Vault Size 1 to be Used on Runs of 1 to 3 Ducts of Conduit when
not intersected

straight runs the long dimensions of the vault shall be in the
line of conduit. For intersections the long dimension of the
vault shall be in the line of the heavier run   For different
cross sections of conduit the desirable forms and dimensions
for vaults are shown by Figs 67 to 78 inclusive

In constructing a vault the bottom of the excavation shall
first be tamped and a layer of concrete of the depth shown on
vault drawing, and of sufficient width and length to project
2 ins. beyond the foundation courses of brick, or the bottom

of the concrete wall shall be placed, tamped and graded for
drainage. A sewer connection or other means of drainage
shall be provided wherever possible. If the vault is located on
high, well-drained, sandy soil, drainage may be secured by
placing one or two lengths of 6-in. sewer tile perpendicularly
into the ground from the bottom of the vault   Where possible
the vault shall be drained by a 6-in. sewer "P" trap in the
bottom of the vault with 6-in sewer tile connection to the
sewer   If the water level of the sewer is higher than the bot-

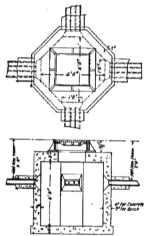

Fig 68 —Vault Size 2 to be Used on Runs of 1 to 3 Ducts of Conduit when
Intersected

tom of the vault, sewer connections may be made through the
wall of the vault using a running sewer trap   A back water
trap shall be installed in all cases where the bottom of the
vault is less than 3 ft above the top of the sewer, by which
the vault is to be drained   All drainage openings shall be provided with cast iron strainers set flush with the floor or wall
of the vault   Where the vault is drained through the floor, the
floor shall be laid so as to drain to the trap with a fall of not
less than 1 in in 10 ft.

In the case of brick vaults, the wall of the vault shall be built up of hard burned sewer brick laid in cement mortar. In dry weather brick shall be well moistened before using. Walls shall be 9 ins thick. The wall shall be built up, every sixth course being laid as headers, to the height required. The top course shall be laid as stretchers. The horizontal mortar joints shall not exceed ½ in. and the vertical joints ⅜ in. in thickness.

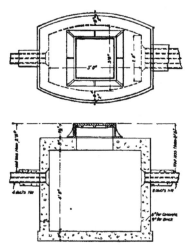

Fig ˉ69 —Vault Size 3 to be Used on Runs of 4 to 8 Ducts of Conduit when not Intersected.

The brick work shall be racked away around the entrance of the ducts to afford room for turning cables when installed. As the walls are built up cable support nipples of approved type shall be installed in all vaults   No less than two supports shall be set in the walls parallel to the conduit run on a level with each layer of ducts in non-intersected vaults. The supports shall not be nearer than 1 ft. from the end of the conduit and shall be placed symmetrically   All pipes entering the vaults shall be well cemented into the brick work and the inside of the vault walls well pointed up

When vaults are intersected at least one support nipple shall be set in each wall between conduit runs on a level with each layer of ducts and set as nearly as practicable at the central point.

The walls of all concrete vaults shall be 6 ins thick. The concrete in the roof and floor shall be thoroughly tamped The concrete in the walls shall be uniformly and equally distributed within the forms, in layers not exceeding 6 ins in

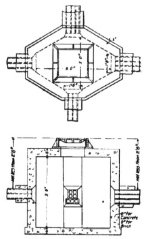

Fig 70 —Vault Size 4 to be Used on Runs of 4 to 8 Ducts of Conduit when Intersected

thickness, each layer being thoroughly tamped in place   After this the succeeding layer shall be at once applied, and the operation continued until the walls have reached the required height.

When the walls of the vault are finished and filled in and around the outside, the wood form for the concrete top shall be placed   The form shall be placed so as to make the center of the manhole opening as nearly as possible over the center line of the ducts, going both ways, and midway between the ends of the vault; the long edge of the opening being parallel to the main line of conduit.

In case a vault top is 7 ft or more in length it shall be strengthened by ⅜-in. x 3 x 3-in. T-iron, or other equivalent reinforcing irons, placed approximately 2 ft. apart and parallel to the short side of the vault top   Where T-irons are used they shall be imbedded in the concrete with the stem of the T up and the bottom of the bar within 1 in. of the lower side

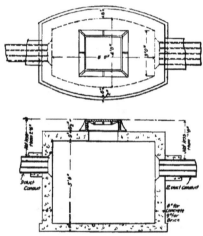

Fig 71 —Vault Size 5 to be Used on Runs of 9 to 12 Ducts of Conduit when not Intersected

of the concrete.   An alternative method for reinforcing concrete roofs of vaults shall be as follows   ½-messenger strand shall be cut to the outside width and length of the vault roof and shall be set in the concrete on 4-in centers about 1 in from the bottom of the concrete roof, both across the length and width of the roof.   Immediately under the center of the bearing surface of the vault frame shall be placed two pieces of ½-in. strand side by side both lengthwise and across the width of the vault roof.

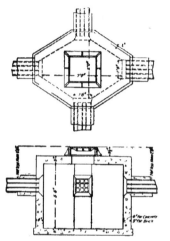

Fig 72 —Vault Size 6 to be Used on Runs of 9 to 12 Ducts of Conduit when Intersected

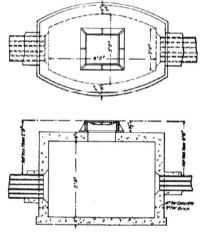

Fig 73 —Vault Size 7 to be Used on Runs of 13 to 24 Ducts of Conduit when not Intersected

The forms used for building vault tops are shown by Fig
81. In the case of concrete vaults, openings for the entrance
of the ducts shall be made with the forms shown by Fig 82.
These forms are made in two styles, collar and block. The
collar form shall be used where the ducts are already installed,
and the block form, where it is desired to leave an opening for
the entrance of future ducts The collar form shall be placed
just over the ducts and against the vault form as shown on
Fig. 81, and shall be removed after the vault form has been
removed.

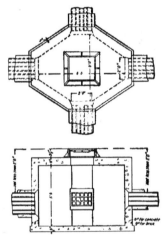

Fig. 74 —Vault Size 8 to be Used on Runs of 13 to 24 Ducts of Conduit when
Intersected

The forms shown by Fig. 83 shall be used to form openings
for the entrance of sewer tile where it is desirable to have a
beveled opening as in some cases where large cable is to be
installed in the sewer tile These forms are also used to form
openings for the entrance of circular ducts.

The method of mixing concrete shall be the same as described for conduit. The proportions of concrete mixtures for
vaults shall be as follows: If crushed stone concrete is used:
For floors of vaults, 1 part American Portland cement, 4

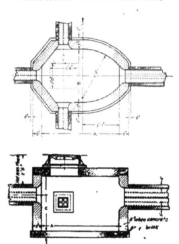

Fig. 75.—Vault Size 9, to be Used on Conduit Runs when Intersected.

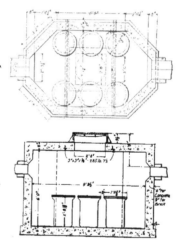

Fig. 76.—Vault Size 10, Used for Installing 6 Loading Pots on Conduit Runs
when not Intersected.

parts ¼-in. screenings and 8 parts No. 3 (¾-in) stone; for roofs and sides of vaults, 1 part American Portland cement, 3 parts ¼-in. screenings, and 5 parts No. 3 (¾-in.) stone. If gravel concrete is used: For floors of vaults, 1 part American Portland cement, 4 parts sand and 8 parts of gravel; for roofs and sides of vaults, 1 part American Portland cement, 3 parts sand and 5 parts gravel.

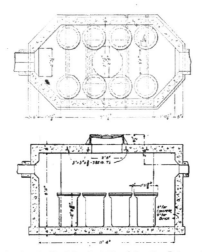

Fig. 77.—Vault Size 11, Used for Installing 8 Loading Pots on Conduit Runs when not Intersected.

Cement mortar shall be mixed on a closely laid timber platform or in a wood box. The sand shall be spread on the mixing platform to a thickness of 2 ins., the cement added and evenly distributed and the materials turned over 3 times with hoes. Sufficient water to make the mortar into a stiff paste shall then be carefully added and the mixture turned over 3 times with hoes to thoroughly mix the material and dampen every particle of cement. Mortar shall be used within 30 mins. of the time of adding the water. Cement mortar shall be mixed in the proportion of 1 part American Portland cement to 3 parts sand.

FORMS FOR RECORDING COSTS OF CONDUIT WORK.

The forms used for reporting the costs of underground conduit construction are shown by Forms 40 to 44, inclusive.

In explanation of Form 40 it will be noted that separate divisions are not made for handling and mixing concrete, and

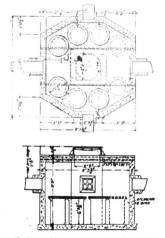

Fig. 78.—Vault Size 12, Used for Installing 6 to 8 Loading Pots on Conduit Runs when Intersected.

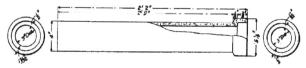

Fig. 79.—3-in, Sewer Tile.

dumping into trench, as in the method of accomplishing the work it is not often practicable to separate the mixing from the wheeling and dumping. On all conduit forms the division for the cost of filling in includes the cost of the labor in loading surplus earth on wagons, reinforcing the trench and cleaning up. The cost of laying tile, plank and placing concrete is

included in one division, as their separation would be difficult
and, on account of the manner in which this work is done, the

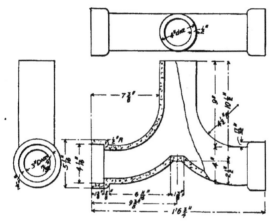

Fig 80 —3-in St Louis "Y"

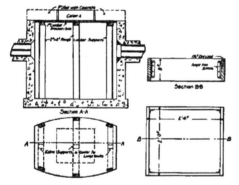

Fig 81 —Forms for Building Vault Tops

separation would considerably increase the work of cost men
without essentially increasing the value of the data. The di-

vision for laying tile, on the form used for reporting sewer tile lateral construction, includes mixing concrete or mortar, this being such a small item that its separation would be of no value On the form shown in Form 43 the cost of laying brick includes the cost of mixing mortar and tending bricklayer.

The division for the cost of placing floor, on both the concrete and the brick vault forms, includes mixing and placing

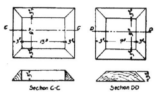

Section C-C   Section D-D

Fig 82 —Forms for Constructing Openings for the Entrance of Ducts into Concrete Vaults

concrete and the division for the cost of placing top includes mixing and placing concrete, filling in and resurfacing, labor in loading surplus earth, and placing frame and cover On the form used for concrete vault construction, the cost of placing sides includes the cost of mixing and placing concrete and filling in around the sides, when necessary

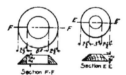

Section F-F   Section E-E

Fig 83 —Forms for Constructing Openings for the Entrance of Circular Ducts Into Concrete Vaults

As in underground construction, generally the building of vault, main conduit and sometimes laterals are carried on at the same time, and large gangs are worked, it is not practicable to make more divisions of vault construction than those shown in these forms, unless several cost men are employed in taking data on the job This may be readily seen from the following description of the usual method used in constructing concrete vaults, which is very much the same for brick vault construction.

A vault gang is generally composed of about 12 or 15 men, an assistant foreman and a team   This gang either builds vaults in advance or following the conduit gang   In either case the two gangs are often widely separated   Six or eight men are detailed to excavate vault, 2 or 3 being assigned to each vault, depending on size and soil

When several vaults are excavated, the balance of the vault gang follow up the men excavating, and mix and lay the concrete bottoms   By the time they have caught up to the men excavating, the concrete bottom of the first vault will be sufficiently dry for placing the sides   The forms are then set up and concrete mixed and placed for all the vault sides. The vault gang will then either start at the first vault and complete same by placing the form for the concrete top, mixing and placing the concrete, setting the iron frame while the concrete is still wet, filling in around the top, resurfacing the street and loading surplus earth ; or will place bottoms on vaults which have been excavated since the sides were placed

METHOD OF KEEPING UNDERGROUND CONDUIT CONSTRUCTION COSTS.

In the method described for keeping costs of line and cable construction, cable splicing, removing material and reconstruction it is required that account shall be kept of the work accomplished by each man in a gang. This is readily done, as the gangs rarely exceed 12 or 15 men. In conduit work, however, this system is impracticable, as the gangs worked are generally composed of 50 to 75 men, and sometimes are as large as 125 men   The following system is therefore used for keeping conduit construction costs:

A report of each day's work is entered on a conduit, vault or lateral form, as the case may be. These reports are either sent to the office each day or at the end of a job, depending upon whether or not cost men are required to keep time as well as costs, and whether the job is large or small   The reports are tabulated and when the job is completed are totaled and averaged

The costs of unloading cars and distributing material, i. e., teaming, labor, and supervision, board and carfare, if any, are added together and entered on the conduit, vault or lateral form, as the case may be, in the column headed "Cost of Unloading and Distributing Material" This cost is not included in the total cost of each day's work, but is kept separate until the job is completed on account of it being generally the case where conduit and vaults are built on the same job that the cost of unloading and distributing the concrete material for the conduit and the vaults cannot be separated as cement, sand or gravel, as the case may be, is not separated when shipped.

The cost of unloading and distributing cement, sand, gravel or stone is kept separate from other unloading and distributing charges and entered on the conduit form in the column reserved for the cost of unloading and distributing material with the word cement, sand, gravel or stone written alongside of it in the "Remark" column Upon completion of the job this cost is prorated and included in the total cost of unloading and distributing material for vaults and for conduit. The volume of concrete as shown in the specifications for building vaults and for building conduit is used as a basis for prorating such cost of unloading and distributing concrete material.

Where mortar or concrete material is unloaded and distributed on job which includes conduit, vaults and lateral construction no attention need be paid to the proportion of such unloading and distributing cost to be charged to lateral construction, as the quantity of cement, sand or gravel used is so small that it is of no importance in estimating The quantity of cement required for a lateral rarely exceeds ¾ of a bag.

When material has once been distributed on the work, any labor in moving material from one part of the job to another part is charged, if tile, to laying tile, if concrete material, to mixing concrete, and the team used in such rehandling is included in the cost of teaming on conduit, vaults, or lateral construction, as the case may be.

In taking cost data, the divisions should be the same as the form shown in Forms 40 to 44, inclusive Costs are taken every ½ hour except when in the judgment of cost keepers the conditions of the work require that costs shall be taken at more frequent intervals, where the gang is small or where a foreman continually shifts his men, where they are taken every 10 or 15 minutes.

Separate data are kept for each section of conduit built where soil, pavement or cross section changes, where the location changes from street to alley, or where on asphalted streets the relative position of the conduit and curb changes

Memorandum books ruled so that there is a column for each ½ hour of a working day and a column on the extreme left of the page for the date, as shown by Form 45, are used for keeping costs of conduit or lateral construction   For conduit construction, there should be a page each for teaming, excavating, handling and mixing concrete and dumping into trench, laying tile, plank and concrete; and filling in   Similar pages are used for lateral construction

In each ½ hour column, under the proper time heading and on the line opposite the proper date on their respective page is entered, every ½ hour, the number of teams working, or the number of men excavating, etc.   The driver is included with the team.

A blue print plan of the work is kept on hand by cost men for reference.   Each vault on the plan is numbered consecutively, and in making reports the space on the form reserved for location shall be filled out with the numbers of the vaults between which the conduit work was installed

In filling out the location on lateral forms the vault from which the lateral runs and the direction in which it runs from the vault is stated   The location on vault forms is filled out with the vault number shown on the blue print plan

For vault construction, the memorandum books are ruled with columns and headings as shown in Form 46   The column on the extreme of the page is used for vault number instead of date   The cost of each vault is kept separate.

Form 40.

Conduit Cross Section...................

McRoy Tile Conduit Construction.

Located Between Vaults No....and No.... at.........Est. No....Class A or B

Date	No. of Lin. Trench Feet Opened	No. of Duct Feet Laid	Cost of Teaming	Cost of Excavating	Cost of Handling and Mixing Concrete and Putting into Trench	Cost of Laying Tile, Plank and Concrete	Cost of Filling In	Supervision	Board	Car Fare	Total Cost	Kind of Pavement and Soil	Roadway or Parkway	No. of Hrs. Worked by Laborers	No. of Men not including Supervisors	No. of Teams	Cost of Unloading and Distributing Material	Remarks

Form 41.

Conduit Cross Section.................

Pump Log Conduit Construction.

Located Between Vaults No...... and No....... at ....Est. No.......

Date	No. of Lin. Trench Feet Opened	No. of Duct Feet Laid	Cost of Teaming	Cost of Excavating	Cost of Laying Pump Log & Plank	Cost of Filling In	Supervision	Board	Car Fare	Total Cost	Kind of Pavement and Soil	Roadway or Parkway	No. of Hrs. Worked by Laborers	No. of Men not including Supervisors	No. of Teams	Cost of Unloading and Distributing Material	Remarks

Form 42.

Conduit Cross Section...................

Sewer Tile Lateral Construction.

Location From Vault No..... North South East West .... Ft. At........... Est. No......

Date	No. of Lin. Trench Feet Opened	No. of Duct Feet Laid	Cost of Teaming	Cost of Excavating	Cost of Laying Tile, Plank and Concrete or Cement	Cost of Filling In	Supervision	Board	Car Fare	Total Cost	Kind of Pavement and Soil	Roadway or Parkway	No. of Hrs. Worked by Laborers	No. of Men not including Supervisors	No. of Teams	Cost of Unloading and Distributing Material	Remarks

Note:—This form is also used for Pump Log Lateral Construction.

Form 43

BRICK VAULT CONSTRUCTION

Location
No of Vault   Size of Vault   Est No

Date	Cost of Teaming	Cost of Excavating	Cost of Placing Floor	Cost of Laying Brick	Cost of Placing Top	Cost of Supervision	Board	Car Fare	Total Cost	Cost of Sewer Connection	Kind of Pavement and Soil	Cost of Unloading and Distributing Material	Remarks

Form 44

CONCRETE VAULT CONSTRUCTION

Location
No of Vault   Size of Vault   Est No ..

Date	Cost of Teaming	Cost of Excavating	Cost of Placing Floor	Cost of Placing Sides	Cost of Placing Top	Supervision	Board	Car Fare	Total Cost	Cost of Sewer Connection	Kind of Pavement and Soil	Cost of Unloading and Distributing Material	Remarks

Form 45

EXCAVATING

Date	7 30 to 8	8 to 8 30	8 30 to 9	9 to 9 30	9 30 to 10	10 to 10 30	10 30 to 11	11 to 11 30	11 30 to 12	1 to 1 30	1 30 to 2	2 to 2 30	2 30 to 3	3 to 3 30	3 30 to 4	4 to 4 30	4 30 to 5	5 to 5 30	Total ½ Hours Work d
June 3	18	20	22	20	21	19	23	23	22	19	20	20	21	21	21	20	20	20	370

Form 46

PLACING BOTTOM

Vault No	7 30 to 8	8 to 8 30	8 30 to 9	9 to 9 30	9 30 to 10	10 to 10 30	10 30 to 11	11 to 11 30	11 30 to 12	1 to 1 30	1 30 to 2	2 to 2 30	2 30 to 3	3 to 3.30	3 30 to 4	4 to 4 30	4 30 to 5	5 to 5 30	Total ½ Hours Work d
1						6	6												12
2							6	6											12
3										6	6	6							18
4													6	6	5				17
5															6	8			14

METHOD OF FIGURING UNDERGROUND CONDUIT CONSTRUCTION COSTS.

In figuring the costs of underground conduit construction the total ½ hours worked on each division of construction as shown in the memorandum books is divided by 2 and multiplied by the rate of wages per hour This will give the cost of excavating, mixing concrete, etc

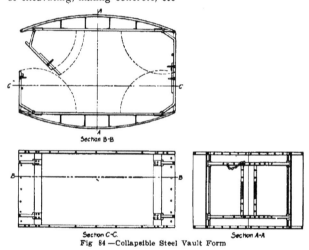

Fig 84 —Collapsible Steel Vault Form

When during the day more than one kind of construction was worked on, or where more than one vault has been built, the method of finding the cost of supervision and expense, board and carfare is as follows

Assuming that 100 men (not including supervisors) have worked 9 hrs each, and that the memorandum book shows:

600 hrs	worked	on	conduit
100 "	"	"	lateral
100 "	"	"	vault No. 1.
100 "	"	"	vault No. 2.

900 hrs. worked

Divide the total hours worked (900) into the cost of super vision and expense, which assume to be $9 00. This will give the cost per man-hour ($0 01) Multiplying the cost of supervision per man-hour ($0 01) by the number of hours spent on each kind of construction, we have as follows:

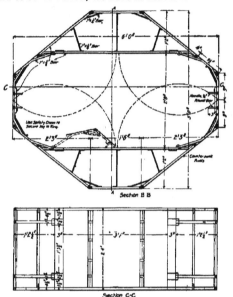

Fig 85.—Collapsible Steel Vault Form for Octagonal Vaults

Kind of Const.	No Hrs Worked		Supervision per Man-Hour.		Cost of Supervision.
Conduit ..	600	×	$ 01	=	$6 00
Lateral . .	100	×	.01	=	1.00
Vault No 1		×	.01	=	1.00
Vault No. 2.. ...	100	×	.01	=	1.00

Carfare and board may be found in the same way

UNDERGROUND CONDUIT COST DATA.

The schedules shown herein comprise data on the labor cost of constructing over 250,000 ft of conduit and lateral, and over 550 vaults.

The rates of wages on which the data given in Tables LXXXI to XCVII are based are as follows:

	Per day of 9 hrs
Foreman	$3 50 to $4 00
Assistant foreman . ..	2 50 to 3.00
Timekeeper	2 00 to 2 50
Watchmen	2 00
Waterboy	1 00
Laborers	2 00
Teams	5.00
	Per hour.
Bricklayers	$0 65 to $0 75

The regular hourly rate was paid for overtime

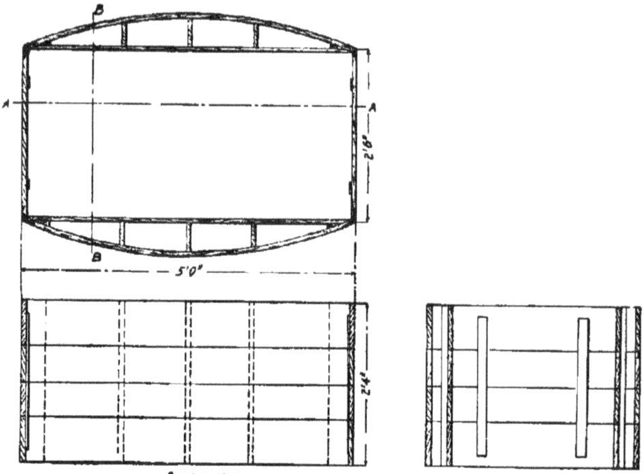

Section A-A   Section B B
Fig 86 —Wooden Vault Form

In the work on which these costs were taken, Mc Roy tile, cement, vault frames and cover, creosoted plank and pump log was shipped in cars and unloaded and distributed by the conduit gang. All other material was bought delivered on the job. The cost of unloading and distributing material, therefore, does not include sand, gravel, stone, brick or sewer tile

As in excavating almost any trench of more than a few hundred feet, there are small portions where nature or kind of soil varies, in drawing up these schedules, if a small percentage of the soil on a job was sand, wet clay, or hard clay, etc, and the balance clay, it is considered clay No separation is made in the schedules showing the average cost of installing the different cross sections of conduit in cities, between the conduit built in roadways and parkways, as there is very little difference in the cost, because, in cities, the surface of parkways is usually grass and it is about as expensive to remove and replace as the pavement of roadways, with the exception of asphalt, which is replaced by paving contractors and not included in the labor costs of resurfacing. The cost of unloading and distributing material is not included in the schedules showing the average cost of each different cross section of conduit in cities, as in many cases cost men were not assigned to a job until after material was distributed.

The data given in Table LXXXVI show the average cost of 68 concrete vaults, size 3, the walls of which were built with the collapsible steel vault form shown by Fig. 84

It will be seen that the cost of these vaults was considerably lower than the cost of the concrete vaults, size 3, given in Table LXXXV. This lower cost is accounted for by the use of the steel form, which proved to be much cheaper to set up and remove than the form shown by Fig 86, which was used in building the vaults on which the data given in Table LXXXV are based

The form is made in two sections, each section forming one side of the vault wall and one-half of each end wall   The end parts are hinged well back on the side parts so that they swing inward immediately, and do not scrape or catch against the concrete when opening   One of the two sections has its end parts fitted with overlapping bars which are fastened as shown, and hold the form rigid so that the use of braces is not required   Two of these forms are used for building a vault to the standard height.

Although no data on the cost of building vaults with the form shown by Fig. 85 were available, it is given to show the style of form used for building octagon shape concrete vaults. The style of the form is similar to that shown by Fig. 84, the end pieces and method of locking being the same.

In connection with the tables of averages given above records of cost of several individual jobs are given in Tables LXXXVII to XCVII

TABLE LXXXI—AVERAGE COST OF McROY TILE CONDUIT CONSTRUCTION IN CITIES

Conduit Cross Section No Ducts	Class	Kind of Soil	Cost of Teaming Per Lin. Ft.	Cost of Excavating Per Lin. Ft.	Cost of Handling and Mixing Concrete Dumping into Trench Per Lin. Ft.	Cost of Laying Plank and Concrete Per Lin. Ft.	Cost of Filling In Per Lin. Ft.	Supervision Per Lin. Ft.	Total Cost Per Lin. Ft.	Total Cost Per Duct Ft.
2	A	Clay	$0 0267	$0 0629	$0 0297	$0 0131	$0 0440	$0 0310	$0 2074	$0 1037
		Hard Clay	0 0438	0 0705	0 0386	0 0133	0 0640	0 0432	0 2634	0 1317
		Average ..	0 0352	0 0667	0 0342	0 0132	0 0490	0 0371	0 2354	0 1177
3	A	Sand ..	0 0160	0 0588	0 0441	0 0294	0 0147	0 0515	0 2145	0 0715
		Clay . ..	0 0174	0 0663	0 0536	0 0169	0 0503	0 0367	0 2412	0 0804
		Hard Clay	0 0223	0 0770	0 0425	0 0125	0 0415	0 0314	0 2272	0 0757
		Average	0 0186	0 0674	0 0467	0 0196	0 0355	0 0398	0 2276	0 0759
3	B	Sand	0 0167	0 0593	0 0173	0 0178	0 0254	0 0380	0 1744	0 0581
		Clay	0 0163	0 0652	0 0189	0 0193	0 0492	0 0406	0 2094	0 0698
		Hard Clay	0 0198	0 0781	0 0166	0 0199	0 0521	0 0372	0 2237	0 0746
		Average .	0 0176	0 0675	0 0176	0 0190	0 0422	0 0386	0 2025	0 0675
4	A	Sand	0 0298	0 0904	0 0529	0 0296	0 0201	0 0426	0 2654	0 0664
		Clay ...	0 0381	0 1291	0 0490	0 0322	0 0384	0 0447	0 3315	0 0829
		Hard Clay	0 0259	0 1547	0 0560	0 0330	0 0602	0 0671	0 3969	0 0992
		Average	0 0313	0 1247	0 0526	0 0316	0 0346	0 0515	0 3313	0 0825
4	B	Sand	0 0253	0 0917	0 0294	0 0190	0 0350	0 0382	0 2386	0 0597
		Clay	0 0276	0 1194	0 0282	0 0201	0 0521	0 0416	0 2890	0 0722
		Hard Clay	0 0801	0 1601	0 0201	0 0242	0 0572	0 0574	0 3491	0 0873
		Average	0 0277	0 1237	0 0259	0 0211	0 0481	0 0457	0 2922	0 0731
5	A	Sand	0 0800	0 1121	0 0649	0 0342	0 0501	0 0417	0 3330	0 0666
		Clay	0 0291	0 1507	0 0620	0 0387	0 0604	0 0481	0 3890	0 0778
		Average	0 0296	0 1314	0 0635	0 0364	0 0552	0 0449	0 3610	0 0722
6	A	Sand	0 0234	0 0911	0 0614	0 0428	0 0514	0 0591	0 3292	0 0549
		Clay	0 0301	0 1348	0 0603	0 0212	0 0820	0 0713	0 3997	0 0666
		Hard Clay	0 0397	0 1602	0 0533	0 0330	0 0834	0 0698	0 4394	0 0732
		Average	0 0311	0 1287	0 0583	0 0323	0 0723	0 0667	0 3894	0 0649
6	B	Sand	0 0315	0 1127	0 0227	0 0343	0 0576	0 0601	0 3189	0 0532
		Clay	0 0296	0 1483	0 0259	0 0360	0 0801	0 0662	0 3861	0 0643
		Hard Clay	0 0380	0 1587	0 0204	0 0313	0 0740	0 0742	0 3966	0 0661
		Average .	0 0330	0 1399	0 0230	0 0339	0 0706	0 0668	0 3672	0 0612
7	A	Clay	0 0307	0 1429	0 0693	0 0341	0 0701	0 0768	0 4239	0 0606
8	A	Sand	0 0246	0 1196	0 0686	0 0302	0 0717	0 0612	0 3759	0 0470
		Clay	0 0384	0,1547	0 0702	0 0366	0 0642	0 0708	0 4349	0 0544
		Hard Clay	0 0401	0 1704	0 0603	0 0327	0 0823	0 0796	0 4654	0 0582
		Average	0 0344	0 1482	0 0664	0 0332	0 0727	0 0705	0 4254	0 0532
9	A	Sand	0 0311	0 1257	0 0743	0 0287	0 0733	0 0711	0 4042	0 0449
		Clay	0 0299	0 1605	0 0728	0 0402	0 0839	0 0605	0 4678	0 0520
		Hard Clay	0 0471	0 1782	0 0696	0 0423	0 0876	0 0673	0 4921	0 0547
		Average	0 0360	0 1548	0 0722	0 0371	0 0816	0 0730	0 4547	0 0505
11	A	Sand	0 0402	0 1464	0 0884	0 0493	0 0812	0 0804	0 4859	0 0442
		Clay ..	0 0501	0 1848	0 0779	0 0501	0 0934	0 0903	0 5465	0 0497
		Average	0 0452	0 1656	0 0831	0 0497	0 0873	0 0853	0 5162	0 0469
12	A	Sand	0 0422	0 1457	0 0787	0 0522	0 0786	0 0781	0 4755	0 0396
		Clay	0 0517	0 1911	0 0824	0 0498	0 0948	0 0829	0 5527	0 0461
		Hard Clay	0 0476	0 2127	0 0760	0 0517	0 1014	0 0887	0 5781	0 0482
		Average	0 0472	0 1832	0 0790	0 0512	0 0916	0 0832	0 5354	0 0446

TABLE LXXXII—AVERAGE COST OF PUMP LOG CONDUIT CONSTRUCTION IN CITIES

Kind of Soil	Conduit Cross Section No. Ducts	Cost of Teaming	Cost of Excavating.	Cost of Laying Pump Log and Plank.	Cost of Filling in.	Supervision	Total Cost per Lin. Ft.	Total Cost per Duct Ft.
Sand and Water	1	$0 0304	$0 0612	$0 0177	$0 0314	$0 0240	$0 1647	$0 1647
Clay .	1	0 0281	0 0574	0 0189	0 0247	0 0262	0 1553	0 1553
Clay and Water	1	0 0331	0 0818	0 0213	0 0386	0 0341	0 2089	0 2089
Average	1	0 0305	0 0668	0 0193	0 0316	0 0281	0 1763	0 1763
Sand and Water	2	0 0334	0 0843	0 0278	0 0397	0 0299	0 2151	0 1076
Clay and Water .	2	0 0317	0 1054	0 0262	0 0411	0 0352	0 2396	0 1198
Average	2	0 0327	0 0949	0 0270	0 0404	0 0326	0 2274	0 1137
Sand and Water	4	0 0412	0 1401	0 0411	0 0519	0 0496	0 3239	0 0810
Clay	4	0 0487	0 1482	0 0490	0 0537	0 0512	0 3508	0 0877
Average	4	0 0449	0 1442	0 0451	0 0528	0 0504	0 3374	0 0844

TABLE LXXXIII —Average Cost of Sewer Tile Lateral Construction in Cities

Kind of Soil	Conduit Cross Section No. Ducts	Cost of Teaming	Cost of Excavating	Cost of Laying Tile, Plank and Concrete	Cost of Filling In	Supervision	Total Cost per Lin Ft	Total Cost per Duct Ft
Sand	1	$0 0099	$0 0364	$0 0201	$0 0219	$0 0291	$0 1174	$0 1174
Clay	1	0 0167	0 0467	0 0156	0 0260	0 0327	0 1377	0 1377
Hard Clay	1	0 0234	0 0581	0 0198	0 0293	0 0302	0 1608	0 1608
Very Hard Clay	1	0 0408	0 0720	0 0178	0 0311	0 0414	0 2031	0 2031
Average	1	0 0227	0 0533	0 0183	0 0271	0 0333	0 1547	0 1547
Clay	2	0 0201	0 0709	0 0223	0 0502	0 0390	0 2025	0 1013

TABLE LXXXIV —Average Cost of Brick Vault Construction in Cities

Kind of Soil	Size No. of Vaults	Cost of Teaming	Cost of Excavating	Cost of Placing Floor	Cost of Laying Brick	Cost of Placing Top	Cost of Supervision	Total Cost
Sand	1	$2 80	$3 69	$0 94	$11 23	$3 18	$2 87	$24 71
Clay	1	3 28	4 56	0 73	11 39	3 69	3 04	26 69
Hard Clay	1	3 27	5 64	1 04	10 86	3 82	3 16	27 79
Average	1	3 12	4 63	0 90	11 16	3 56	3 02	26 39
Sand	2	2 97	3 81	1 15	10 71	3 34	3 01	24 99
Clay	2	3 47	4 48	0 92	11 22	3 48	3 41	26 98
Hard Clay	2	3 49	5 52	1 14	11 46	3 67	3 28	28 56
Average	2	3 31	4 60	1 07	11 13	3 50	3 23	26 84
Sand	3	2 62	3 85	1 12	12 63	2 55	3 10	25 87
Clay	3	3 64	4 52	1 26	11 47	3 76	3 56	28 31
Hard Clay	3	3 01	5 71	1 34	13 89	3 58	2 93	30 46
Average	3	3 09	4 69	1 24	12 66	3 30	3 20	28 18
Sand	4	3 62	4 54	1 82	14 41	4 07	4 12	32 58
Clay	4	4 06	5 78	1 76	14 28	5 83	4 57	36 2b
Hard Clay	4	4 85	7 51	2 23	14 12	4 32	4 98	38 01
Average	4	4 17	5 94	1 94	14 27	4 74	4 56	35 62
Sand	5	3 48	4 69	2 04	14 47	4 16	4 21	33 05
Clay	5	4 17	5 54	1 93	14 32	5 94	4 86	36 76
Average	5	3 83	5 12	1 98	14 39	5 05	4 54	34 91
Sand	6	4 01	4 76	2 33	14 35	4 34	4 51	34 30
Clay	6	3 90	5 71	2 04	14 57	5 66	4 22	36 10
Hard Clay	6	4 46	7 42	2 11	13 86	5 81	4 91	38 57
Average	6	4 12	5 96	2 16	14 26	5 27	4 55	36 32
Sand	8	6 27	6 27	3 06	18 27	5 98	5 64	45 49
Clay	8	6 90	8 04	2 87	18 94	6 40	6 87	50 02
Average	8	6 59	7 15	2 97	18 60	6 19	6 25	47 75
Sand	9*	2 40	4 01	1 19	11 63	3 43	3 12	26 32
Clay	9*	3 57	4 72	1 21	11 22	3 59	3 44	27 75
Hard Clay	9*	3 68	5 43	1 07	11 56	3 86	3 52	29 12
Average	9*	3 40	4 72	1 16	11 47	3 62	3 36	27 73
Sand	9†	3 19	4 27	1 26	12 04	4 01	3 61	28 38
Clay	9†	3 39	4 63	1 19	12 83	4 32	3 97	30 33
Average	9†	3 29	4 45	1 23	12 43	4 17	3 79	29 36
Sand	10	7 94	16 43	3 96	26 14	7 27	10 74	72 48
Clay	10	9 12	18 74	4 67	24 82	8 02	12 02	77 39
Hard Clay	10	9 53	22 04	4 09	25 32	7 73	13 81	82 52
Average	10	8 86	19 07	4 24	25 43	7 67	12 19	77 46
Clay	11	10 52	26 02	5 34	30 96	8 52	15 11	96 47
Clay	12	9 93	25 64	5 83	32 11	8 36	14 04	95 91
Hard Clay	12	10 14	28 89	5 16	31 07	8 84	14 41	98 50
Average	12	10 03	27 27	5 49	31 59	8 60	14 23	97 21

*For 8 ducts or less †For 9 ducts to 12 ducts

TABLE LXXXV —Average Cost of Concrete Vault Construction in Cities

Kind of Soil	Size No of Vaults	Cost of Teaming	Cost of Excavating	Cost of Placing Floor	Cost of Placing Sides	Cost of Placing Top	Supervision	Total Cost
Sand	1	$2 44	$3 79	$1 02	$4 41	$2 44	$2 11	$16 21
Clay	1	3 16	4 38	0 87	4 58	2 83	2 46	18 28
Average	1	2 80	4 08	0 95	4 50	2 63	2 29	17 25
Sand	3	2 78	3 91	1 22	5 79	2 22	2 51	18 43
Clay	3	3 21	4 60	1 14	5 48	3 51	2 57	20 83
Hard Clay	3	3 54	5 83	1 18	5 64	3 42	2 82	22 43
Average	3	3 18	4 78	1 18	5 64	3 05	2 73	20 56

TABLE LXXXVI.—AVERAGE COST OF 68 CONCRETE VAULTS, SIZE 3

Kind of Soil	No of Vaults Built	Cost of Teaming	Cost of Excavating	Cost of Placing Floor	Cost of Placing Sides	Cost of Placing Top	Cost of Supervision	Total Cost
(In)	49	$2 76	$4 42	$1 08	$3 66	$3 20	$2 58	$17 70
Hard (In)	19	3 21	5 69	1 03	3 79	3 11	2 67	19 40

Note—These vaults were built after the conduit was installed.

TABLE LXXXVII.—COST OF McROY TILE CONDUIT CONSTRUCTION ON JOB 1

Conduit Cross Section	No of Lin Trench Feet Opened	No of Duct Feet Laid	Cost of Teaming Per Lin Ft	Cost of Excavating Per Lin Ft	Cost of Handling, Mixing and Dumping Concrete into trench Per Lin Ft	Cost of Laying Tile Plank and Concrete Per Lin Ft	Cost of Filling in Per Lin Ft	Supervision Per Lin Ft
McROY TILE CONDUIT								
3 Duct	660	1,980	$ .0194	$ .0751	$ .0400	$ .0127	$ .0382	$ .0291
6 Duct	1,004	6,024	.0324	.1581	.0514	.0315	.0602	.0654
9 Duct	2,212	19,908	.0429	.1740	.0880	.0412	.0843	.0666
Average Cross Section 7 20	3,876	27,912	.0362	.1530	.0589	.0338	.0754	.0599
PUMP LOG CONDUIT								
1 Duct	822	822	.0250	.0543		.0186	.0320	.0224
4 Duct	426	1,704	.0444	.1421		.0451	.0326	.0482
Average Cross Section, 2 02	1,248	2,526	.0316	.0843		.0277	.0390	.0310
ALL CONDUIT								
Average Cross Section, 5 94	5,124	26,428						
9 Vaults.								
CONDUIT AND VAULTS								
Average Cross Section, 5 94	5,124	30,438						

Conduit Cross Section	Total Cost Per Lin Ft	Per Duct Ft	Kind of Pavement and Soil	Roadway or Parkway	No Hours Worked by Laborers	No of Men not including Supervisors	No of Teams
McROY TILE CONDUIT							
3 Duct	$ .2145	$ .0715	Hard Clay	Parkway	487	57	3
6 Duct	.4190	.0398		Parkway	1,456	170	6
9 Duct	.4770	.0530	Cinders on Hard Clay	Roadway	3,625	425	19
Average Cross Section, 7 20	.4172	.0579		Roadway	5,568	652	28
PUMP LOG CONDUIT							
1 Duct	.1520	.1520	Macadam on Clay	Roadway	425	49	5
4 Duct	.3324	.0831	No Pavement—Clay	Alley	482	565	4
Average Cross Section, 2 02	.2136	.1055			907	614	9
ALL CONDUIT							
Average Cross Section, 5 94	.3677	.0619					
CONDUIT AND VAULTS.							
Average Cross Section, 5 94	.4529	.0762					

TABLE LXXXVIII.—COST OF BRICK VAULT CONSTRUCTION ON JOB 1.

Location as shown on Blue Print Plans	Cost of Teaming	Cost of Excavating	Cost of Placing Floor	Cost of Laying Brick	Cost of Placing Top	Cost of Supervision	Board	Car Fare	Cost of Sewer Connection	Total Cost	Kind of Pavement and Soil
					Size No 2 VAULTS						
No 1	$2 86	$5 22	$1 14	$11 34	$3 00	$2 84			$3 14	$29 63	No Pav'mt. Hard Clay.
No 2	3 14	5 14	1 11	10 82	3 22	2 68			2 66	28 70	No Pav'mt. Hard Clay.
Total	6 00	10 86	2 26	22 16	6 31	5 52			5 82	55 42	
Average	3 00	5 18	1 12	11 08	3 16	2 76			2 91	29 21	
					Size No 5 VAULTS						
No 3	3 54	6 24	1 86	14 20	5 42	4 38			3 78	39 42	No Pav'mt Hard Clay.
No 5	3 42	5 22	1 77	13 80	5 27	4 14			3 88	33 62	No Pav'mt Clay
No 6	3 67	5 44	1 98	14 54	5 36	4 26			7 16	38 63	
Total	10 63	16 90	5 61	42 54	16 05	12 78			2 39	111 67	
Average	3 54	5 63	1 87	14 18	5 35	4 26			2 39	37 22	
					Size No 8 VAULTS						
No 4	9 00	24 86	4 92	29 50	8 24	14 24	.		3 86	94 62	No Pav'mt Clay
					Size No 12 VAULTS						
No 9	9 24	27 04	5 04	30 64	8 36	14 04	.		3 54	97 90	Cedar on Hard Clay.
					Size No 6 VAULTS						
No 7	3 90	6 77	1 92	13 20	5 40	4 10		:	2 94	38 23	Cedar on Hard Clay
No 8	4 10	7 14	2 08	13 20	5 32	4 26		:	2 94	36 10	
Total	8 00	13 91	4 00	26 40	10 72	8 36			1 47	74 33	
Average	4 00	6 96	2 00	13 20	5 36	4 18			1 42	37 17	
Total of all	42 87	93 07	21 83	151 34	44 68	54 94			23 22	436 94	
Average of all	4 76	10 34	2 43	16 81	5 53	6 11			2 69	48 55	

TABLE LXXXIX.—COST OF McROY TILE CONDUIT CONSTRUCTION ON JOB 2

AVERAGE COST OF CONDUIT CONSTRUCTION

Conduit Cross Section	No of Lin Trench Feet Opened	No of Duct Feet Laid	Cost of Teaming, Per Lin Ft	Cost of Excavating Per Lin Ft	Cost of Handling, Mixing and Dumping into trench Concrete Per Lin Ft	Cost of Laying Tile and Concrete Per Lin Ft	Cost of Filling in Per Lin Ft	Supervision Per Lin Ft	Board Per Lin Ft
4 Duct	486	1,944	$ 0226	$ 1548	$ 0516	$ 0226	$ 0669	$ 1303	$ 0094
4 Duct	1,866	7,464	0259	1547	0564	0189	0812	0634	0041
7 Duct	1,282	8,974	0297	1404	0533	0330	0831	0651	0035
2 Duct with 2 Sewer Tile Laterals in same trench	446	1,784	0384	0949	0451	0238	0575	0550	0029
Average Cross Section 4.94	4,080	20,166	0248	1437	0538	0243	0775	0710	0044
CONDUIT AND VAULTS 8 Vaults									
Average Cross Section 4.94	4,080	20,166							

AVERAGE COST OF CONDUIT CONSTRUCTION

Conduit Cross Section	Car Fare Per Lin Ft	Total Cost Per Lin Ft	Total Cost Per Duct Ft	Kind of Pavement and Soil	Roadway or Parkway	No of Hours Worked by Laborers	No of Men not including Supervisors	No of Teams
4 Duct	$ 0014	$ 4596	1149	Macadam on Hard Clay	Roadway	583	08	4
4 Duct	0012	4058	1014	Brick on Hard Clay		229	242	14
7 Duct	0007	4089	0584	Macadam on Clay	..	1,641	204	14
2 Duct with 2 Sewer Tile Laterals in same trench	0009	2885	0721	Macadam on Hard Clay	..	280	53	1
Average Cross Section 4.94	0011	4004	0810			4,843	617	33
CONDUIT AND VAULTS		4771	0965					

TABLE LXXXIXa — COST OF BRICK VAULT CONSTRUCTION ON JOB 2

Location as shown on Blue Print Plan	Cost of Teaming	Cost of Excavating	Cost of Placing Floor	Cost of Laying Brick	Cost of Placing Top	Cost of Supervision	Board	Car Fare	Cost of Sewer Connection	Total Cost	Kind of Pavement and Soil
No 1	$2 80	$5 75	$1 70	$15 00	$3 53	8 35	$0 20	$0 05	None	$32 38	Macadam on Hard Clay
No 2	2 86	5 75	1 75	13 86	3 08	2 83	18	02	$17 50	47 65	"
No 3	2 98	5 38	1 80	11 88	3 00	2 58	18	05	17 32	45 77	"
No 4	3 05	4 55	1 50	11 90	4 25	2 71	12	02	16 58	44 68	"
No 5	3 30	7 65	1 65	12 50	4 40	2 86	45	02	17 00	49 25	"
No 6	2 95	5 60	1 35	18 30	3 15	3 10	22	04	None	37 21	"
No 7	3 10	5 40	1 75	10 85	1 30	3 23	30	06		37 24	"
No 8	3 10	5 10	1 30	10 85	20 46	2 75	15	03		26 91	.
Total	24 14	46 18	13 30	105 64	20 46	23 41	1 80	36	68 40	313 09	
Average	3 01	5 77	1 66	13 25	3 68	2 93	23	05	8 55	39 14	

TABLE XC.—COST OF McROY TILE CONDUIT CONSTRUCTION ON JOB 3

Conduit Cross Section	No of Lin Trench Feet Opened	No of Duct Feet Laid	Cost of Teaming, Per Lin Ft	Cost of Excavating into trench Per Lin Ft	Cost of Handling Mixing and Dumping Concrete Per Lin Ft	Cost of Laying Tile and Concrete Per Lin Ft	Cost of Filling in Per Lin Ft	Supervision Per Lin Ft	Board Per Lin Ft	Car Fare Per Lin Ft	Total Cost Not inc Unload'g and Dist Material Per Lin Ft
3 Duct	34	102	$ 0199	$ 0688	$ 0441	$ 0294	$ 0147	$ 0441	$ 0274	$ 0001	$ 1915
4 Duct	42	168	0323	0664	0536	0357	0296	0357	0083		2295
4 Duct	1,278	5,112	0235	0476	0316	0239	0360	0197	0037		1815
2 Duct	271	742	0238	0795	0441	0305	0635	0415	0081		2995
5 Duct	868	4,340	0041	0346	0297	0219	0245	0207	0043	0010	1602
6 Duct	1,290	6,450	0244	0648	0426	0320	0533	0421	0069	0006	2661
6 Duct	1,310	7,860	0226	0427	0347	0223	0294	0204	0044		1580
7 Duct	1,162	6,972	0047	0423	0274	0247	0407	0226	0034	0010	1864
8 Duct	1,744	9,424	0105	0484	0356	0252	0408	0337	0071	0009	2133
9 Duct	1,178	5,208	0101	0412	0322	0257	0400	0278	0049	0007	1663
11 Duct	1,855	16,695	0150	0908	0542	0289	0278	0230	0035	0002	1699
	447	4,917		0495	0351	0456	0485	0718	0196		3406
Average Cross Section, 6 43	10,579	67,990				0271	0375	0285	0054	0005	1995
SEWER TILE LATERAL CONSTRUCTION											
1 Duct	2,736	2,736	0084	0400	0106	0188	0296	0203	0034	0006	1317
MAIN CONDUIT AND LATERALS											
Average Cross Section 5 31	13,315	70,726	0144	0476	0300	0264	0359	0268	0049	0005	1856
MAIN CONDUIT, INCLUDING VAULTS											
Average Cross Section, 6 43	10,579	67,990	14 Vaults.								2339
MAIN CONDUIT VAULTS AND LATERALS											
Average Cross Section, 5 31	13,215	70,726	14 Vaults								2130

TABLE XC (CONTINUED)—COST OF McROY TILE CONDUIT CONSTRUCTION ON JOB 3

Conduit Cross Section	Total Cost Not inc Unload'g and Dist Material Per Duct Ft	Kind of Pavement and Soil	Roadway or Parkway	No of Hours Worked by Laborers	No of Men not including Supervisors	No of Teams	Cost of Unloading and Distributing Material Per Lin Ft	Per Duct Ft	Total Cost including Unloading and Distributing Material Per Lin Ft	Per Duct Ft
3 Duct	$ 0662	Sand	Roadway	18	2		$ 0118	$ 0035	2103	$ 0701
4 Duct	0574	"	"	27	3		0133	0033	2428	0607
4 Duct	0464	Clay	Parkway	684	77	4	0189	0047	2904	0501
2 Duct	1498	Macadam on Clay	Roadway	385	43	3	0161	0080	3156	1578
5 Duct	0320	Macadam on Sand	"	478	53½	4	0269	0054	1871	0374
5 Duct	0532	Clay	Parkway	1,092	155	6	0269	0054	2930	0586
6 Duct	0263	Clay and Loam	Roadway	779½	83½	3	0240	0040	1820	0303
5 Duct	0311	Clay	Parkway	702	78	4	0201	0033	2965	0344
6 Duct	0305	Clay and Loam	"	542	63	3	0329	0047	2462	0362
7 Duct	0233	Macadam on Clay	"	857½	94	5	0342	0043	2305	0276
8 Duct	0189	Sandy Loam	"	1,196½	121½	5	0399	0044	2088	0233
9 Duct	0309	Sand	Roadway	380	44		0504	0046	3910	0365
11 Duct	0311						0288	0045	2283	0356
Average Cross Section, 6 43				7,081½	819½	42				
SEWER TILE LATERAL CONSTRUCTION										
1 Duct	1317	Clay	Alley	1,171	139	4				
MAIN CONDUIT AND LATERALS										
Average Cross Section, 5 31	0349						0229	0043	2085	0392
MAIN CONDUIT, INCLUDING VAULTS										
Average Cross Section, 6 43							0302	0047	2641'	0411
MAIN CONDUIT, VAULTS AND LATERALS										
Average Cross Section, 5 31	0401	...	...				0240	0045	2270	0446

TABLE XCI—COST OF BRICK VAULT CONSTRUCTION ON JOB 3

Location	Cost of Teaming	Cost of Excavating	Cost of Placing Floor	Cost of Laying Brick	Cost of Placing Top	Cost of Supervision	Board	Car Fare	Total Cost Not inc Unloading and Distribut'g Material	Kind of Pavement and Soil	Cost of Unloading and Distribut'g Material	Total Cost including Unloading and Distribut'g Material
Size No 3 Vaults												
No 18	$5 75	$4 00	$1 50	$10 50	$2 75	$3 26	$0 25	$0 75	$28 76	Clay	$1 04	$29 80
No 21	4 10	4 00	1 75	9 00	2 75	3 60	1 05		26 25		1 04	27 29
No 22	1 75	4 00	1 40	12 00	2 30	3 65	1 50		26 60	..	1 04	27 64
No 25	1 75	4 00	1 50	12 00	2 75	3 25	1 25	15	27 65	..	1 04	28 69
No 27	1 50	4 00	1 25	10 25	2 75	3 25	1 00	10	24 35	Sand	1 04	25 39
No 26	2 00	4 00	1 25	10 50	2 50	3 60	1 00		24 60		1 04	25 64
No 24	2 10	4 00	1 50	12 00	2 75	4 25	1 50		28 10		1 04	29 14
Size No 4 Vaults												
No 23	2 25	4 00	1 60	9 00	2 51	6 95	2 10		28 41	Macadam on Loam & Clay	1 04	29 45
No 16	2 25	4 00	1 00	11 00	1 75	3 80	1 00	10	24 90	Loam & Clay	1 04	25 94
No 17	3 05	4 00	1 00	10 95	2 75	2 45	1 25		25 45	Loam ..	1 04	26 49
No 20	2 50	4 00	1 25	8 00	2 75	2 31	0 25		21 06	..	1 04	22 10
Total*	29 64	44 00	15 00	115 20	28 31	41 02	12 40	1 10	286 03		11 44	297 47
Average	2 64	4 00	1 36	10 47	2 57	3 73	1 13	10	26 00		1 04	27 04
Size No 9 Vaults												
No 15†	3 90	4 00	1 05	11 25	3 18	2 60	75	15	22 18	Macadam	1 04	23 22
No 19	4 15	4 00	1 05	12 00	2 50	3 53	75		27 73	Clay	1 04	28 77
Total	8 05	8 00	2 10	23 25	5 68	6 13	1 50	15	49 91		2 08	51 99
Average	4 02	4 00	1 05	11 63	2 84	3 07	75	07	24 95		1 04	25 99
No 5	2 90	4 00	2 00	12 00	1 50	3 25 *(For 8 Ducts or Less)*	2 25	1 25	27 90	Clay	1 04	28 94
Total of all Vaults	36 05	56 00	18 05	150 45	35 49	50 40	16 15		363 84		14 56	378 40
Average	2 57	4 00	1 29	10 75	2 54	3 60	1 15	1 09	25 99		1 04	27 03

* Two men dug one vault each day and bricklayers built one vault per day

† Old vault torn out and old floor used

TABLE XCII — COST OF McROY TILE CONDUIT CONSTRUCTION ON JOB 4

Conduit Cross Section	No of Lin Trench Feet Opened	No of Duct Feet Laid	Cost of Teaming, Per Lin Ft	Cost of Excavating into trench Per Lin Ft	Cost of Handling, Mixing and Dumping Concrete into trench Per Lin Ft	Cost of Laying Tile and Concrete Per Lin Ft	Cost of Filling in Per Lin Ft	Supervision Per Lin Ft	Board Per Lin Ft	Car Fare Per Lin Ft	Total Cost Not inc Unload'g and Dist Material Per Lin Ft
McROY TILE CONDUIT											
6 Duct	3,999	23,994	$ 0573	$ 0878	$ 0390	$ 0191	$ 1332	$ 0556	$ 0051	$ .0004	$ 3975
2 Duct	1,301	2,602	0267	0539	0392	0145	0612	0393	0043	0007	2498
3 Duct	2,598	7,794	0314	0747	0337	0147	0563	0308	0028	0008	2542
Average Cross Section, 4 35	7,898	34,390	0437	0796	0370	0169	0994	0448	0042	0004	3260
SEWER TILE LATERAL											
1 Duct	269	269	0420	0660		0157	0311	0843	0239	0011	2651
1 Duct	1,352	1,362	0231	0572		0133	0231	0254	0045	0003	1459
2 Duct	168	336	0161	0720		0223	0634	0368	0030		2136
Average Cross Section 1 09	1,789	1,967	0254	0599		0145	0281	0353	0073	0004	1709
Average Cross Section, 3 75 — MAIN CONDUIT AND LATERALS	9 687	36,347	0404	0756	0301		0862	0430	0048	0004	2973
Average Cross Section, 4 35 — MAIN CONDUIT AND LATERALS AND VAULTS (17 Vaults)	7,898	34,390									4046
Average Cross Section, 3 76 — MAIN CONDUIT LATERALS AND VAULTS (17 Vaults)	9,687	36,347									3614

Conduit Cross Section	Total Cost Not inc Unload'g and Dist Material Per Duct Ft	Kind of Pavement and Soil	Roadway or Parkway	No of Hours Worked by Laborers	No of Men not including Supervisors	No of Teams	Cost of Unloading and Distributing Material Per Lin Ft	Cost of Unloading and Distributing Material Per Duct Ft	Total Cost Including Unloading and Distributing Material Per Lin Ft	Total Cost Including Unloading and Distributing Material Per Duct Ft
McROY TILE CONDUIT										
6 Duct	$ 0662	Cdr Blk on Hard Clay	Roadway	4,213	494	111	$ 0964	$ 0161	$ 4939	$ 0823
2 Duct	1249		McRoy	1,017	120	9	0642	0321	3140	1570
3 Duct	0847		Parkway	2,018	228	35	0758	0253	3300	1100
Average Cross Section, 4 35	0749	Clay		7,278	842	155	0843	0193	4103	0942
SEWER TILE LATERAL										
1 Duct	$ 2651	Mac'm & Very Hd Cl'y	Roadway	120	17	8				
1 Duct	1459	Clay	Parkway	480	51	11				
2 Duct	1068		Roadway	106	18	2				
Average Cross Section 1 09	1502	Macadam on Clay		706	86	21				
Average Cross Section, 3 75 — MAIN CONDUIT AND VAULTS	0793						0088	0183	3661	0976
Average Cross Section, 4 35 — MAIN CONDUIT AND LATERALS	0929						0925	0213	4971	1142
Average Cross Section, 3 75 — MAIN CONDUIT, LATERALS AND VAULTS	0963						0754	0201	4368	1164

TABLE XCIII—COST OF BRICK VAULT CONSTRUCTION ON JOB 4

Location as shown on Blue Print Plan	Cost of Teaming	Cost of Excavating	Cost of Placing Floor	Cost of Laying Brick	Cost of Placing Top	Cost of Supervision	Board	Car Fare	Cost of Sewer Connection included in Total Cost	Total Cost Not inc Unloading and Distribut'g Material	Kind of Pavement and Soil	Cost of Unloading and Distribut'g Material	Cost of Vault including Unloading and Distribut'g Material
No 1	$3 02	$5 18	$0 60	$12 38	$1 40	$ 96	$0 08	$0 01	$22 21	$45 84	Brick on Clay	$3 81	$49 65
No 2	2 80	5 62	75	11 65	1 50	80	05		22 21	45 38		3 81	49 19
Size No 1 Vaults													
No 3	2 88	3 80	80	11 50	69	58	06		22 21	43 72	Cedar Bl ck on Clay	3 81	47 53
No 5	3 05	5 60	58	11 30	48	75	05		22 21	44 97		3 81	48 78
No 7	3 03	4 90	77	11 18	63	80	03	01	22 21	44 68	::	3 81	48 49
No 8	3 10	4 15	73	12 21	61	91	15		22 21	44 71		3 81	48 52
No 9	20 75	4 00	01	12 40	1 00	72	41	02	22 21	46 50	Clay	3 81	50 31
Total	20 63	34 00	5 01	82 62	10 82	6 96			155 47	315 70		26 67	342 37
Average	2 95	4 86	71	11 80	1 55		06	02	22 21	45 10		3 81	48 91
Size No 2 Vaults													
No 4	2 85	4 25	60	12 40	1 45	1 04	06	02	None	22 67	Clay	3 81	26 48
No 6	3 00	4 75	62	11 29	52	92	07	01		22 12		3 62	25 93
Total	5 85	9 00	1 22	23 69	1 97	1 96	01	03		44 79		7 62	52 41
Average	2 93	4 50	61	11 84	1 49	98	03	01		22 39		3 81	26 21
Size No 3 Vaults													
No 10	3 10	3 25	80	14 25	3 95	1 98	16	01	1 04	27 49	Cedar Bl ck on Hd Clay	3 81	31 30
No 11	2 95	4 25	75	13 50	3 98	1 30	07		7 37	28 85		3 81	32 66
No 12	3 05	4 50	73	13 75	3 46	2 26	05	03	7 37	34 16		3 81	37 97
No 13	3 05	3 50	84	13 60	3 60	2 21	21		7 20	34 42	:	3 81	38 23
No 14	2 97	6 00	75	15 00	3 80	2 54	18	04	3 10	32 44	:	3 81	36 25
No 15	2 93	4 25	82	18 40	3 00	2 95	29	01	1 25	37 36	:	3 81	41 17
No 16	2 95	4 25	70	14 83	4 05	2 85	13	01	4 51	31 97	:	3 81	35 78
No 17	3 00	5 45	2 17	13 77	27 93	1 80	1 21	11		33 99		30 48	35 90
Total	24 00	35 63	8 17	116 10	27 93	19 59	1 21	11	26 84	259 78		30 48	290 28
Average	3 00	4 45	1 02	14 51	3 49	2 48	15	01	3 36	32 47		3 81	36 28
Total of all Vaults	50 48	78 63	14 40	222 41	41 72	28 47	1 69	16	182 31	620 27		64 77	685 04
Average	2 97	4 62	85	13 08	2 45	1 67	10	01	10 73	36 48		3 81	40 29

* Sewer Connections were made by Maywood Public Works Dept

TABLE XCIV—COST OF McROY TILE CONDUIT CONSTRUCTION ON JOB 5

Conduit Cross Section	No of Lin Trench Feet Opened	No of Duct Feet Laid	Cost of Teaming Per Lin Ft	Cost of Excavating Per Lin Ft	Cost of Handling, Mixing and Dumping Concrete into trench Per Lin Ft	Cost of Laying Tile and Concrete Per Lin Ft	Cost of Filling in Per Lin Ft	Supervision Per Lin Ft
McRoy Tile Conduit								
4 Duct	75	100	$ .0065	$ .04	$ .02	$ .02	$ .02	$ .01
5 Duct	781	3,095	.0130	.0475	.0320	.0266	.0252	.0383
9 Duct	1,042	9,378	.0093	.0783	.0392	.0285	.0262	.0297
6 Duct	2,745	16,470	.0118	.0484	.0367	.0205	.0230	.0286
12 Duct	2,303	27,636	.0167	.0787	.0465	.0377	.0206	.0342
12 Duct	1,936	23,232	.0117	.0722	.0551	.0384	.0444	.0507
Average Cross Section 9 14	8,832	80,721		.0650	.0400	.0304	.0310	.0350
Sewer Tile Lateral								
1 Duct	1,723	1,723	.0074	.0357	.0126	.0134	.0213	.0234
Main Conduit and Laterals								
Average Cross Section 7 81	10,555	82,444	.0110	.0602	.0345	.0276	.0295	.0331
Main Conduit and Vaults								
Average Cross Section 9 14	8,832	80,721						
Main Conduit, Laterals and Vaults								
Average Cross Section 7 81	10,555	82,444	15 Vaults					

Conduit Cross Section	Board Per Lin Ft	Car Fare Per Lin Ft	Total Cost Per Lin Ft	Per Duct Ft	Kind of Pavement and Soil	Roadway or Parkway	No of Hours Worked by Laborers	No of Men not including Supervisors	No of Teams
McRoy Tile Conduit									
4 Duct	$ .0054	$ .0001	$ .1100	$ .0275	Sand	Alley	10	1	4
5 Duct	.0050	.0009	.1716	.0343	..	Roadway	313	55	9
9 Duct	.0053	.0009	.2308	.0255	..	"	875	95	10
6 Duct	.0052	.0006	.1612	.0269	..	Alley	1,297	151	16
12 Duct	.0075	.0011	.2453	.0204	..	Roadway	1,966	202	5
12 Duct	.0057	.0007	.2801	.0258			1,542	171	
Average Cross Section 9 14			.2195	.0240			5,063	675	44
Sewer Tile Lateral									
1 Duct	.0041	.0009	.1188	.1188	Sand	Roadway	543	96	3
Main Conduit and Laterals									
Average Cross Section 7 81	.0065	.0007	.2031	.0260					
Main Conduit and Vaults									
Average Cross Section 9 14			.2698	.0295					
Main Conduit Laterals and Vaults									
Average Cross Section 7 81			.2451	.0314					

TABLE XCV.—COST OF BRICK VAULT CONSTRUCTION ON JOB 5

Location as shown on Blue Print Plans	Cost of Teaming	Cost of Excavating	Cost of Placing Floor	Cost of Laying Brick	Cost of Placing Top	Cost of Supervision	Board	Car Fare	Total Cost	Kind of Pavement and Soil
SIZE NO. 6 VAULTS										
	$1 20	$4 00	$1 00	$14 00	$1 50	$2 10	$0 50	15	$23 10	Sand and Water
	1 20	4 00	1 00	15 05	1 50	3 10	1 50	18	26 40	"
	40	5 20	1 00	14 00	1 50	1 60	1 00	25	25 60	
Total		13 20	3 10	43 05	4 50	6 80	3 00	08	75 10	
Average	40	4 40	1 03	14 35	1 50	2 27	1 00		25 03	
SIZE NO. 6 SPECIAL VAULT										
Average	1 00	4 00	1 00	14.00	1 50	1 00	50		23 00	Sand
SIZE NO. 5 VAULTS										
		6 00	1 00	14 00	1 50	2 50	1 25	10	26 35	Sand
		8 00	1 00	14 00	1 50	1 50	1 25	10	26 35	"
	1 00	4 00	1 00	12 00	1 50	1 20	50		21 20	"
		4 00	1 00	14 00	1 60	1 00			21 50	
Total	1 00	22 00	4 00	54 00	6 00	6 20	2 00	20	95 40	
Average	25	5 50	1 00	13 50	1 40	1 55	50	05	23 35	
SIZE NO. 3 VAULTS										
	1 20	4 00	1 00	14 00	1 50	2 60	75	15	24 95	Sand and Water
	1 20	4 00	1 00	14 00	1 00	75	75		24 35	"
	1 20	4 00	1 00	14 00	2 00	1 65	1 00		24 00	"
	1 20	4 00	1 00	14 00	1 50	1 50	50		23 70	"
Total	6 00	20 00	5 00	70 00	7 50	9 00	4 75	15	123 30	
Average	1 20	4 00	1 00	14 00	1 50	1 98	95	03	24 66	
SIZE NO. 10 VAULTS										
	2 70	22 95	1 50	28 00	4 00	7 50	3 00		69 65	Sand
	20	17 75	1 75	24 00	2 50	8 22	1 00	60	57 42	"
Total	90	40 70	8 00	52 00	6 50	15 72	2 00		127 07	
Average	45	20 35	1 82	26 00	3 25	7 86	2 00	04	63 53	
Total of all Vaults	14 10	20 90	16 35	223 05		39 62	14 25		443 87	
Average	94	6 66	1 00	15 64	1 73	3 04	1 95		29 59	

TABLE XCVI.—COST OF McROY TILE CONDUIT CONSTRUCTION ON JOB 6.

Conduit Cross Section	No of Lin Trench Feet Opened	No of Duct Feet Laid	Cost of Teaming, Per Lin Ft	Cost of Excavating into trench Per Lin Ft	Cost of Handling, Mixing and Dumping Concrete into trench Per L in Ft	Cost of Laying Tile and Concrete Per Lin Ft	Cost of Filling in Per Lin Ft	Super-vision Per Lin Ft	Board Per Lin Ft
McROY TILE CONDUIT									
2 Duct	430	860	$ 0251	$ 0694	$ 0352	$ 0126	$ 0520	$ 0362	$ 0030
3 Duct	1,032	3,096	0253	0752	0414	0129	0531	0378	0032
8 Duct	841	6,728	0380	1680	0591	0322	0795	0780	0046
11 Duct	466	5,126	0471	1812	0752	0510	0882	0840	0060
12 Duct	1,210	14,520	0602	1877	0796	0472	0905	0833	0071
Average Cross Section, 7 62	3,979	30,330	0381	1408	0600	0319	0740	0654	0058
SEWER TILE LATERAL									
1 Duct	1,280	1,280	0212	0602		0182	0390	0324	0012
PUMP LOG LATERAL									
2 Duct	294	688	0392	1020		0261	0396	0361	0016
MAIN CONDUIT AND VAULTS									
Average Cross Section, 5 80	5,553	32 198							
11 Vaults									
Average Cross Section, 7 62	3 979	30 330							
MAIN CONDUIT, LATERALS AND VAULTS									
11 Vaults									
Average Cross Section, 5 80	5,353	32,198							

Conduit Cross Section	Car Fare Per Lin Ft	Total Cost Per Lin Ft	Cost of Duct Ft	Kind of Pavement and Soil	Roadway or Parkway	No Hours Worked by Laborers	No of Men not including Supervisors	No of Teams	Cost of Unloading and Distributing Material
McROY TILE CONDUIT									
2 Duct	$ 0006	$ 2341	$ 1170	Macadam on Hard Clay	Roadway	333	36	2	
3 Duct	0010	2499	0833	Hard Clay	Parkway	855	91	6	
8 Duct	0011	4605	0576	Asphalt on Hard Clay	Roadway	1,266	139	7	
11 Duct	0015	5342	0486	Asphalt on Clay		824	90	5	
12 Duct	0018	5474	0454	Macadam on Clay		2 198	240	13	
Average Cross Section, 7 62	0013	4165	0546			5 476	596	33	
SEWER TILE LATERAL									
1 Duct	0010	1732	1732	Hard Clay	Parkway	709	77	6	4 Laterals
PUMP LOG LATERAL									
2 Duct	0008	2344	1172	Clay and Water	Alley	230	25	2	2 Laterals
MAIN CONDUIT AND LATERALS									
Average Cross Section, 5 80		3507	0605						
MAIN CONDUIT AND VAULTS									
Average Cross Section, 7 62		5128	0673						
MAIN CONDUIT, LATERALS AND VAULTS									
Average Cross Section, 5 80		4198	0724						

TABLE XCVII.—Cost of Brick Vault Construction on Job 6

Location as shown on Blue Print Plans	Cost of Teaming	Cost of Excavating	Cost of Placing Floor	Cost of Laying Brick	Cost of Placing Top	Cost of Supervision	Board	Car Fare	Cost of Sewer Connection	Total Cost	Kind of Pavement and Soil	Remarks
					Size No 1 Vaults							
No 1	$2 86	$6 71	$1 22	$11 15	$3 42	$2 83	$0 20	$0 05	$ 2 40	$29 84	Hard Clay	Brick-layer, 76c per hour
No 2	3 04	5 30	1 18	11 30	3 64	2 76	28	12	2 22	29 84	Hard Clay	
Total	5 90	11 01	2 40	22 45	7 06	5 59	48	17	4 62	59 68		
Average	2 95	5 50	1 20	11 23	3 53	2 79	24	09	2 31	29 84		
				Size No 9 Vaults—For 8 Duct or Less								
No 3	3 22	5 49	1 24	11 40	4 00	3 10	26	04	2 94	31 78	Hard Clay	
No 4	3 46	6 64	1 26	11 88	4 12	2 89	40	07	2 50	32 92	''	
No 5	3 40	5 59	1 18	11 85	4 40	3 25	35	10	2 42	31 94		
Total	10 08	17 72	3 68	34 23	12 61	9 24	1 01	21	7 86	96 64		
Average	3 36	5 91	1 22	11 41	4 20	3 08	34	07	2 62	32 21		
				Size No 9 Vaults—For 9 to 12 Duct								
No 6	4 01	4 86	1 34	12 46	5 03	3 54	50	08	2 64	34 46	Clay	
No 7	3 30	5 09	1 22	12 80	4 59	3 28	42	11	2 24	33 05	''	
Total	7 31	9 95	2 56	25 26	9 62	6 82	92	19	4 88	67 51		
Average	3 65	4 98	1 28	12 63	4 81	3 41	46	09	2 44	33 75		
					Size No 9 Vaults							
No 8	4 22	6 08	1 92	15 08	6 14	4 10	54	02	3 12	41 22	Clay	
No 9	3 80	5 70	1 87	14 30	5 43	3 74	48	10	3 40	35 42	''	
No 10	4 34	6 18	2 06	15 34	6 22	4 22	66	04	3 22	42 80	''	
No 11	4 12	6 12	2 07	14 80	5 70	4 16	40	20	9 14	40 76		
Total	16 48	24 18	7 89	59 82	23 87	16 22	1 98	05	9 14	159 70		
Average	4 12	6 05	1 97	14 88	5 87	4 06	49	77	2 46	39 95		
Total all	39 77	62 86	16 53	141 46	52 78	37 44	4 39	27 10		383 93		
Average	3 62	5 72	1 50	12 86	4 80	3 44	40	67	2 46	34 87		

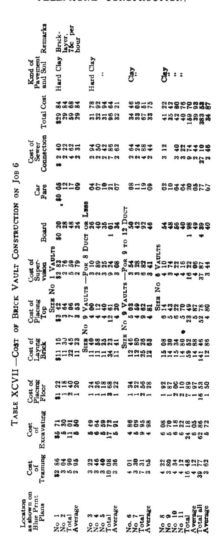

CHAPTER VI.

DETAILED COST OF CONSTRUCTING 824,862 DUCT FEET OF UNDERGROUND CONDUIT AND 318 VAULTS IN ONE JOB.

The following data give the costs of one of the largest multiple duct conduits ever installed It comprises 824,862 duct feet of conduit and 318 vaults. In securing these data special attention was paid to accuracy and uniformity. A competent cost man was assigned to each gang, and in some cases, where gangs were large, two men were engaged in keeping costs. Reports were made daily to the cost statistician who had an office on the ground and who personally supervised the taking of the costs The work was divided into three divisions, each division being subdivided into two or three sections with a separate gang for each section The work commenced in June, and with the exception of a small part, delayed on account of right of way trouble, was completed by November 1st.

The system of figuring these costs and the forms used differ in some respects from the forms and system already explained The form used for reporting the cost of concrete vaults has a division for setting up and removing forms and a division for mixing and placing concrete; while on the form shown by Form 44, the cost of setting up and removing forms is included in both the cost of placing side and in the cost of placing top, and the cost of mixing and placing concrete is included in the three divisions—placing the bottom, the side and the top.

On the form used for reporting the cost of brick vaults, the cost of mixing concrete and mortar is included in one division, and the cost of placing floor and top is included in another, whereas, on the form shown by Form 43, the cost of mixing mortar is included in cost of laying brick, the cost of mixing

129

concrete is separated and included in both the cost of placing floor and in the cost of placing top; and cost of placing floor and top are separate divisions.

The divisions for entering the cost of placing floor and top on the form used for reporting the cost of brick vaults, and the divisions for entering the cost of mixing concrete on the form used for reporting the cost of concrete vaults include the cost of setting up the frame and resurfacing the street.

It was necessary to make an extra division for entering the cost of erecting and painting posts which were used to mark the site of vaults built in country roads

On all the forms supervision and expense includes carfare and board, and it is entered in a column on the right of the column used for the total cost, because it has been included in the total cost by prorating and adding it to the cost of each division by the following method:

Assuming the cost of supervision and expense per man-hour, having been found by the method explained in Chapter V, was $0.01, and that the memorandum book shows·

> 300 hrs. worked on excavating
> 100 hrs worked on mixing concrete, etc.
> 100 hrs. worked on laying tile, etc
> 100 hrs. worked on filling in.

Multiplying the cost of supervision and expense per man-hour ($0.01) by the number of hours worked on excavating, mixing concrete, laying tile and filling in, we have the following:

Division of Const.	No. Hrs Worked		Supervision and Expense per Man-Hour	Cost of Supervision
Excavating	300	×	01	$3.00
Mixing concrete, etc...	100	×	.01	1 00
Laying tile, etc.......	100	×	.01	1.00
Filling in	100	×	.01	1.00

Adding these proportions of supervision and expense to the labor cost of the excavating, mixing concrete, etc., will give the total cost of excavating, etc.

The proportion of supervision and expense for each division of vault or lateral construction is found by the same method.

The rates of wages paid on this work were the same as those given in the previous chapter

Table XCVIII is a summary of the entire work, showing in detail average costs of each of the three divisions of the job. The unloading and distributing cost on Divisions 1 and 3 were higher than Division 2 on account of having been further away from the freight depot. The freight on material for Division 1 was high on account of being further away from the shipping point than either Divisions 2 or 3, and also on account of the quantity of creosote plank used, on which freight rates are high. The supervision, traveling and livery under the heading of expense were incurred by right of way men, superintendent of construction and assistant superintendents.

Tables XCIX to CIV, inclusive, show the average labor costs for installing each class and cross section of conduit by the various foremen.

Table CV is a summary of the total and average labor costs of each kind and class of vault built, and Tables CVI to CXVI, inclusive, show the average labor costs of each class of vault built by the various foremen.

Table CXVII is a summary of all the work done by each foreman, comparing the total and average labor costs. This, as well as the succeeding Tables CXVIII to CXXII, inclusive, which show the average labor costs in detail of all the work done by each foreman, and Tables CXXIII to CXXVII, inclusive, which show the average labor costs in detail of all the vaults built by each foreman, are interesting comparisons of the ability of foremen and are of value in proving the advisability of system in laying out work and handling men

Table CXXVIII shows the labor cost of both classes of 3-duct conduit, with vault corresponding, built on Division 1, and is a comparison of the cost of the work completed by the two foremen in charge. Both of these foremen had practically the same soil and physical conditions to contend with.

Foreman B mixed concrete by hand and had a gang averaging about 50 men, composed of Italians; whereas, Foreman

E mixed concrete by machine, had a gang averaging about 100 men, composed almost entirely of Americans, ranging in age from 20 to 70 years, collected in a city settled by a religious sect. The gang was collected in this city under an agreement made with the officials in order to secure right of way for the conduit. It will be seen that it cost Foreman E more to handle, mix and dump concrete than Foreman B, although the former mixed by machine where the latter mixed by hand. This difference in cost is accounted for by the high cost of handling and wheeling concrete incident to a poor class of labor such as employed by Foreman E.

The difference in the cost of excavation, and laying tile and placing concrete is accounted for by the same reasons The lower cost of filling in on the work done by Foreman E is accounted for by the method he used of filling in without tamping and then running a 5-ton roller over the trench; whereas, on the work done by Foreman B the trench was filled in and tamped by hand.

As weekly reports of the costs and work completed by each foreman were made, great rivalry existed between the various foremen in an endeavor to make a record This tended to increase the amount of work accomplished and to develop ability in the foremen.

Foreman A had more technical knowledge of conduit work than any of the other foremen, but had no system in handling men or laying out work He continually shifted both laborers and assistant foremen, used too many men in mixing and handling concrete, and built vault far in the rear of the conduit work. He mixed concrete by machine He had a gang averaging 100 men, but could have accomplished more, proportionately with a gang of 50 men.

Foreman B was formerly assistant to Foreman C. While he used very much the same system of handling men and laying out work as Foreman C, he was lacking in self-confidence and in ability to drill men in the work. He frequently went into a trench or a vault in order to show the method of accomplishing a task, whereas another foreman could explain the work from the bank of the trench He had gangs for mixing concrete, laying tile and placing concrete, and for building vaults These gangs he rarely shifted, but the balance of the men he continually changed from one part of the work to another He put little responsibility on his assistant foremen and relied on himself to supervise the entire work. He built vaults a short distance in the rear of the conduit work. His gang was composed of about 50 men. He mixed concrete by hand.

Foreman C, although having practically no education, was a genius in handling men and laying out work. While too erratic to handle a large gang, this foreman with 50 men could accomplish more and cheaper work than any other foreman He built vaults along with the conduit, thereby economizing in labor and cost He mixed concrete by hand.

Foreman D was a competent foreman and had considerable system in his method of working his men, but was inclined to stretch out the gang over a great distance making it almost impossible to supervise all the work. The vault, corresponding to conduit built by Foreman D, were built by Foreman E, but are included in the cost of building his section of conduit for the purpose of comparison The average gang employed by Foreman D was 90. He used a machine mixer.

Foreman E had at times a gang of 140 men, which he handled with the same facility as most foremen would a gang of 10 men. He did everything systematically He divided his gang into divisions corresponding with the work, put each division under an assistant foreman, and assigned them to a certain branch of the work and kept them on this branch day by day, never shifting either a man or a gang except when required by the conditions of the work. He used a machine mixer. He built vault as close behind the conduit work as possible, it being not practical to build them along with the trench on account of the amount of conduit installed each day forcing the vaults—which take several days to build—in the rear. This foreman installed 12,947 lin ft. of 3-duct conduit in one week with an average gang of 112 men. His highest run for any one day being 2,808 lineal trench feet opened and 7,851 duct feet of 3-duct laid He rarely gave orders to laborers direct, as he held his assistants responsible for the men and the work accomplished. He completed more work in less time than any other foreman, although having the hardest conditions of soil to contend with and having had a gang composed of a poor class of labor, as explained before.

When it is considered that other things equal, the smaller the cross section the more the cost, it will be seen that Foreman E, conditions notwithstanding, installed his part of the work almost as cheap as any foreman, and he installed 6-duct, Class A, where fair conditions were encountered, at a much lower cost than any other foreman.

Foreman F built only vaults. For the purpose of comparison these vaults are included in the schedules with the sections of conduit to which they correspond

In these data the conduit built in parkways crosses intersecting roadways, but no separation was made of the part built in roadways, as it was not practicable. There were also sections where the soil varied for a short distance, but separate data were not kept, on account of the very small difference in cost which it made, and also as explained before, a percentage of variation is always incident to a trench of any considerable length.

The vaults, the costs of which are given in these tables, were built with sectional wood forms shown by Fig. 86. It will be seen that these forms are made in four sections, two side and two end sections, both side and end sections being fitted with grooved iron ends. For convenience in handling, these forms are made one-half the height of the vault walls, so that two forms are required for building the walls to the standard height. The form shown is used for building size 1 vaults; a similar form, of larger size, is used for building size 3 vaults. In constructing vaults with these forms it is necessary to place braces between the two side sections. O'Leary ditch braces are used for this purpose.

The method and forms used for building vault tops and opening for the entrance of ducts were the same as explained in the previous chapter.

Table XCVIII—Cost of Toll Conduit
(Divisions 1, 2 and 3)
Cost of Constructing Conduit and Vaults.

Division Number	Average Cross Section	No of Lin Trench Ft	No of Duct Feet Laid	Cost of Teaming Per Lin. Ft	Per Duct Ft	Cost of Excavating Per Lin Ft	Per Duct Ft	Cost of Handling Mixing and Dumping Concrete Per Lin Ft	Per Duct Ft	Cost of Laying Tile Concrete and Plank Per Lin Ft	Per Duct Ft	Cost of Filling in Per Lin Ft	Per Duct Ft	Total Cost of Duct Per Lin Ft	Per Duct Ft	Cost of Vaults Per Lin Ft	Per Duct Ft	Cost of Vaults and Trench Per Lin Ft	Per Duct Ft
1	3.31	76,262	252,759	0200	0061	0747	0226	0199	0057	0175	0053	0340	0102	1653	0499	0490	0147	2142	0646
2	6.77	53,372½	261,271	0449	0056	1548	0228	0448	0016	0411	0001	0774	0114	3625	0535	0385	0102	4310	0637
3	4.78	44,104	210,832	0233	0046	1478	0209	0332	0069	0209	0065	0435	0091	2787	0583	0374	0120	3361	0703
Total	4.75	173,738½	824,862	0285	0060	1177	0248	0305	0064	0282	0059	0497	0105	2546	0535	0371	0120	3117	0656

Placing Material on Job

Division Number	Unloading and Distributing Material Per Lin Ft	Per Duct Ft	Freight Per Lin Ft	Per Duct Ft	Total Cost of Placing on Job Per Lin Ft	Per Duct Ft	Repaving Per Lin Ft	Per Duct Ft	Right of Way Supervision, Traveling, Livery Incidental Per Lin Ft	Per Duct Ft	Total Expense Per Lin Ft	Per Duct Ft	Total Labor and Expense Per Lin Ft	Per Duct Ft	Material Per Lin Ft	Per Duct Ft	Total Cost Per Lin Ft	Per Duct Ft
1	0277	0084	0152	0046	0429	0130	0013	0004	0378	0114	0391	0118	2962	0893	4735	1429	7697	2322
2	0271	0040	0139	0021	0410	0061	0005	0001	0600	0088	0605	0089	5325	0787	5082	0750	10407	1537
3	0499	0105	0073	0015	0572	0120			0396	0083	0396	0083	4329	0906	4878	1020	9207	1926
Total	0332	0070	0128	0027	0460	0097	0007	0002	0451	0095	0458	0097	4035	0850	4878	1037	8913	1877

TABLE XCIX—Average Labor Cost of Nine-Duct Class A McRoy Tile Conduit Construction

(Division 2, Clay Soil, Roadway Unpaved)

Foreman	No of Lin Trench Feet	No of Duct Feet Laid	Cost of Teaming Per Lin Ft	Cost of Excavating Per Lin Ft	Cost of Hauling Mixing and Dumping Concrete Per Lin Ft	Cost of Laying Tile and Concrete Per Lin Ft	Cost of Filling in Per Lin Ft	Total Cost of Duct Per Lin Ft	PerDuctFt	Cost of Unloading & Distributing Material Per Lin Ft	Total Cost Per Lin Ft	Per Duct Ft
			$	$				$	$	$	$	$
A	3,004	27,036	0395	1793	1741	0.48	2102	6679	0742	0361	7040	0782

TABLE C—Average Labor Cost of Eight-Duct McRoy Tile Conduit Construction

(Division 2, Hard Clay Soil, Parkway and Private Property)

Foreman	No of Lin Trench Feet	No of Duct Feet Laid	Cost of Teaming *	Cost of Excavating *	Cost of Hauling Mixing and Dumping Concrete*	Cost of Laying Tile and Concrete *	Cost of Filling in *	Total Cost of Duct Per Lin Ft	PerDuctFt	Cost of Unloading and Distributing Material*	Total Cost *	†
			$					$	$		$	$
A	10,326	82,608	0640	1707	0717	0697	1086	4847	0606	0320	5167	0646
B	1,385	11,080	0509	2125	0440	0366	0476	3916	0490	0320	4236	0529
C	4,301	34,408	0302	1351	0298	0202	0384	2537	0317	.0320	2857	0357
Total	16,012	128,096	0538	1647	0580	0536	0845	4146	0518	0320	4466	0558

*Per Lin Ft   †Per Duct Ft

TABLE CI—Average Cost of Six-Duct Class A McRoy Tile Conduit Construction

(Divisions 1, 2 and 3, Hard Clay Soil, Parkways)

Foreman	No of Lin Trench Feet	No of Duct Feet Laid	Cost of Teaming *	Cost of Excavating *	Cost of Hauling Mixing and Dumping Concrete*	Cost of Laying Tile and Concrete *	Cost of Filling in *	Total Cost of Duct Per Lin Ft	PerDuctFt	Cost of Unloading and Distributing Material*	Total Cost *	†
			$					$	$		$	$
A	1,053	6,318	0387	1308	1095	0560	1923	.5276	0879	0240	5516	0919
C	4,991‡	29,949	0620	1549	0479	0468	0687	3803	0634	0240	4043	0674
E	21,325	127,950	0242	1381	0384	0284	0490	2781	0464	0580	3351	0559
Aver Cost	27,369‡	164,217	0316	1409	0429	0329	0581	3064	0510	0505	3569	0594

*Per Lin Ft   †Per Duct Ft

Kinds of soil and pavement { Foreman A, clay parkway. Foreman C, hard clay parkway, Foreman E, hard clay, roadway, unpaved

TABLE CII—Average Cost of Six-Duct Class B McRoy Tile Conduit Construction

(Divisions 2 and 3, Hard Clay Soil, Parkways)

Foreman	No of Lin Trench Feet	No of Duct Feet Laid	Cost of Teaming *	Cost of Excavating *	Cost of Hauling Mixing and Dumping Concrete*	Cost of Laying Tile and Concrete *	Cost of Filling in *	Total Cost of Duct Per Lin Ft	PerDuctFt	Cost of Unloading and Distributing Material*	Total Cost *	†
			$					$	$		$	$
B	24,692	148,152	0382	1436	0211	0302	0602	2933	0489	0240	.3173	0529
C	3,620	21,720	0345	1665	0176	0276	0324	2786	0464	0240	3026	0504
D	3,874	23,244	0287	1699	0292	0420	0600	3278	0546	0626	3904	0650
Aver Cost	32,186	193,116	0364	1493	0217	0313	0371	2958	0493	0286	3244	0540

*Per Lin Ft   †Per Duct Ft

TABLE CIII — AVERAGE COST OF FOUR-DUCT CLASS A McROY TILE CONDUIT CONSTRUCTION

(Division 3, Wet Clay Soil, Parkway)

Foreman	No of Lin Trench Feet	No of Duct Feet Laid	Cost of Teaming *	Cost of Excavating *	Cost of Hauling Mixing and Dumping Concrete *	Cost of Laying Tile and Concrete *	Cost of Filling in *	Total Cost of Duct Per Lin Ft	Total Cost of Duct Per Duct Ft	Cost of Unloading and Distributing Material *	Total Cost *	Total Cost †
			$	$	$	$	$	$	$	$	$	$
D	50	200		1574	0250	0322	0224	2370	0592	0418	2788	0697
E	3,047	12 188	0182	0864	0381	0414	0409	2250	0562	0418	2668	0667
Aver Cost	3,097	12,388	0179	0875	0379	0413	0406	2252	0563	0418	2670	0667

*Per Lin Ft †Per Duct Ft

TABLE CIV — AVERAGE COST OF FOUR-DUCT CLASS B McROY TILE CONDUIT CONSTRUCTION

(Division 3)

Foreman	No of Lin Trench Feet	No of Duct Feet Laid	Cost of Teaming*	Cost of Excavating *	Cost of Hauling Mixing and Dumping Concrete *	Cost of Laying Tile and Concrete *	Cost of Filling in *	Total Cost of Duct Per Lin Ft	Total Cost of Duct Per Duct Ft	Cost of Unloading and Distributing Material *	Total Cost *	Total Cost †
			$	$	$	$	$	$	$	$	$	$
D	7,335	29,340	0074	1552	0244	0331	0295	2496	0624	0417	2913	0728
E	16,464	65,856	0371	1515	0295	0243	0531	2955	0739	.0418	3373	0843
Aver Cost	23,799	95,196	0279	1526	0280	0270	0458	.2813	0703	0418	3231	0808

*Per Lin Ft, †Per Duct Ft

Kind of soil and pavement { Foreman D, hard clay, parkway
Foreman E, very hard clay, macadam roadway

TABLE CV — LABOR COSTS OF BRICK AND CONCRETE VAULT CONSTRUCTION

(Divisions 1, 2 and 3)

Kind	Size No	Total Cost	Average Cost	No Built	Size of Vaults
Concrete	3	$2 553 16	$22 39	114	5′ x 3′ 6″ x 4′ 6″
Concrete	1	1 567 05	15 07	104	3′ 6″ x 4′ 6″ x 4′ 6″
Brick	4	1 528 21	36 39	42	6′ x 5′ ″ x 5′ 6″
Brick	2	156 99	26 17	6	4′ 6″ x 4′ 6″ x 4′ 6″
Brick	6	25 41	25 41	1	7′ x 5′ x 5′ 6″
Brick	Special	75 27	75 27	1	11′ x 9′ x 7″
Brick	Special	65 91	65 91	1	7′ x 5′ x 5′ 6″
Brick	Class A	182 46	36 49	5	6′ x 5′ 6″ x 3′ 6″
Brick	12	104 12	104 12	1	10′ x 10′ x 5′ 6″
Brick	10	3 549 22	80 09	42	6′ x 9′ 2½″x 7′1″
Brick	11	115 85	115 85	1	6′ x13′ 5′ x 7′ 1″
Concrete and Brick	Total	$9,923 65	$ 31 21	318	

TABLE CVI — AVERAGE LABOR COSTS OF CONCRETE VAULT CONSTRUCTION SIZE NO 3

(Hard Clay Soil Size of Vault, 5′ x 3′ 6″ x 4′ 6″—Divisions 2 and 3)

Foreman	Cost of Teaming	Cost of Excavating	Cost of Setting up and Removing Frame	Cost of Mixing and Placing Concrete and Setting Frame	Marking Vaults	Total Cost	Supervision and Expense Included in Total Cost	No of Men Worked	No of Hours Worked	No Built
A	$9 46	$11 50	$4 30	$18 46	$	$43 72	$9 35	15	132¼	11
B	4 08	6 49	2 32	7 73	1 21	21 83	5 92	5¼	50 [illegible]	14
C	1 42	4 63	1 12	3 30	1 22	11 69	2 41	4	35	6
F	5 02	5 97	1 37	9 32	1 21	22 89	6 25	6 [illegible]	53 [illegible]	25
E	3 57	5 56	1 42	7 59	1 24	19 38	3 59	9 [illegible]	47 [illegible]	58
Av Cost of all	4 41	6 29	1 77	8 81	1 11	22 39	4 95	8 [illegible]	56 [illegible]	114

TABLE CVII—Average Labor Costs of Concrete Vault Construction
Size No. 1
(Sand Soil   Size of Vault, 3′ 6″ x 4′ 6″ x 4′ 6″—Division 1)

Foreman	Cost of Teaming	Cost of Excavating	Cost of Setting up and Removing Frame	Cost of Mixing and Placing Concrete and Setting Frame	Marking Vaults	Total Cost	Supervision and Expense Included in Total Cost	No. of Men Worked	No. of Hours Worked	No. Built
B	$3 10	$3 82	$0 87	$4 41	$2 19	$14 39	$2 69	4	35½	47
E	3 76	3 66	1 84	5 17	1 20	15 63	2 12	4½	38½	57
Av of all	3 46	3 73	1 40	4 83	1 65	15 07	2 38	4½	37½	104

TABLE CVIII—Average Labor Costs of Brick Vault Construction,
Size No 4
(Hard Clay Soil   Size 6′ x 5′ x 5′ 6″—Divisions 1, 2 and 3)

Foreman	Cost of Teaming	Cost of Excavating	Cost of Mixing Concrete and Mortar	Cost of Laying Brick	Cost of Placing Floor, Top and Frame	Marking Vaults	Total Cost	Supervision and Expense Included in Total Cost	No. of Men Worked	No. of Hours Worked	No. Built
A	$11 68	$15 26	$5 46	$19 68	$3 39	$	$55 47	$14 84	17	128½	1
B	5 55	8 75	2 06	23 80	3 61	1 22	44 99	7 97	10½	90	9
C	2 00	6 09	2 31	17 31	4 57	1 22	33 50	6 36	8	69½	2
F	6 50	9 46	5 08	10 92	4 63	1 22	37 81	10 74	10½	81¼	7
E	5 84	6 22	3 18	11 71	4 52	54	32 01	6 48	7½	67½	23
Av Cost of all	5 85	7 51	3 27	14 62	4 32	82	36 39	7 69	8½	76¾	42

TABLE CIX—Average Labor Costs of Brick Vault Construction,
Size No 2
(Sand Soil   Size of Vault, 4′ 6″ x 4′ 6″ x 4 6″—Division 1)

Foreman	Cost of Teaming	Cost of Excavating	Cost of Mixing Concrete and Mortar	Cost of Laying Brick	Cost of Placing Floor Top and Frame	Total Cost	Supervision and Expense Included in Total Cost	No. of Men Worked	No. of Hours Worked	No. Built
E.	$2 97	$5 40	$1 45	$13 01	$3 34	$26 17	$1 77	8½	74½	6

TABLE CX—Labor Costs of Brick Vault Construction, Size No 6
(Clay Soil   Size of Vault, 7′ x 5′ x 5′ 6″—Division 2)

Foreman	Cost of Excavating	Cost of Mixing Concrete and Mortar	Cost of Laying Brick	Cost of Placing Floor Top and Frame	Total Cost	Supervision and Expense Included in Total Cost	No. of Men Worked	No. of Hours Worked	No. Built
A	$6 81	$3 33	$10 61	$4 66	$25.41	$1 00	11	91	1

TABLE CXI—Labor Costs of Special Brick Vault Construction
(Hard Clay Soil   Size of Vault, 11′ x 9′ x 7′—Division 3)

Foreman	Cost of Teaming	Cost of Excavating	Cost of Mixing Concrete and Mortar	Cost of Laying Brick	Cost of Placing Floor, Top and Frame	Marking Vaults	Total Cost	Supervision and Expense Included in Total Cost	No. of Men Worked	No. of Hours Worked	No. Built
E	$4 98	$36 99	$3 71	$19 50	$8 85	$1 24	$75 27	$9 84	29	286½	1

TABLE CXII—LABOR COSTS OF SPECIAL BRICK VAULT CONSTRUCTION
(Hard Clay Soil Size of Vault, 7' x 5' x 5' 6"—Division 3)

Foreman	Cost of Teaming	Cost of Excavating	Cost of Mixing Concrete and Mortar	Cost of Laying Brick	Cost of Placing Floor Top and Frame	Marking Vaults	Total Cost	Supervision and Expense Included in Total Cost	No of Men Worked	No of Hours Worked	No Built
E	$1 50	$24 47	$7 91	$18 19	$12 60	$1 24	$65 91	$20 48	19	163½	1

TABLE CXIII—AVERAGE LABOR COSTS OF CLASS A BRICK VAULT CONSTRUCTION
(Clay Soil Size, 6' x 5½' x 3½"—Division 2)

Foreman	Cost of Teaming	Cost of Excavating	Cost of Mixing Concrete and Mortar	Cost of Laying Brick	Cost of Placing Floor Top and Frame	Total Cost	Supervision and Expense Included in Total Cost	No of Men Worked	No of Hours Worked	No Built
A	$3 05	$9 53	$5 65	$12 90	$5 36	$36 49	$3 79	14½	105½	5

TABLE CXIV—LABOR COSTS OF BRICK VAULT CONSTRUCTION, SIZE NO 12
(Hard Clay Soil Size of Vault, 10' x 10' x 5' 6"—Division 2)

Foreman	Cost of Teaming	Cost of Excavating	Cost of Mixing Concrete and Mortar	Cost of Laying Brick	Cost of Placing Floor, Top and Frame	Total Cost	Supervision and Expense Included in Total Cost	No of Men Worked	No of Hours Worked	No Built
A	$7 90	$30 99	$15 40	$24 75	$25 08	$104 12	$28 61	39	326	1

TABLE CXV—AVERAGE LABOR COSTS OF BRICK VAULT CONSTRUCTION, SIZE NO 10
(Hard Clay Soil Size of Vault, 6' x 9' 2½" x 7' 1"—Divisions 1, 2 and 3)

Foreman	Cost of Teaming	Cost of Excavating	Cost of Mixing Concrete and Mortar	Cost of Laying Brick	Cost of Placing Floor, Top and Frame	Marking Vaults	Total Cost	Supervision and Expense Included in Total Cost	No of Men Worked	No of Hours Worked	No Built
A	$16 31	$40 97	$15 87	$25 60	$9 97		$106 62	$33 77	29	220½	1
F	20 54	30 46	7 17	27 05	14 88	$1 22	101 32	25 90	25½	228½	5
B	8 20	23 10	2 07	39 26	7 49	33	80 45	10 85	21½	199½	11
C	17 50	40 85	2 27	60 93	3 99	1 22	126 76	13 19	32	293	1
E	11 97	26 27	5 52	26 82	9 00	52	80 10	14 70	21½	196½	24
Av Cost of All	12 24	26 64	4 98	30 88	9 21	56	84 51	13 56	22½	203½	42

TABLE CXVI—LABOR COSTS OF BRICK VAULT CONSTRUCTION, SIZE NO 11
(Very Hard Clay Soil Size of Vault, 6' x 13' 5" x 7' 1"—Division 2)

Foreman	Cost of Teaming	Cost of Excavating	Cost of Mixing Concrete and Mortar	Cost of Laying Brick	Cost of Placing Floor, Top and Frame	Marking Vaults	Total Cost	Supervision and Expense Included in Total Cost	No of Men Worked	No of Hours Worked	No Built
F	$17 00	$36 94	$8 53	$35 63	$16 53	$1 22	$115 85	$22 12	33	310½	1

TABLE CXVII.—LABOR COSTS OF DUCT AND VAULTS, McROY TILE CONDUIT CONSTRUCTION
(Divisions 1, 2 and 3)

Foreman	No of Lineal Trench Ft	No of Duct Ft Laid	Average Cross Sect	No Vaults built	Total cost of Duct and Vaults	Average Cost of Duct and Vaults Per Lin ft	Per Duct ft
A	14,383	115,962	8.06	21	$8,552.93	$.5947	$.0738
B	56,637	250,612	4.43	106	16,286.17	.2704	.0610
C	12,912½	86,077	6.67	22	4,916.14	.3807	.0571
D	11,259	52,784	4.69	14	3,548.82	.3152	.0672
E	78,647	319,427	4.06	156	21,858.05	.2179	.0684
Av Cost of all	173,738½	824,882	4.75	318	54,162.22	.3117	.0657

TABLE CXVIII.—AVERAGE LABOR COSTS OF CONDUIT WORK DONE BY FOREMAN A

Conduit Cross Section	No of Lin Trench Feet	No of Duct Feet Laid	Cost of Teaming Per Tr Ft	Cost of Excavating Per Tr Ft	Cost of Handling, Mixing and Dumping into trench Per Tr Ft	Cost of Concrete Laying Tile and Plank Per Tr Ft	Cost of Filling in Per Tr Ft	Total Cost Per Lin Tr Ft	Per Duct Ft	Kind of Soil and Pavement
Nine Duct Class A	3,004	27,036	.0395	.1793	.1741	.0648	.2102	.6679	.0742	Clay, Road'y, unpaved
Eight	10,326	82,608	.0640	.1707	.0717	.0697	.1086	.4847	.0606	Hard Clay, Parkway
Six	1,063	6,318	.0387	.1808	.1098	.0560	.1923	.5276	.0879	Clay, Parkway
Av. Cost of all Duct & Vaults	14,383	115,962	.0570	.1696	.0958	.0678	.1359	.5947	.0738	

TABLE CXIX.—AVERAGE LABOR COSTS OF CONDUIT WORK DONE BY FOREMAN B

Conduit Cross Section	No of Lin Trench Feet	No of Duct Feet Laid	Cost of Teaming Per Tr Ft	Cost of Excavating Per Tr Ft	Cost of Handling, Mixing and Dumping into trench and Plank Per Tr Ft	Cost of Concrete Laying Tile Per Tr Ft	Cost of Filling in Per Tr Ft	Total Cost Per Lin Tr Ft	Per Duct Ft	Kind of Soil and Pavement
Eight Duct, Class A	1,385	11,080	.0509	.2125	.0440	.0386	.0473	.3316	.0400	Hard Clay, Parkway
Six ,, B	24,692	148,152	.0382	.1436	.0211	.0302	.0602	.2933	.0489	,, ,, Parkway
Three ,, A	1,680	5,040	.0153	.0760	.0273	.0188	.0416	.1790	.0597	Sand, Parkway
,, B	28,780	86,340	.0200	.0575	.0157	.0157	.0354	.1443	.0481	Quicksand and Water, Parkway
Av Cost of all Duct Duct & Vaults	56,537	250,612	.0285	.0994	.0191	.0227	.0467	.2704	.0610	Clay, Parkway

TABLE CXX — AVERAGE LABOR COSTS OF CONDUIT WORK DONE BY FOREMAN C

Conduit Cross Section	No of Lin Trench Feet	No of Duct Feet Laid	Cost of Teaming Per Tr Ft $	Cost of Excavating Per Tr Ft	Cost of Handling, Mixing and Dumping Concrete into trench Per Tr Ft	Cost of Laying Tile Concrete and Plank Per Tr Ft	Cost of Filling in Per Tr Ft	Total Cost Per Lin Tr Ft $	Total Cost Per Duct Ft $	Kind of Soil and Pavement
Eight Duct, Class A	4,301	34,408	0302	1351	0298	0202	0384	2537	0317	Hard Clay, Priv Prop
Six " " A	4,991½	29,949	0619	1849	0479	0468	0888	3803	0634	Hard Clay, Parkway
" " B	3,620	21,720	0345	1665	0176	0276	0324	2786	0464	
Av " Cost of all Duct	12,912½	86 077	0437	1816	0333	0326	0484	3006	0464	
Duct & Vaults								3307	0571	

TABLE CXXI — AVERAGE LABOR COSTS OF CONDUIT WORK DONE BY FOREMAN D

Conduit Cross Section	No of Lin Trench Feet	No of Duct Feet Laid	Cost of Teaming Per Tr Ft $	Cost of Excavating Per Tr Ft	Cost of Handling, Mixing and Dumping Concrete into trench Per Tr Ft	Cost of Laying Tile Concrete and Plank Per Tr Ft	Cost of Filling in Per Tr Ft	Total Cost Per Lin Tr Ft $	Total Cost Per Duct Ft $	Kind of Soil and Pavement
Six Duct, Class B	3,874	23 244	0267	1699	0292	0420	0600	3278	0546	Hard Clay, Parkway
Four " A	50	200		1574	0250	0322	0224	2370	0592	Wet Clay
Four " B	7,335	29,340	0074	1552	0244	0331	0296	2496	0624	Hard Clay
Av " Cost of all Duct	11,259	52,784	0140	1603	0261	0361	0399	2764	0590	
Duct & Vaults								3152	0672	

NOTE —1138 Lin Ft of trench excavated, refilled and abandoned on account of right-of-way trouble, is included in total cost of Four Duct Class B, shown above.

Table CXXII — Average Labor Costs of Conduit Work Done by Foreman E.

Conduit Cross Section	No of Lin Trench Feet Per Tr Ft	No of Duct Feet Laid	Cost of Teaming Per Tr Ft	Cost of Excavating Per Tr Ft	Cost of Handling Mixing and Dumping Concrete into trench Per Tr Ft	Cost of Laying Tile Concrete and Plank Per Tr Ft	Cost of R'fling in Per Tr Ft	Total Cost Per Lm Tr Ft	Total Cost Per Duct Ft	Kind of Soil and Pavement
			$	$	$	$	$	$	$	
Six Duct, Class A	21.325	127.950	.0242	.1881	.0385	.0284	.0489	.2781	.0464	Hard Clay Par'y, unn
Four A	3.047	12.188	.0182	.0864	.0381	.0114	.0409	.2250	.0562	Wet Clay, Parkway
" B	16.464	65.856	.0371	.1515	.0295	.0043	.0531	.2955	.0739	Very Hd Cl, Mac'in R
Three A	.419	1.257	.0239	.0655	.0803	.0310	.0269	.2277	.0759	Sand Parkway
Av.. Cost of all Duct	37.392	112.176	.0160	.0776	.0179	.0177	.0245	.1537	.0512	Quicksand and Water, Parkway
" " Duct & Vaults	78.647	319.427	.0228	.1097	.0370	.0230	.0378	.2779	.0684	

Note — 1,322 Lin Ft of trench excavated refilled and abandoned on account of right-of-way trouble is included in the total cost of Four Duct, Class B, shown above.

Table CXXIII — Average Labor Costs of Brick and Concrete Vaults Built by Foreman A

Kind	Size No	Total Cost of Vaults	Included in Total Cost Supervision and Expense	Number of Men Worked	Number of Hours Worked	Number Built	Size of Vaults	Kind of Soil
Concrete	3	$43 72	$9 35	15	132½	11	5' x 3' 6" x 4' 6"	Hard Clay
Brick	4	55 47	14 34	17	128½	11	6' x 6' x 6' 6"	Hard Clay
Brick	10	108 62	33 77	29	220½		6' x 9' 2½' x 7' 1"	Hard Clay
Brick	A"	36 49	3 79	14½	105½	5	6' x 5' x 3' 6"	Clay
Brick	6	25 41	1 00	11	91	1	7' x 5' x 5' 6"	Clay
Brick	12	104 12	28 61	39	326	20	10' x 10'	Hard Clay
Concrete and Brick	Average Cost of all	47 85	9 98	15½	137½			

Table CXXIV — Average Labor Costs of Brick and Concrete Vaults Built by Foreman B

Kind	Size No	Total Cost of Vaults	Included in Total Cost Supervision and Expense	Number of Men Worked	Number of Hours Worked	Number Built	Size of Vaults	Kind of Soil
Concrete	3	$21 83	$5 92	5½	59½	14	5' x 3' 6" x 4' 6"	Hard Clay
Concrete	1	14 39	2 70	4½	35½	47	3' 6" x 4' 6" x 4' 6"	Sand
Brick	10	44 90	7 97	10½	90	9	6' x 9'	Hard Clay
Brick		80 45	10 86	21½	199 ½	11	6' x 9' x 21' x 7' 1"	Hard Clay
Concrete and Brick	Average Total Cost	28 05	4 95	7¾	66 ½	81		

TABLE CXXV.—AVERAGE LABOR COSTS OF BRICK AND CONCRETE VAULTS BUILT BY FOREMAN F

Kind	Size No	Total Cost of Vaults	Included in Total Cost Supervision and Expense	Number of Men Worked	Number of Hours Worked	Number Built	Size of Vaults	Kind of Soil
Concrete	3	\$22 87	\$6 25	6$\frac{2}{25}$	53$\frac{29}{50}$	25	5′ x 3′ 6″ x 4′ 6″	Hard Clay
Brick	4	37 81	10 74	10$\frac{1}{7}$	81$\frac{13}{14}$	7	6′ x 5′ x 5′ 6″	Hard Clay
Brick	10	101 32	25 20	25$\frac{3}{5}$	228$\frac{4}{5}$	5	6′ x 9′ 2½″ x 7′ 1″	Hard Clay
Brick	11	115 85	22 12	33	310$\frac{1}{2}$	1	6′ x 13′ 5″ x 7′ 1″	Very Hard Clay.
Concrete and Brick	Average Cost of all	38 40	9 99	10$\frac{2}{19}$	88$\frac{47}{76}$	38		

TABLE CXXVI.—AVERAGE LABOR COSTS OF BRICK AND CONCRETE VAULTS BUILT BY FOREMAN C

Kind	Size No	Total Cost of Vaults	Included in Total Cost Supervision and Expense	Number of Men Worked	Number of Hours Worked	Number Built	Size of Vaults	Kind of Soil
Concrete	3	\$11 69	\$2 41	4	35	6	5′ x 3′ 6″ x 4′ 6″	Hard Clay.
Brick	4	33 50	6 36	8	69$\frac{1}{4}$	2	6′ x 5′ x 5′ 6″	Hard Clay.
Brick	10	126 76	13 19	32	293	1	6′ x 9′ 2½″ x 7′ 1	Hard Clay.
Concrete and Brick	Average Cost of all	29 32	4 48	8	71$\frac{1}{4}$	9		

TABLE CXXVII.—AVERAGE LABOR COSTS OF BRICK AND CONCRETE VAULTS BUILT BY FOREMAN E

Kind	Size No	Total Cost of Vaults.	Included in Total Cost Supervision and Expense	Number of Men Worked	Number of Hours Worked	Number Built	Size of Vaults.	Kind of Soil
Concrete	3	\$19 38	\$3 59	9$\frac{23}{33}$	47$\frac{11}{16}$	58	5′ x 3′ 6″ x 4′ 6″	Hard Clay
Concrete	1	15 63	2 12	4$\frac{1}{7}$	38$\frac{1}{2}$	57	3′ 6″ x 4′ 6″ x 4′ 6″	Sand
Brick	4	32 01	6 48	7$\frac{21}{46}$	67$\frac{13}{16}$	23	6′ x 5′ x 5′ 6″	Hard Clay
Brick	2	26 17	1 77	8$\frac{1}{12}$	74$\frac{1}{2}$	6	4′ 6″ x 4′ 6″ x 4′ 6″	Sand
Brick	10	80 10	14 70	21$\frac{5}{12}$	196$\frac{1}{8}$	24	6′ x 9′ 2½″ x 7′ 1″	Hard Clay
Brick	Special	75 27	9 85	29	236$\frac{1}{2}$	1	11′ x 9′ x 7′	Hard Clay
Brick	Special	65 91	20 47	19	163$\frac{1}{2}$	1	7′ x 5′ x 5′ 6″	Hard Clay
Concrete and Brick	Av Cost of all	29 24	5 13	9$\frac{1}{2}$	70$\frac{187}{316}$	170		

TABLE CXXVIII — LABOR COSTS, INCLUDING VAULTS, OF THREE-DUCT CLASSES A AND B McROY TILE CONDUIT

(DIVISION I)

CONSTRUCTION

(Class B, Sand Soil, Parkway, Class A, Quicksand and Water, Parkway)

Foreman	No. of Lin. Trench Ft.	No. of Duct Ft. Laid	Cost of Teaming	Cost of Excavating	Cost of Mixing, Handling and Dumping Concrete	Cost of Laying Tile Concrete and Plank	Cost of Filling in	Total Cost of Duct	Supervision and Expense Included in Total Cost of Duct	No. Hours Worked	No. Men Worked	Teams Worked	Class	No. of Vaults Built	Size of Vaults	Cost of Unloading and Distributing Material	Total Cost
B	28,790	86 340	$ 576 53	$ 1 653 08	$ 453 05	$ 453 47	$ 1 017 70	$ 4 153 13	$ 780 11	12 827½	1 474½	125	B			$ 722 46	4,875 59
E	37,382	112,176	599 37	2 899 63	668 18	663 61	915 51	5 746 62	635 43	20 436	2 319½	121	B			938 91	6,864 83
Total Class B	66,172	198 516	1 176 21	4 552 61	1 130 23	1 116 48	1 933 21	9 988 75	1 415 54	33 959	2 794	246	B			1,661 37	11,590 12
B	1,680	5 040	25 78	127 72	45 83	31 61	69 98	300 92	72 78	904½	100	6	A			42 18	343 10
E	419	1,257	10 00	27 80	33 60	13 00	11 25	95 41	9 62	344	38	4	A			10 52	105 93
Total Class A	2,099	6,297	35 78	155 52	79 49	44 61	81 23	396 33	82 30	1 264	128	7	A			52 70	449 03
B	30 460	91,380	602 31	1 780 80	497 88	485 08	1 087 68	4 454 05	852 99	13 483	1 574½	130	A & B			764 64	5,218 69
E	37,811	113 433	609 37	2 927 03	701 84	676 61	925 03	5 841 03	644 95	20 780	2 357½	123	A & B			940 43	6,780 46
Total Class A & B	68 271	204,813	1 212 08	4 707 83	1 199 72	1 161 09	2 014	10 295 08	1 497 94	34 218	3 932	253	A & B			1,714 07	12,000 15
Total of Vaults														55 $\{$ 8, 147 $\}$ 6 2, 74 $\{$ 57, 11 $\}$		No 1 10 1 10	
														129		1,714 07	

Total Cost of Vaults
1 297 81
1 801 88
3 098 89

Total Cost of Duct and Vaults

B	30,460	91,380						5 751 98								764 64	6,516 50
E	37,811	113,433						7 642 11								940 43	8,561 54
Total of Duct & Vlt	68 271	204,813	..					13,393 97								1,714 07	15,108 04

TABLE CXXVII (CONTINUED) —LABOR COSTS, INCLUDING VAULTS, OF THREE-DUCT CLASSES A AND B MCROY TILE CONDUIT CONSTRUCTION

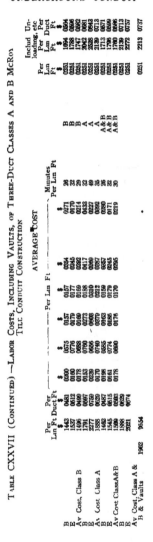

	Per Lin Ft	Per Duct Ft	AVERAGE COST $			Per Lin Ft				Minutes Per Lin Ft		Per Lin Ft	Includ Un-loading, etc Per Lin Duct Ft
	$	$	$	$	$	$	$	$	$			$	$
B	1443	0481	0200	0575	0157	0157	0204	0271		36	B	0251	1094	0594
B	1357	0512	0160	0776	0170	0177	0245	0170		32	B	0251	1788	0596
Av Cost, Class B	1496	0499	0178	0688	0169	0169	0202	0214		29	B	0251	1747	0652
B	1791	0697	0153	0700	0273	0188	0417	0438			A	0251	2042	0681
A	2277	0759	0239	0656	0908	0310	0266	0227		49	A	0251	2528	0843
Av Cost, Class A	1588	0529	0170	0740	0970	0212	0087	0092		35	A	0251	2139	0713
B	1482	0487	0198	0585	0163	0159	0357	0280		26	A & B	0251	1713	0571
B	1545	0615	0161	0774	0198	0179	0245	0171		32	A & B	0251	1796	0599
Av Cost Class A&B	1598	0533	0178	0680	0176	0170	0256	0219		30	A & B	0251	1780	0596
B	1588	0529										0251	2139	0713
B	2021	0674										0251	2272	0757
Av Cost, Class A & B & Vaults	1982	0654										0251	2213	0737

CHAPTER VII.

MISCELLANEOUS COSTS AND SPECIAL DATA

The tables given in this chapter are a collection of data covering many kinds of telephone construction both aerial and underground. Some of these tables were drawn up to facilitate estimating and others were used in deciding as to the expediency of different methods. With the exception of those showing the cost of certain jobs, the tables are based on data collected and records kept on several thousand jobs Only the results of actual records are given, and as exemplified in the case of the shrinkage of mortar and concrete shown herein the percentage is much greater in the actual mixing than in the theoretical mixing

In the previous chapters the specifications explained in a general way the quantities of materials used in the various kinds of telephone construction These quantities are usually familiar to men engaged in constructing and estimating, but there are some cases where there is a great difference of opinion as to the average amount of material required In the case of a mile of toll line or farm line, although the general specifications may require that poles be set 130 ft or 150 ft apart, as the case may be, on account of road crossings and corners making it necessary to shorten spans, it rarely happens that a mile of line is built which does not require more poles, cross-arms and other equipment than the number based on poles set an equal distance apart The question, therefore, how many poles, cross-arms or anchors to a mile, requires a knowledge of the records of many lines The tables are based on average quantities of materials and present prices of standard materials of the best grade

In gathering the cost data which form the subject of the previous chapters, some remarkably cheap work was, from time to time, reported by cost men and, with the object of reducing the cost of construction without lowering the standard, special circular letters containing these data were sent to the various foremen They had the effect of spurring foremen on to make a "record" for cheapness in construction, as shown by results of the work of some foremen after the receipt of these circular letters

Tables CXXIX and CXXX are examples of work of which special reports were made, they show the labor costs of constructing some farm lines. Although these jobs were very cheaply built considering the nature of the soil and other conditions, no effort was made by the foremen in charge to make a "record," or no special kind of tool was used In the case of the jobs shown in Table CXXIX the frozen ground was loosened with digging-bars and the balance of the hole excavated by means of spoon and shovel Spoon and shovel was used for excavating holes on the jobs shown in Table CXXX Where quicksand was encountered, sand barrels were used All the work was one or more miles distant from the stations of the gangs, and on that account considerable time was lost each day in getting to the jobs This time is included in the cost of the work Both tables represent the record of consecutive days' work.

TABLE CXXIX —COST OF LINE CONSTRUCTION ON JOB 1

20 ft —4 in top Farm Line Poles

No Poles	Cost Teaming Labor in Hauling	Cost Framing	Cost Dig and Locating	Cost Setting	Cost Super and Exp	Total Cost Per Pole	Kind of Soil	No Hours Worked	Mi to job	Remarks
7	$ 23	$ 04	$ 24	$ 13	$ 08	$ 72	Soft Clay	9⅞	1	6″ frost
10	26	04	23	10	11	74	"	13½	4	6″ "
8	21	04	26	10	08	69	"	10½	1	12″ "
49	25	03	26	09	09	72	'	63	7	16″
41	.30	05	28	06	10	79	'	58½	3½	6″

25 ft —5 in top Farm Line Poles

8	15	04	36	13	15	83	Soft Clay	5⁷₁₂	1	6″ frost
19	26	06	35	15	20	1 02	"	35⅜	1	6″ "
5	33	04	40	11	11	99	'	9⁴₁₅	3½	16″
8	26	03	37	12	11	89		11¼	6	16″

STOMBAUGH ANCHORS

No Anchors	Cost Teaming and Labor in Hauling	Cost Setting	Cost Placing Guys	Cost Super and Exp	Total Cost Per Anchor	Kind Soil	No Hours Worked	Mi to job	Remarks
1	$ 07	$ 33	$ 18	$ 06	$ 64	Clay	1⁴₅	2	30″ frost
11	07	19	13	06	45	"	8¼	7	12″ "
6	95	13	00	08	35	'	3⅚	5	12″ "

No 12 STEEL WIRE

Miles Wire Strung	Cost Teaming and Labor in Hauling	Cost Stringing and Equip	Cost Super and Exp	Total Cost Per Mi	No Hours Worked	No Line Orders	Remarks
6½	$ 76	$2 01	$ 39	$3 16	43⅜	3	2½ Miles to job.
5½	58	2 69	64	3 91	40½	4	'
4¼	64	2 88	60	4 12	33⅝	4	8 " "

TABLE CXXX—COST OF LINE CONSTRUCTION ON JOB 2, FARM LINE.

No of Poles	Cost of Teaming Labor in Hauling	Cost of Framing	Cost of Digging and Locating	Cost of Setting	Cost of Super and Exp	Total Cost Per Pole	Kind of Soil	No Hours Worked	Remarks
				30 ft —6 in top Poles					
1	$ 43	$.06	$ 48	$ 36	$ 15	$1 33	Clay & Wat	3½	3 Mi. to job
				25 ft —6 in. top Poles					
22	41	09	44	24	.18	1 36	Clay & Wat	45 1/12	1½ Mi to job
8	26	08	.33	14	09	90	Loam & Wat	15 1/12	1 " "
4	40	.06	.55	32	23	1 56	Quicksand	12	1½ " "
6	.32	.10	43	.24	14	1 23	Coarse Grav	11¾	used bbls 2 Mi to job
				5 in top Poles					
45	36	06	24	.18	.11	95	Sand & Wat	74½	2 " "
				20 ft —5 in top Poles					
16	24	.03	17	11	05	60	Sand & Wat	19¾	3½ " "
22	22	.03	24	12	08	69	Sand & Wat	31 1/12	3½ " "
22	25	03	23	09	06	66	Sand & Wat	32¼	3½ " "
5	41	.03	.83	13	17	1 57	Quicksand	15 11/12	3½ " "
				4 in top Poles					
14	.21	.02	13	10	05	51	Sand & Wat	14	used bbls 3½ Mi to job

STOMBAUGH ANCHORS

No of Anchors	Cost of Teaming	Cost of Setting	Cost of Placing Guy	Cost of Super & Exp	Total Cost Per Anchor	Kind of Soil	No of Hours Worked	Remarks
2	$.02	$.03	$.06	$ 02	$ 13	Sand.	1/2	3½ Mi to job

Table CXXXI shows the labor cost in detail of pulling in 120 pr one-half 14-gage and one-half 16-gage toll cable The expense of hauling reels was large as the distance from the freight depot averaged 3 miles, the roads were deep in clay mud, and on account of their great weight a special team and wagon at $7 per day was used to haul the reels The expense of pumping water was high on account of the vaults being full of water In one section of conduit, cable was pulled in twice as the first cable had flaws in the armor. The cable was pulled in by horsepower.

TABLE CXXXI.—COST OF PULLING UNDERGROUND CABLE (MAIN)

120 Pr, ½ - 14 Ga and ½ - 16 Ga

No Ft. Pulled	Cost of Pulling	No Men Used in Pulling	Cost of Rodding	Cost of Pumping Water	No Sections Pulled	Cost of Pulling, Rodding and Pumping
18,992	$333 40	93	$90 90	$79 60	38	$503 90
	Per Ft	Per Day	Per Ft	Per Ft	Per Day	Per Ft
Average	$ 0175	6 1-5	$ 0048	$ 0042	2 8-15	$ .0265

HAULING REELS				RETURNING REELS		
No Reels Hauled	Cost of Hauling	No Men Used in Hauling	No Reels Returned	Cost of Returning.	No Men Used in Returning	Total Cost of All Work
39	$ 211 60	67	39	$65 10	23	$ 780 60
	Per Reel,	No Men Per Reel,		Per Reel,	No Men Per Reel	
Average	$5 40	2		$1 67	23-39.	$ 0411

Table CXXXII shows in detail the total and average material, including poles, cross-arms, wire and other equipment, used in constructing line orders in several districts during periods of from one month to 1½ years. They also show the total and average cost of completed line orders for the several districts, and the total and average cost in all districts. As the cost of a line order is the part of a telephone installation on which the most guessing is done, by reason of the indefiniteness of material and labor required, a table of this nature will be found to be very valuable in drawing up new rate schedules and telephone prospectives

On account of the greater number of lines per square mile already installed in District No 2, new line orders required less poles, cross-arms, wire and other materials than in any other district. This accounts for the comparatively small cost of line order in this district. The increase in the cost of material for line orders in District No 3 for 1907 over 1906 is accounted for by the increase in the amount of material used per line order, caused by a larger percentage of line orders being installed in thinly settled sections where comparatively few poles existed. An increase of 7 per cent in wages taken in connection with the greater quantity of material installed accounts for the increase in labor cost. The line orders built in District No. 4 were mostly farm lines, which, although requiring a larger amount of material, cost less for material than city lines on account of the smaller size poles and cross-arms and cheaper kind of wires used. The labor cost is higher than for the city line orders on account of the greater quantity of material installed

The average length of drops in the different districts was as follows:

District No. 1.... .. .. 201 ft
District No. 2 . . .. 170 ft
District No 3. .. .. 106 ft
District No. 3.. . . . . 99 ft
District No 4 .. . . 244 ft

TABLE CXXXII—TOTAL AND AVERAGE LABOR AND MATERIAL COSTS OF LINE ORDERS, INCLUDING POLES, CROSS-ARMS, WIRE AND MISCELLANEOUS MATERIAL

	Dist No 1 July 1907		Dist No 2 April and May, 1907		Dist No 3 Jan to July, 1907		Dist No 3 Jan 1 to Dec 31, 1906		Dist No 4 April & May, 1907		All Locations	
	Totals	Averages Per Line Order	Totals	Averages Per Line Order	Totals	Averages Per Line Order	Totals	Averages Per Line Order	Totals	Averages Line Per Order	Totals	Averages Per Line Order
No Line Orders	77	77	246	246	421	421	668	668	14	14	1,426	1,426
Ft 080 Bare Copper Wire	70,760	918 83	117,580	477 97	491,366	1 167 13	555,745	831 95	2,000	142 86	1,237,440	867 77
Ft 080 Insulated Copper Wire	18,300	237 66	56,610	230 12	69,140	164 23	101,395	151 79	1,300	92 86	246,745	173 03
Ft No 12 Galv Steel Wire	6,900	89 61	12,269	49 87	0	0	0	0	12,400	885 71	31,859	22 14
Ft No 12 Insulated Steel Wire	1,080	14 03	1,250	5 08	0	0	0	0	2,350	167 85	1,880	3 28
Ft No 18 Bridle Wire	542	7 04	684	2 78	7,483	17 77	14,075	21 07		227 84	22,784	15 98
Ft ¼" Strand	140	1 82	280	1 14	520	1 24	804	1 20	0		1,744	1 22
No 20 Ft Poles	2	1 01	4	02	0		0		21	1 50	26	02
No 25 Ft Poles	1	03			0		0		3	21	54	04
No 30 Ft Poles	30	39	49	20	43	10	92	14	1	07	184	13
No 35 Ft Poles	8	10	18	07	23	05	36	05	1		67	05
No 40 Ft Poles					2	01	7	01			14	01
No 6-Pin Cross-Arms	31	01	5	02	0		0		1	07	12	01
No 10-Pin Cross-Arms	25	38	100	41	528	1 25	405	61			1,062	74
No Brackets		03	34	14			10	02	97	6 93	166	12
No Porcelain Knobs	154	2 00	18	07	34	08	48	07	62	4 43	102	07
No Test Connectors	141	1 83	684	2 78	940	2 23	1,136	1 70			2,976	2 09
No Fuses	83	1 08	448	1 82	721	1 71	1,054	1 58	28	2 00	2,384	1 66
No Full Joints	6	08	203	83	396	94	581	87	1	07	1,291	91
No Half Joints					24	06	36	05			67	05
No Pony Glass	694	9 01	2,043	8 30	3,987	9 47	5,126	7 67	204	14 57	12,054	8 45
No Transposition Glass	31	40	241	98	408	97	642	96	18	1 29	1,340	94
No Window Irons	62	81	323	1 31	501	1 19	728	1 09	7	50	1,621	1 14
No Cleats	72	93	46	19	214	51	301	45			633	44
No Steps	64	84	28	11	189	45	251	38			517	36
No Anchors	5	06	6	02	12	03	15	02	2	14	40	03
Material Cost	$839 66	$10 90	$1,638 74	$8 66	$4,387 56	$10 37	$5,140 19	$7 69	$75 80	$5 41	$12,061 95	$8 46
Labor Cost	444 64	5 78	939 43	3 82	3,084 55	7 33	3,619 45	5 42	122 80	8 77	8,210 87	5 76
Total Cost	1,284 30	16 68	2,578 17	10 48	7,452 11	17 70	8,759 64	13 11	198 60	14 18	20,272 82	14 22

TABLE CXXXIII—Comparison of Costs to Erect Drop Wires on Basis of 100-ft Drop Length and Four Drops on a Short Buck Arm with Capacity for Five Drops Each Way

	A		B		C		D		E	
	Material	Labor	Material	Labor	Material	Labor	Material	Labor	Material	Labor
Buck Arm in Place	$0 23	$0 06	$0 23	$0 06	$0 23	$0 06	$0 23	$0 06	$0 23	$0 06
Drop Wire in Place	1 81	17	1 22	17	62	17	2 10	17	1 70	17
House Fixtures in Place	18	07	18	07	18	07	18	07	22	07
Fuses Outside House in place	16	01	16	01	16	01	16	01	16	01
	$2 18	$0 31	$2 39	$0 31	$1 19	$0 31	$2 67	$0 31	$2 31	$0 31
Teaming Facilities and Lost Time	31		31		31		31		31	
	1 00		1 00		1 00		90		90	
	$3 49		$3 70		$2 50		$3 88		$3 52	

A—Cost per drop .080 copper, one bare, one insulated
B—Cost per drop No .080 copper, both insulated
C—Cost per drop No. 14 steel, both insulated
D—Cost per drop No. 14 Twisted pair copper insulated
E—Cost per drop, Twisted pair Monotte insulated

Omitting the cost of fuses at sub-station, namely 17c, in order of first cost expense it then follows

C (per above) $2 33   D (per above) $3 35
B (per above) 3 32   B (per above) 3 53
A (per above)

Table CXXXIII compares several methods of erecting drop wires Method "A" is the one generally used for erecting drops for the line orders in the city districts, on which the data in the previous table were based   Method "E" is based on the use of comparatively new material, the qualities of which have not yet been proven

The fuses used are known as No. 46 critical current 8½ amperes, and are installed between the drop wire and rubber-covered leading-in wire

Table CXXXIV shows the comparative cost of 15-pair terminals   The wooden style has been found to be more accessible in sleety weather when "trouble" is most frequent, as ice does not form as readily on wood as metal.

TABLE CXXXIV —COMPARATIVE COST TO ERECT 15-PAIR TERMINAL, NOT INCLUDING FUSING OR POLE BALCONY

	Wooden	No 14 (grace) Iron	No 8 Can	Comparative Cost Per Pair	
Pole Terminal Box	$3 90	$4 00	$2 88	No 8 Can .	$0 51
Splicing Material	70	70	70	Wooden	57
All Labor, including lost time	4 01	4 01	4 01	No 14 Iron .	58
	$8 61	$8 71	$7 59		

NOTE —The wooden style permits fusing in the box   This will increase the cost if fuses are added $0 14 per pair

The cost of fusing for exchange protection is shown in Table CXXXIV   The style of fuses used is known as No 7-F—critical current 8½ amperes

TABLE CXXXIV — COST OF FUSING FOR EXCHANGE PROTECTION
INSTALLING FUSE AT JUNCTION OF AERIAL AND UNDERGROUND

	Material	Labor
One 50 pr box in place	$31 00	$1 60
One Splicing	1 50	3 10
One Balcony	1 50	
Pole Changing		3 00
	$35 00	$7 70
	7 70	
Total	$42 70	
Cost per pair	0 85	
Fuses per pair	0 14	
	$ 0 99 Say $1 00	

The miscellaneous data composing Table CXXXVI will be found useful in estimating labor costs and material quantities for conduit and vault construction

The cost of unloading and distributing material is based on data collected on many separate jobs   The average cost of teams and labor was respectively $5.00 and $2 00 per day of 9 hours

The data on the average load carried in a wheelbarrow are based on actual tests made on numerous jobs without either foremen or laborers having previous knowledge that the tests were to be made. They show the average load carried by the average day laborer on conduit work

The shrinkage of mortar and concrete shown in this table is based on data secured on many conduit jobs. A certain percentage of this shrinkage is caused by loss of material while mixing, incident to mixing on paved streets, rough boards and windy days

The quantity of mortar used per 1,000 bricks is based on building vaults of sewer brick averaging 8 x 3¼ x 2½ ins. in size; the wall of the vaults being two bricks thick and every sixth course being laid as headers, the horizontal mortar joints being ½ in. and the vertical joints ⅜ in. in thickness. Some of the mortar is lost over the back of the wall, some is lost in handling and some is used in incidental work, such as cementing in a sewer trap, etc   Where these figures have been used in estimating the variance in quantity of mortar actually used was less than 2 cu ft per vault

The cost of mortar is based on the use of American Portland cement, washed gravel and torpedo sand delivered on the work.

TABLE CXXXVI — MISCELLANEOUS DATA

COST OF UNLOADING AND DISTRIBUTING MATERIAL

Cement, per bag	$ 0228
Frames and Covers, each	38

COST OF UNLOADING AND DISTRIBUTING TILE, PLANK AND CONCRETE PER LINEAL FOOT OF CONDUIT

Conduit Cross Section	Class A	Class B
2	$ 0092	
3	0116	$ 0100
4	0134	0116
6	0180	0160

DATA ON AVERAGE LOAD CARRIED IN A WHEEL BARROW

Capacity of wheel barrow	3 Cu Ft
Sand, Gravel or Stone, average load to wheel barrow	2¼ to 2½ Cu Ft
Finished Concrete, average load to wheel barrow	1½ to 1¾ Cu. Ft

DATA ON SHRINKAGE OF MORTAR AND CONCRETE

Shrinkage of Mortar, 3 to 1	33 76 Cu Ft = 1 Yd
Shrinkage of Concrete 1–4–8	40 60 Cu Ft = 1 Yd {based on washed
Shrinkage of Concrete, 1–3–5	38 63 Cu Ft = 1 Yd {gravel concrete

DATA ON QUANTITY AND COST OF MORTAR FOR 1,000 BRICKS

Quantity of Mortar to 1,000 Bricks	0 90 Cu Yds
Cost 2 to 1 Mortar for 1,000 Bricks	$5 81*
Cost 3 to 1 Mortar for 1,000 Bricks	4 88*

* Based on Cement $0 43½ per bag, and sand $1 90 per yard, delivered on work

Table CXXXVII shows the comparative labor cost of mixing concrete by hand and by machine These data were collected on conduit work where 6-duct or 8-duct was installed, and
where the mixing gang worked all day. They show the cost
of mixing by several different foremen on five or six jobs each.
The data were secured without the knowledge of the foremen,
so that no attempt would be made to accomplish more than
average work   The days on which these data were taken were
selected without regard to any other conditions than that concrete be mixed all day and the weather be fair. The cost of
moving mixing boards and time consumed in getting tools
when starting work is included in the cost   Supervision and
expense are not included

The advantage of mixing by machine when the work requires the mixing of more than a small quantity of concrete
is clearly shown by these data

TABLE CXXXVII.—COMPARATIVE COST OF MIXING CONCRETE BY HAND AND
BY MACHINE

| | | | MIXING BY MACHINE | | | | Average | |
Foreman	No of Mixings	Proportions to a Mixing Cu Ft	No Cu Yd Concrete Mixed	No of Men Used	No Hours Worked	No of Mixings per Hour	Time used to Mix 1 Cu Yd Concrete Minutes	Average Cost per Cu Yd Concrete.
A	1 586	½-3-6	380 87	5	120	13	19	$0 385
B	960	½-3-6	230 54	6	61	26	16	0 382
C	528	½-3-6	126 80	5	27	19½	13	0 260
D	1,140	½-3-6	273 77	5	79	14½	17	0 353
E	1,804	½-3-6	433 23	7	75	24	10	0 289
Aver'gs	6 018		1,445 21	5¾	362	17	15	0 339

Rates   Engineer, $3 00 for 9 hours, Laborers, $2 00 for 9 hours

		MIXING BY HAND						
A	135	9–36–72	389 04	5	172	78	27	$0 491
B	211	3–12–24	202 68	4	133	1 59	39	0 583
C	604	3–12- 24	580 20	5	283	·2 13	29	0 542
D	161	6–24–48	309 31	6	·118	1 36	23	0 51
Aver'gs	1,111		1 481 23	5	706	1 57	29	0 53

Wages of Laborers $2 00 for 9 hours

In Tables CXXXVIII to CXL are shown in detail the
quantities of materials required for different size vaults and
various cross sections of conduit, as well as the labor and material costs   The labor figures are based on the average cost of
installing over 1,500,000 duct feet of conduit and over 550

vaults The material figures are based on the quantities as shown in the specifications in Chapter V on "Underground Conduit Construction Costs " To these quantities, shown by these tables, should be added 3 per cent to 5 per cent. for waste of material, depending upon the size of the job. As a general rule the larger the job the smaller the percentage of waste.

These tables have been used in estimating conduit work and have been found to greatly facilitate the work, especially when quick estimates were desired The prices of materials include freight, and in the case of sand and gravel include the average cost of delivering on the job

The comparative cost of a mile of farm line and a mile of toll line are shown in Tables CXLI and CXLII, respectively The material quantities used in figuring these tables are based on average quantities actually used in constructing a mile of line as shown by records kept of many miles of both toll and farm line. The prices of poles include the cost of freight and labor cost of unloading and piling in pole yards The specifications require that poles used in toll construction shall weigh 540 lbs. each. The labor cost is based on averages shown in Chapter I.

Tables CXLIII and CXLIV show respectively the comparative cost of 1,000 ft. of underground cable and 1,000 ft. of aerial cable, including splicing These tables, as in the previous tables, are based on average quantities of material actually used in installing a thousand feet of cable as shown by records kept of many miles of cable. The averages shown in the chapters on "Cable Construction Costs" and "Cable Splicing Costs" are used as basis for figuring labor. The number of splices per 1,000 ft is based on the average number shown by records kept of cable installation. The labor of splicing does not include the cost of cutting in subsidiary boxes and cables, as they are cut in from time to time as the demands of distribution may require, some of the cable boxes and subsidiary cable not being cut in until several years after the installation of the main cable.

TABLE CXXXVIII—QUANTITIES AND COST OF MATERIALS AND LABOR REQUIRED IN CONCRETE VAULT CONSTRUCTION

Quantities and Cost of Material	Size No	Kind of Vault 1	Kind of Vault 3
Bags Cement for bottom @ 4325		1¼	1¼
Yds Sand for bottom @ 1 90		2222	2222
Yds Gravel for bottom @ 1 90		4444	4444
Total Cement, Sand, Gravel for bottom		7221	7221
Yds Concrete for bottom		4814	4814
Cost of Concrete for bottom @ 3 98		$1 92	$1 92
Bags Cement for sides and tops @ 4325		7 60	8 02
Yds Sand for sides and top @ 1 90		8368	8820
Yds Gravel for sides and top @ 1 90		1 3908	1 4670
Total Cement, Sand and Gravel for sides and tops		2 5091	2 6460
Yds Concrete for sides and top.		1 7656	1 8518
Cost of Concrete for sides and top @ 4 20		$7 55	$7 94
Cost Frame and Cover		$11 74	$11 74
Total Cost Material per Vault		$21 21	$21 60

	Kind of Vault 1	Kind of Vault 3
Cost of Unloading and Distributing Material		
Cost of unloading and distributing cement	$0 21	$0 22
Cost of unloading and distributing frame and cover	38	38
Total cost unloading and distributing material	59	60
Labor Cost.		
Cost of teaming	2 80	3 18
Cost of excavating	4 08	4 78
Cost of mixing and placing bottom	95	1 18
Cost of mixing and placing sides	4 50	5 64
Cost of mixing and placing top and frame	2 63	3 05
Supervision and expense	2 11	2 73
Total Labor Cost per Vault	16 21	20 56
Total	$28 01	$42 76
Total Cost per Vaults.		

TABLE CXXXIX — QUANTITIES AND COST OF MATERIAL AND LABOR REQUIRED IN BRICK VAULT CONSTRUCTION

Size No	1½	2	1½	2	1½	2	2	2½	3	4	5	6
Quantities and Cost of Material												
Bags Cement for bottom @ 4325												
Yards Sand for bottom @ 1 90												
Yards Gravel for bottom @ 1 90												
Total Cement, Sand and Gravel for bottom												
Cost of Concrete for bottom												
Bags Cement for top @ 4325												
Yards Sand for top @ 1 90												
Yards Gravel for top @ 1 90												
Total Cement, Sand and Gravel for top												
Yards Concrete for top												
Cost of Concrete for top @ 4 29												
Bags Cement for Mortar @ 4325												
Yards Sand for Mortar @ 1 90												
Total Yards Sand and Cement												
Yards of Mortar												
Cost of Mortar @ 5 12												
No of Brick												
Cost of Brick @ 8 50												
Cost of Frame and Cover												
Total Cost of Material per Vault												
Cost of Unloading and Distributing Material												
Cost of Unloading and Distributing Cement												
Cost of Unloading and Distributing Frame and Cover												
Total Cost Unloading and Distributing Material												
Labor Costs												
Cost of Teaming												
Cost of Excavating												
Cost of Mixing and Placing bottom												
Cost of Laying Brick												
Cost of Mixing and Placing Top and Frame												
Supervision and Expense												
Total Labor Cost per Vault												
Total Cost per Vault												

TABLE CXL.—QUANTITIES AND COST OF MATERIAL AND LABOR REQUIRED IN McROY TILE CONDUIT CONSTRUCTION

Class	Conduit Cross Section							
	8 Duct A	6 Duct A	6 Duct B	4 Duct A	4 Duct B	3 Duct A	3 Duct B	2 Duct A
Quantities and Cost of Material								
Bags Cement @ 4325	1578	1327	0456	1147	0360	1147	0456	0955
Yds Sand @ 1 90	0236	0198	0068	0171	0054	0171	0068	0143
Yds Gravel @ 1 90	0471	0397	0136	0343	0107	0343	0136	0285
Total Yd Cement, Sand and Gravel	0764	0642	0221	0555	0174	0555	0221	0462
Yds Concrete	0509	0427	0147	0370	0116	0370	0147	0308
Cost of Concrete @ 3 98	$ 2026	$ 1704	0585	1463	0462	1463	0585	1226
No of Dowel Pins per duct	3	2	37			2		1
Cost of Dowel Pins @ 00325	00325	00217	00217	00109	00109	00325	00325	00163
Inches Burlap 61" wide, per duct	616	37	37	33	33	29	29	25
Cost of Burlap @ 014	0086	0048	0048	0043	0043	0057	0057	0049
Cost of Duct @ 0396	$ 3168	$ 2376	2376	1584	1684	1188	1188	0792
No inches 1½ x 9 Creosote Plank	0	0	131	0	134	0	194	0
Cost of Creosote Plank	0	0	0597	0	0597	0	08619	0
Total Cost Material, not including waste, etc								
Per Lineal Ft	5313	4150	3628	3101	2887	2741	2724	2083
Per duct Ft	0884	0692	0605	0775	0672	0914	0908	1041
Cost Unloading and Distributing Material								
Cost of Unloading and Distributing—Duct and Cement	0268	0180	0160	0134	0116	0116	0100	0092
—Creosote Plank			0051		0029		0051	
Total Cost of Unloading and Dist Material—Per Lin Ft	0268	0180	0211	0134	0145	0116	0151	0092
—Per Duct Ft	0034	0030	0035	0034	0036	0039	0050	0046
Labor Cost								
Cost of Excavating	0344	0311	0330	0313	0277	0186	0176	0352
Cost of Foaming	1482	1287	1399	1247	1237	0674	0675	0607
Cost of Mixing Handling and Dumping Concrete	0884	0583	0230	0626	0259	0467	0176	0342
Cost of Laying Tile and Plank	0332	0323	0339	0316	0211	0190	0190	0133
Cost of Filling in	0705	0667	0706	0396	0481	0355	0422	0490
Supervision and Expense	4254	3894	0668	3313	0457	2376	2886	2341
Labor Cost—Per Lineal Ft	0532	0649	3672	0828	2942	0759	2085	2314
—Per Duct Ft			0612		0731		0675	1177
Total Cost								
Per Lineal Ft	9835	8224	7511	6548	5754	5133	4900	4529
Per Duct Ft	$ 1230	$ 1371	$ 1252	$ 1637	$ 1439	$ 1712	$ 1633	$ 2264

TABLE CXLI—COMPARATIVE COST OF A MILE OF FARM LINE ON A BASIS OF 30 POLES TO A MILE

20-ft Poles, 4-in Tops, Bracket Line, 2 Wires

30 poles @ 75 (freight paid and unloaded)	$ 22 50
2 mi No 12 galvanized steel wire @ $4 65	9 30
4 Stombaugh anchors @ 50	2 00
No 4 wire for anchor guys, No 6 wire for lightning rods, tie wire, joints, glass, staples, spikes, brackets	2 27
Total cost material	$ 36 07
Labor	39 30
Total cost	$ 75 37

20-ft. Poles, 5-in Tops, 1 Cross-Arm, 2 Wires.

30 poles @ 95 (freight paid and unloaded)	$ 28 50
2 mi No 12 galvanized steel wire @ $4 65	9 30
4 Stombaugh anchors @ 50	2 00
30 6-pin cross-arms @ 41 (complete)	12 30
No 4 wire for anchor guys, No 6 wire for lightning rods, tie wire, joints, glass, staples, spikes	2 51
Total cost material	$ 54 61
Labor	45 80
Total cost	$100.41

20-ft Poles, 5-in Tops, 1 Cross-Arm, 4 Wires

30 poles @ 95 (freight paid and unloaded)	$ 28 50
4 mi No 12 galvanized steel wire @ $4 65	18 60
4 Stombaugh anchors @ 50	2 00
30 6-pin cross-arms @ 41 (complete)	12 30
No 4 wire for anchor guys, No 6 wire for lightning rods, tie wire, joints, glass, staples, spikes	3 81
Total cost material	$ 65 21
Labor	55 46
Total cost	$120 67

25-ft Poles, 5-in Tops, 1 Cross-Arm, 2 Wires

30 poles @ $1 35 (freight paid and unloaded)	$ 40 50
2 mi No 12 galvanized steel wire @ $4 65	9 30
4 Stombaugh anchors @ 50	2 00
30 6-pin cross-arms @ .41 (complete)	12 30
No. 4 wire for anchor guys, No 6 wire for lightning rods, tie wire, joints, glass, staples, spikes	2 51
Total cost material	$ 66 61
Labor	60 80
Total cost	$127 41

25-ft. Poles, 5-in Tops, 1 Cross-Arm, 4 Wires

30 poles @ $1 35 (freight paid and unloaded)	$ 40 50
4 mi No 12 galvanized steel wire @ $4 65	18 60
4 Stombaugh anchors @ 50	2 00
30 6-pin cross-arms @ 41 (complete)	12 30
No 4 wire for anchor guys, No 6 wire for lightning rods, tie wire, joints, glass, staples, spikes	3 81
Total cost material	$ 77 21
Labor	70 46
Total cost	$147 67

TABLE CXLII.—COMPARATIVE COST OF A MILE OF TOLL LINE ON A BASIS
OF 43 POLES TO A MILE

30-ft. Poles, 7-In. Tops, 36-In Butt Circum , 1 Cross-Arm, 2 Wires.

43 poles @ $6 70 (freight paid and unloaded)	$288 10
43 10-pin cross-arms @ 65 (complete)	27 95
2 mi 104 bare copper wire @ $35 70	71 40
4 log anchor rods @ 35	1 40
200' ⅜" strand for anchor guys @ 0091	1 82
04 mi No 6 steel wire for head guys @ $15 42	62
Guy lugs, pole protectors, glass, joints, staples, No 6 wire for lightning rods, tie wire	4 46
Total cost material	**$395 75**
Labor	120.74
Total cost	$516 49

30-ft Poles, 7-In. Tops, 36-In. Butt Circum., 1 Cross-Arm, 4 Wires.

43 poles @ $6 70 (freight paid and unloaded)	$288 10
43 10-pin cross-arms @ 65 (complete)	27 95
4 mi 104 bare copper wire @ $35 70	142 80
4 log anchor rods @ .35	1 40
200' ⅜" strand for anchor guys @ 0091	1 82
04 mi No 6 steel wire for head guys @ $15 42	62
Guy lugs, pole protectors, glass, joints, staples, No 6 wire for lightning rods, tie wire	6 93
Total cost material	**$469 62**
Labor	132 00
Total cost	$601 62

30-ft Poles, 7-In. Tops, 36-In Butt Circum , 1 Cross-Arm, 6 Wires.

43 poles @ $6 70 (freight paid and unloaded)	$288 10
43 10-pin cross-arms @ 65 (complete)	27 95
6 mi 104 bare copper wire @ $35 70	214 20
4 log anchor rods @ 35	1 40
200' ⅜" strand for anchor guys @ 0091	1 82
04 mi No 6 steel wire for head guys @ $15 42	62
Guy lugs, pole protectors, glass, joints, staples, No 6 wire for lightning rods, tie wire	9 30
Total cost material	**$543 39**
Labor	141 50
Total cost	$684 89

30-ft. Poles, 7-In. Tops, 36-In Butt Circum , 1 Cross-Arm, 8 Wires

43 poles @ $6 70 (freight paid and unloaded)	$288 10
43 10-pin cross-arms @ 65 (complete)	27 95
8 mi 104 bare copper wire @ $35 70	285 60
4 log anchor rods @ 35	1.40
200' ⅜" strand for anchor guys @ 0091	1 82
04 mi No 6 steel wire for head guys @ $15 42	62
Guy lugs, pole protectors, glass, joints, staples, No 6 wire for lightning rods, tie wire	11 67
Total cost material	**$617 16**
Labor	150 50
Total cost	$767 66

30-ft. Poles, 7-In. Tops, 36-In Butt Circum , 1 Cross-Arm, 10 Wires.

43 poles @ $6 70 (freight paid and unloaded)	$288 10
43 10-pin cross-arms @ 65 (complete)	27 95
10 miles 104 bare copper wire @ $35 70	357 00
4 log anchor rods @ 35	1 40
200' ⅜" strand for anchor guys @ 0091	1 82
04 miles No 6 steel wire for head guys @ $15 42	62
Guy lugs, pole protectors, glass, joints, staples, No 6 wire for lightning rods, tie wire	13 94
Total cost material	**$690 83**
Labor	159.50
Total cost	$850 33

TABLE CXLIII—COMPARATIVE LABOR AND MATERIAL COST TO ERECT 1.000 FEET UNDERGROUND CABLE

1,000 ft 50 Pr —19 Ga

1,000' 50 pr —22 ga paper insulated cable @ 30	$300 00
8 vault cable supports @ 12	96
Soapstone, solder, paraffine wax, muslin, candles, pasters, lead sleeves, paper sleeves, gasoline, pasters and miscellaneous material	5 75
Total cost material	$306 71
Labor, including splicing	42 76
Total cost	$349 47

1,000 ft 100 Pr —22 Ga

1,000' 100 pr —22 ga paper insulated cable @ 31	$310 00
8 vault cable supports @ 12	96
Soapstone, solder, paraffine wax, muslin, candles, pasters, lead sleeves, paper sleeves, gasoline, pasters and miscellaneous material	8 15
Total cost material	$319 11
Labor, including splicing	44 94
Total cost	$364 05

1,000 ft 100 Pr.—19 Ga

1,000' 100 pr —19 ga paper insulated cable @ 60	$600 00
8 vault cable supports @ 12	96
Soapstone, solder, paraffine wax, muslin, candles, pasters, lead sleeves, paper sleeves, gasoline, pasters and miscellaneous material	9 33
Total cost material	$610 29
Labor, including splicing	59 34
Total cost	$669 63

1,000 ft 200 Pr —22 Ga

1,000' 200 pr —22 ga paper insulated cable @ 60	$600 00
8 vault cable supports @ 12	96
Soapstone, solder, paraffine wax, muslin, candles, pasters, lead sleeves, paper sleeves, gasoline, pasters and miscellaneous material	9 94
Total cost material	$610 90
Labor, including splicing	61 70
Total cost	$672 60

1,000 ft 200 Pr —19 Ga

1,000' 200 pr —19 ga paper insulated cable @ 95	$950 00
8 vault cable supports @ 12	96
Soapstone, solder, paraffine wax, muslin, candles, pasters, lead sleeves, paper sleeves, gasoline, pasters and miscellaneous material	10 63
Total cost material	$961 59
Labor, including splicing	69 50
Total cost	$1,031 09

TABLE CXLIV.—COMPARATIVE LABOR AND MATERIAL COST TO ERECT 1,000 FT AERIAL CABLE.

1,000 ft 25 Pr —22 Ga.

2 cable arms (complete) @ 81	\$ 1.62
2 ¾ in by 8 ft log anchor rods @ 48	96
1 25 pr protected cable box .	23 00
4 anchor lugs @ 285 . ..	1 14
16 pole protectors @ 031 .	50
600 Marlin cable hangers @ 00395 .	2 37
1250 ft ⅝-in messenger strand @ .00912	11 40
250 ft. No 18 bridle wire @ .00969 .	2 42
1000 ft 25 pr —22 ga paper insulated cable @ \$10 46 .	104 60
1 balcony or seat .	1 35
25 ft No 6 copper ground wire @ 03	.75
Clamps, cleats, messenger supports, side braces, ground rod, par- affine wax, lead sleeves, solder, pasters, paper sleeves, thim- bles, miscellaneous material	3 88
Total cost material . . .	\$153 99
Labor, including splicing	48 10
Total cost	. \$202 09

1,000 ft 25 Pr —13 Ga

2 cable arms (complete) @ 81 .	\$ 1 62
2 ¾ in by 8 ft log anchor rods @ 48	96
1 25 pr protected cable box	23 00
4 anchor lugs @ 285 . . .	1 14
16 pole protectors @ 031 .	50
600 marlin cable hangers @ 00395 .	2 37
)250 ft ⅝ in messenger strand @ 00912	11 40
250 ft No 18 bridle wire @ 00969 .	2 42
1000 ft 25 pr —19 ga paper insulated cable @ 18 .	180 00
1 balcony or seat	1 35
25 ft No 6 copper ground wire @ 03 .	75
Clamps, cleats, messenger supports, side braces, ground rod, par- affine wax, lead sleeves, solder, pasters, paper sleeves, thim- bles, miscellaneous material . .	3 99
Total cost material . .	\$229 50
Labor, including splicing	48 40
Total cost . .	\$277 90

1,000 ft. 50 Pr —22 Ga.

2 cable arms (complete) @ \$ 81	\$ 1 62
2 ¾ in by 8 ft log anchor rods @ 48	96
1 25 pr protected cable box	23 00
4 anchor lugs @ 285 .	1 14
16 pole protectors @ 031	50
600 marlin cable hangers @ 00395	2 37
1250 ft ⅝ in messenger strand @ 00912	11 40
250 ft No 18 bridle wire @ 00969	2 42
1000 ft 50 pr —22 ga paper insul cable @ 185	185 00
1 balcony or seat .	1.35
25 ft No 6 copper ground wire @ 03	.75
Clamps, cleats, messenger supports, side braces, ground rod, par- affine wax, lead sleeves, solder, pasters, paper sleeves, thim- bles, miscellaneous material	4 08
Total cost material	\$234 59
Labor, including splicing	50 28
Total cost	\$234 87

1,000 ft 50 Pr.—19 Ga.

2 cable arms (complete) @ $ 81	.$ 1 62
2 ¾ in by 8 ft log anchor rods @ 48	96
1 25 pr protected cable box	23.00
4 anchor lugs @ 285	1 14
16 pole protectors @ 031	50
600 marlin cable hangers @ 00435	2 61
1000 ft 50 pr —22 ga paper insul cable @ 30	300 00
250 ft ½ in strand for anchors @ 0135	3 38
250 ft No 18 bridle wire @ 00969	2 42
1000 ft ⅜ in messenger strand @ 00912	11 40
1 balcony or seat	1 35
25 ft No 6 copper ground wire @ 03	75
Clamps, cleats, messenger supports, side braces, ground rod, paraffine wax, lead sleeves, paper sleeves, solder, pasters, thimbles, miscellaneous material	4 32

Total cost material	$353 45
Labor, including splicing	50 33
Total cost	$403 78

1,000 ft 100 Pr —22 Ga.

2 cable arms (complete) @ $0 81	$ 1 62
2 ¾ in by 8 ft log anchor rods @ 48	96
1 25 pr protected cable box	23 00
4 anchor lugs @ 285	1 14
16 pole protectors @ 031	50
600 marlin cable hangers @ 00435	2 61
1000 ft ⅜ in messenger strand @ 00912	11 40
250 ft ½ in strand for anchors @ 0135	3 38
250 ft No 18 bridle wire @ 00969	2 42
1000 ft 100 pr —22 ga paper insul cable @ 31	310 00
1 ft balcony or seat	1 35
25 ft No 6 copper ground wire @ 03	75
Clamps, cleats, messenger supports, side braces, ground rod, paraffine wax, lead sleeves, solder, pasters, paper sleeves, thimbles, miscellaneous material	4 62

Total cost material	$363 75
Labor, including splicing	52 50
Total cost	$416 25

1,000 ft 100 Pr —19 Ga

2 cable arms (complete) @ $81	$ 1 62
2 ¾ in by 8 ft log anchor rods @ 48	96
1 25 pr protected cable box	23 00
4 anchor lugs @ 285	1 14
16 pole protectors @ 031	50
800 marlin cable hangers @ 0048	3 84
1250 ft ¼ in messenger strand @ 0135	16 20
250 ft No 18 bridle wire @ 00969	2 42
1000 ft 100 pr —19 ga paper insul cable @ 60	600 00
1 balcony or seat	1 35
25 ft No 6 copper ground wire @ 03	75
Clamps, cleats, messenger supports side braces, ground rod, paraffine wax, lead sleeves solder, pasters, paper sleeves, thimbles, miscellaneous material	5 28

Total cost material	$657 06
Labor, including splicing	54 85
Total cost	$711 91

CHAPTER VIII.
THE PRACTICE OF ESTIMATING.

In the previous chapters, construction cost data have been shown covering the various branches of telephone work, the system for figuring and keeping costs has been explained in considerable detail, the methods for constructing the work on which the costs were based and the form used for reporting the data have been shown It remains in this chapter to describe the practice of estimating, explaining the origin of estimates in a large corporation, the system by which they are made and handled and the indispensability to estimating of cost data based on a system

Until recent years systematic estimating was practically unknown ; and even now, estimating and guessing are almost synonymous in a great many instances.

The waste caused by inaccurate estimating is great. In the case of a corporation doing its own construction, too liberal estimates result in expensive work, as it being only required that construction men shall keep within the estimates, they have a tendency to lay out work with that object in view, and they believe good results have been achieved if they succeed —no matter how large the estimate may have been On the other hand, estimates which are much too small have a tendency to cause construction men to lose interest in the work, as they know that the overrunning of an estimate never results in any credit to them, no matter how cheap the work is done Naturally construction superintendents and foremen are guided by the estimate, and they believe to a certain extent that the results of their work are shown by the amount of the debit or credit balance In the case of a contractor it needs little argument to show the loss caused by inaccurate estimating If the estimate is too large he may lose the contract, if too small, he loses his profits. In the first instance he often discourages construction , and in the other, he cannot long exist.

In some cases the estimating is done by men whose long experience in construction has given them a kind of intuitive knowledge of costs, and although using no systems or records, they are able to estimate fairly accurately; but such methods, being, as they are, dependent upon the personnel of the estimators—their retirement and health—sooner or later must end in leaving the estimating in a chaotic condition

The practice in estimating may be divided into four classes (1) estimating based on time; (2) estimating based on guess, (3) estimating based on sporadic costs; (4) estimating based on systematic average costs

In the first class, a method of procedure is to divide the proposed work into divisions of construction, as where the work comprises the building of a toll line, the number and sizes of poles, anchors, cross-arms and miles of wire are ascertained, and the time required to set a pole and an anchor, erect a cross-arm and string a mile of wire is used as the basis for figuring the total time and the estimate is then made by using the average cost, per hour, of a line construction gang to find the total cost

Another method, and the one most generally used in time estimating, is to find, by basing the figures on the number of holes a groundman can dig in a day, the number of poles a lineman can frame in a day and the number of cross-arms a lineman can erect, how many poles, cross-arms, etc, a gang composed of a certain number of linemen, combination men, groundmen and a team can install in a day, and use these data to figure the number of days required by a gang to complete the proposed work   The estimated cost is then found by figuring the cost of a gang for the total number of days.

The first method would require that a record of the time expended in setting a pole, erecting a cross-arm, etc, be kept for each gang, or tables be made showing the number of poles that gangs composed of different number and grades of men can set in a day or hour   In one case it is impracticable, as the gangs fluctuate too much, and in other cases, tables of this character are very difficult to collect and always subject to errors, and in both cases it involves more work than the collection of data based on cost

The second method does not take into consideration the fact that both groundmen and linemen dig holes, that combination men sometimes frame poles or erect cross-arms, all of which make considerable difference in cost—if not in time This method might work out if all gangs were composed the same and certain work was always done by the same grade of men

Time data to be accurate bases for estimating would require records of linemen-hours, combination men-hours, groundmen-hours, as well as team-hours and foremen-hours, be kept for each kind and division of line construction, and the lost time be separated in the same manner, as the difference between the wages of the several grades of men is considerable   The collection of data on average time, based on this system is not practical, as the composition of gangs varies—often greatly—and the exigencies of work frequently require that linemen do the work of groundmen or combination men do the work of linemen.

Data of this character may be collected on conduit work where the construction is done almost entirely by men of the same grade and receiving the same wages

These systems are obviously better than no system, and if all conditions such as kind of soil, distance from station and size of job are taken into consideration, an estimate of some value may be made, especially if a record of the time required to accomplish the work has been collected, but too often no records of any kind have been kept, the records are based on time consumed in constructing entire lines, no separation being made of the time spent in setting poles, erecting cross-arms or stringing wire, or the records are based on foremen's work reports, and these reports are known by men experienced in construction costs to be almost valueless, as a foreman will report, for example, that the day's work was 50 holes excavated for 30-ft poles, whereas 40 holes were excavated to the required depth and the balance were in various stages of completion—perhaps not averaging 2 ft where the required depth is 5½ ft   Even a work report of this character is rare   Usually besides holes excavated for poles, there are poles framed. labor spent in hauling poles, etc , and no separation is made of the time spent on each division Any record based on data of this character is worse than useless because it is misleading

No matter how carefully a time system may be devised, the hours and minutes spent in preparing for work, in rehandling materials, in lost time and in contingencies in general are rarely included A matter of a few minutes used on this or that part of construction seems so small that little attention is paid to it, but these minutes mean the expenditure on large jobs of considerable money

The second class of estimates is used almost exclusively by small telephone companies and contractors, and in many cases by large companies and contractors

Small telephone companies doing their own work usually advance the argument that the work is to be done no matter what the cost, and, therefore, there is no use in spending money or time on cost data. They do not take into consideration the value the data will have when contemplating the building of extensions. which, a company in business in a small town where the percentage of telephones per capita is small, or a company in business in a large town where the percentage of plant per telephone is large, often builds although the cost of the extension is frequently not justified by the income or future prospects To estimates based on guess may be attributed the failure of some small companies that have undertaken work which a careful estimate would have shown to be unjustified by the size of their capital or prospective income

Where companies let their work by contract the lack of cost records puts them at the mercy of contractors, besides subjecting them to the same conditions when making extensions and adopting new materials, as explained for a company doing its own work.

Comparatively few large telephone companies or contractors are without some cost system or so-called cost system, but many of these "systems," if used in estimating, make the estimate a guess.

With telephone companies most of these systems are designed with the object of keeping a record of the cost for the auditing department, so that expenditures may be checked, and the value and amount of the increase and displacement of plant may be recorded and charged, and with contractors these systems are designed for keeping records of expenditures which the exigencies of bookkeeping require. In both cases the records of costs are not kept with an idea to facilitate estimating or to collect systematic cost data.

While labor and material costs are generally separated, under these systems, the labor or material costs of any particular kind of equipment cannot be ascertained, and the character of soil and conditions under which the work was done are not recorded

Sometimes the records show the lumped cost of underground conduit including cable and splices, and other times the lumped cost of a job composed of every kind of telephone construction is shown. It is rarely that a record of the cost of only one kind of construction such as a toll line or a run of conduit is shown, and when shown, the only data for future estimates which may be gleaned are the cost of a toll line composed of a certain number of 30-ft., 35-ft. and 40-ft. poles: 10-pin and terminal cross-arms; anchors, and miles of wire; or in the case of a conduit job, the cost of a certain number of feet of conduit including vaults, perhaps composed of different classes of construction, different cross sections and several different sizes of vaults. The average cost of a mile of toll line or a lineal foot of conduit based on such data might be good bases for estimating a similar job, but for general estimating, the fluctuations in size of poles, cost of setting poles in different soils, number of miles and style of wire, number and size of cross-arms, number of anchors and cost of setting them in different soil, and conditions; or the fluctuation in cross sections, percentage of vaults per foot of conduit, size of vaults, character of soil, and conditions, make any attempt to use such data for estimating result in a guess.

There are, however, systems designed for taking costs solely for use in estimating, whose use results in guess. In this class may be put the work report systems already explained, and systems in which the attempt is made to secure costs on arbitrary, infinitesimal, incomplete or insufficient divisions.

An instance of these systems occurred on a job where the cost of excavating per cu. yd. was kept on a run of conduit of different cross sections, each cross section requiring a trench of different dimensions, but no division was made of the cost per cu yd. of each cross section. In another instance, on a job where wire was being strung, "costs" were kept on tying-in, dead ending, putting on test connectors, fuses and glass, making joints, climbing poles, pulling slack and several other divisions, although to secure such costs is obviously impracticable, and, without a stop watch, a field glass and a cost man for each workman, is impossible.

By the usual and most economical method of stringing wire, the act of climbing a pole, putting on glass and tying-in, slide so gradually into each other that any attempt to separate them is like trying to separate the cost of laying brick and the cost of placing mortar in the work of bricklaying

It may be said that the stumbling-block in devising a practical system for taking labor costs is in the tendency to make a division of construction for each different material used

New method of construction and new materials cannot be adopted by telephone companies or contractors basing estimates on guess, unless it is clear that the mechanical or electrical improvement will be great, without hazarding avoidable losses, as it is evident that the question whether the new material costs less to install, or the new method cheapens construction is a matter of speculation when the cost of installing the old material or the cost of the old construction method is a matter of guess

A contractor basing his estimates on guess is much the same as a novice at an auction—neither knows whether he is bidding high or low; and if he gets his bid, does not know whether he made or lost.

With systematic estimating, even a small, unknown contractor is able to secure contracts, and contractors whose plants are large, and consequent expense great, may in times when money is stringent, stimulate business by close estimates

In the third class of estimating may be put estimates that are based on the cost of a single job, parts of jobs or a few hours' work on a job.

When based on a single, large job, if costs of the divisions and subdivisions of construction are separated and accurately collected, an estimate may be made that is fairly correct.

Costs on parts of jobs, whether the part is the start, the middle or the finish of a job, are poor data on which to base estimates, because, in construction, there is certain preliminary labor expense, loss of time, and work to be done at the start; and at the finish there is often more or less loss by reason of a surplus of men, there is cleaning up to be done and surplus material to be returned to yards, all of which cannot be correctly charged to the first or last part of a job, as the case may be, but are charges against the whole work, and, therefore, if the cost of the middle of the job be taken, it will be found to average much less than the average cost of an entire job.

In line construction, for example, the poles may be hauled at the beginning of the work, all anchors and poles may be located at one time, holes may be dug one day and poles set the next, or in the case of conduit construction at the start of a job the gang may be inexperienced, test holes may be dug, there may be mixing boards to be made, the percentage of laborers per supervisor may be larger than at the middle; and at the finish, the streets may be cleaned up, surplus material carted away and numerous other things done

Costs of a few hours' work, whether on one or many jobs, are very crude data for estimating, and being an abridgment of the last explained method of taking costs. they increase its inaccuracies The general method of taking these costs is to keep a record for a few minutes or for a few hours of the amount of lineal feet or cubic yards excavated, the number of feet of tile laid, the cubic yards of concrete mixed, and so on, and on these data base the cost of the entire work.

The fourth class of estimates are based on costs such as have been shown in the previous chapters

Showing the rates of wages and methods of construction, based on a uniform system, small and large jobs, different conditions and seasons; separated for each kind, division and subdivision of construction, each kind of soil and each size and style of material, easily revised for changes in wages or methods, these costs make estimating facile and accurate

The following description of the system used by a large telephone company gives some idea of the methods of originating, handling and making estimates that are based on systematic average cost data when applied to construction or reconstruction

Exchange managers have the authority to authorize work not to exceed a certain specified amount, usually sufficient to string a drop and install a telephone set, or make small repairs and changes. Work requiring a larger outlay but not exceeding an amount usually sufficient to erect a short line of poles including necessary wire, anchors, etc., or make proportionate changes and repairs is authorized by the superintendent of construction If, however, the line is for a new subscriber, and requires more than 2 or 3 poles and 2 or 3 spans of wire, it is rarely authorized until the territory has been canvassed for future prospects and then only if prospects justify. The general manager has jurisdiction in cases requiring an expenditure of a still greater amount not to exceed three hundred dollars, except in the case of repairs such as are sometimes required after a sleet storm or a fire. With these exceptions all work is authorized by the board of directors.

All estimates except those of managers are made by the construction cost department. In the case of managers' estimates, practically no knowledge of costs is required; simply a rough estimate is made by the manager or district foreman and the manager orders the work done In the case of a line order for a new subscriber, requiring over 2 or 3 poles and 2 or 3 spans of wire, a rough estimate is first made for the guidance of the canvassing or special agents' department, and if authorized by that department, it is then carefully estimated and the superintendent of construction orders the line built.

Except in the case of estimates to be submitted to the board of directors or manager's estimates, the district fore-

men or managers send an estimate of the number of poles,
wire and other materials needed for the work in question.
An estimate of the labor cost of installing this material is
then made, based on average costs and taking into consideration previous data secured on work in the vicinity, showing
kind of soil and conditions of work such as distance from station, etc. In event of no data having been taken in the vicinity, the information as to the kind of soil is obtained from the
district foreman or manager. The material is then added to
the estimate using prices based on latest quotations   The
forms used for these estimates are shown by Forms 47 to 52,
inclusive   An order authorizing the construction is then written, showing the lump sums estimated for labor and for material, and two copies are sent to an assistant superintendent
of construction who in turn sends one to the district foreman
The original estimate is filed with the records.

While work authorized by managers, superintendent of
construction or general manager usually originates in lines
for new subscribers, "out orders," "change orders," repairs
and reconstruction, work authorized by the board of directors
generally has its origin in extensions, redistribution, changes
from open wire to cable or changes from aerial to underground, proposed by an exchange manager, the superintendent of construction, the engineer or a combination of all
three officers

When the proposed plan has been submitted, in the rough,
to the general superintendent or general manager, plans on
the style of Fig. 87, showing the proposed work and specifications, are made   The construction cost department on receipt
of the blue print plans has measurements made of the number
of feet of cable, strand, conduit or other materials, the required amount of which are not specified on the blue print;
and the kind of soil and conditions of work are ascertained.
An estimate is then made on forms similar to those shown.

If the estimate is approved by the superintendent of construction it is typewritten on a form like that shown in No. 52,
and sent to the various officials whose approval is required.
The original estimate on the forms like those shown in Nos.
47 to 51, inclusive, are retained in the construction department,

and if the estimate is approved by the board of directors, it is given to the material and tool clerks to order material and tools, and an order authorizing the construction, showing the lump amounts allowed for labor and material is then written. This order is made in triplicate. One copy is filed with the estimate and two copies are sent to an assistant superintendent of construction who in turn forwards one copy to a foreman.

The assistant superintendent to whom the order is addressed, supervises the construction and is responsible to the superintendent for the standard of the work and its completion within the estimated cost.

In event of the estimate being overrun more than 10 per cent. the assistant superintendent must explain the cause to the superintendent of construction and both the latter and the general superinendent must in turn explain the cause to the general manager   The general manager then asks the board of directors for a further authorization to make up the deficit, explaining the reasons for overrunning the estimate.

The expenses occasioned by the supervision of work by an assistant superintendent, such as railroad fare, livery, board and time, are included in the estimate as "general supervision." If the superintendent of construction inspects the works, as is usually the case on a large job, his time and expenses are also charged to the estimate under "general supervision "

The organization of the construction department for the handling and general supervision of work is as follows:

There are three assistant superintendents of construction, with headquarters at the main office, each being in charge of all construction work done in a certain territorial district.

Each is responsible for the standard of the construction in his district and each has an assistant or facility man who usually supervises small jobs. In all districts there are foremen, some stationed in large towns and some "floating," who report to the assistant superintendent of the respective district. There are also a few foremen under the supervision of the first assistant superintendent, that do practically all the conduit construction, irrespective of district, on account of their experience in this line of work.

The usual custom of assistant superintendents is to spend one-half hour or one hour every week inspecting the construction in company with each foreman. The foremen also report each day by telephone and consult with the assistant superintendent or his assistant on matters of construction.

The assistant superintendents and their assistants charge their time spent in the office to general accounts, such as maintenance and district aerial construction, and time spent inspecting and supervising work is charged to the respective job.

General supervision is a small item in an estimate, rarely exceeding 2 per cent or 3 per cent. It fluctuates greatly in amount and only very general rules may be given for estimating its cost. It is, however, a small and comparatively unimportant item and may be very roughly estimated without materially affecting the value of the estimate as a whole.

In estimating its cost it is necessary to take into consideration the size of the job, the kind of construction and the distance from main office to the town in which the work is to be done. If the jobs are small and ordinary city or farm line construction, several are usually inspected on one tour or left for the inspection of the facility man If railroad communication is infrequent or distance from main office great, a job is not often visited unless it is a large conduit job; these are visited almost every day by the assistant superintendent and every three or four days by the superintendent of construction. General supervision is a part of the cost of work which is almost entirely dependent upon the system of supervision and inspection of each individual company

To explain the method used in estimating from a blueprint plan, that shown in Fig 87 will be taken as an example It is divided into several parts in order to minimize the size of the blueprint. The parts having block lines show the proposed line construction, and the other or center part shows the proposed cable construction.

It will be found more facile to estimate first the part or parts showing one class of construction.

For the purpose of avoiding useless repetition, an estimate of the proposed work in the alley south of State street and west of Hohman street. as shown on Fig 87, will be used to show the method of estimating the whole plan.

Starting with the part of the plan showing the proposed line construction and assuming the measurement from the first pole west of Hohman street to the second pole west of Morton place to be 1,000 ft., and assuming further, that the soil is sand, the estimate would be as follows:

Estimated Labor.

24,000 ft. .080 copper wire to be removed.

    27 10-pin cross-arms to be removed

    1 guy and log anchor to be set in sand.

    5 15-pr can terminals to be placed

    5 terminal poles to be wired (say 8 bridle wires to be run on each pole).

Estimated Material.

1 ⅝-in x 8-ft guy rod ⎫

40 ft. ⅜-in strand ⎪

2 guy lugs ⎬ For Guy and Anchor.

6 pole strand protector strips. ⎪

1 thimble. ⎪

2 3-bolt guy clamps. ⎭

5 15-pr. can terminals complete

280 ft. No. 18 twisted pair bridle wire for wiring poles (7 ft. is usually considered the average length required for each connection)

    Cleats and staples.

Estimated Material to Be Removed.

27 10-pin cross-arms complete.

24,000 ft. .080 copper wire

Estimated Original Labor.

27 10-pin cross-arms.

24,000 ft 080 copper wire

Continuing the estimate to the part of the plan showing the cable work and assuming, as above, the distance from the lateral pole just west of Hohman street to the pole just west of Morton place to be 1,000 ft , the estimate would be ·

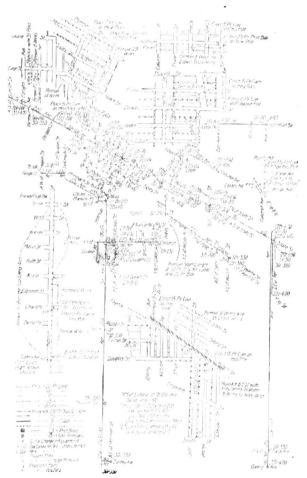

Fig. 87.—Typical Plan of Telephone Work.

Estimated Labor.

1,050 ft 25-pr., 22-ga. cable including strand, to be erected.

   1 straight splice (not tagged), 1—15-pr leg into 1— 25-pr. cable with 10-pr, dead (on the pole just west of Morton place).

   4 straight-bridge splices (tagged), each 1—15-pr. leg into 2—25-pr. cables

   1 straight splice (tagged), 1—25-pr. cable into 1—50-pr cable (on the lateral pole)

   1 change of count (tagged), 1—25-pr leg into 1— 50-pr. cable (on the lateral pole).

Estimated Material.

1,050 ft 25-pr. 22-ga. cable (50 ft. is allowed for splices and sag.)

1,150 ft ⅜-in messenger strand (125 ft. allowed for the span between the pole on which the cable ends and the anchored pole and 25 ft is allowed for wrapping)

   2 3-bolt guy clamps (for dead ending messenger).

   9 ⅜-in messenger supports

  800 marlin cable hangers.

5 1½ x 16-inch lead sleeves	
2 2 x 8-inch lead sleeves	
20 lbs solder	
10 lbs paraffine	} For Splices
4 boxes paper sleeves	
30 pasters.	
10 rolls muslin	
2 gals gasoline	

The style of anchors, wire, messenger and other materials, while not shown on the plans, is familiar to the estimator through his knowledge of general specifications for city, farm and toll line construction

The estimator has lists showing materials required for a log anchor, a thousand feet of cable, a splice of each kind, etc , so that in making up an estimate these quantities need only be multiplied by the total number of anchors, feet of cable, splices, and so on.

It is not always possible to tell what splices will be tagged or not tagged, but an estimator familiar with splicing can judge very closely.

"Estimated Material to be Removed" and "Estimated Original Labor" are separated when estimating and entered on a form like that shown (Form 48), and figured on the basis of present material prices and labor costs. The object of separating these items from, the balance of the estimate is in order to fill in the "Total approximate value plant displaced," shown on Form 52.

The present labor cost of removing materials is included in the estimated cost of new construction on forms like Forms 47 to 51, inclusive

Where more than one form is used the estimated cost of labor for all work may be shown on one form only.

When lists on the style of the above have been made, showing the estimated labor and material required, it is a simple matter to transfer the items to the forms and figure the cost of material from a price list and the cost of labor from the cost records.

Form 53, while not a part of estimating, is shown for the purpose of explaining the method of keeping account of the expenses of the construction cost department. One of these forms is kept for each cost man employed.

FORM 47.

.. . . **190..**

Estimate for City and Farm Line Construction at . . . .

Items · Cost

    Feet   Top Poles
    Feet   Top Poles
    Feet .   Top Poles .
    Feet   Top Poles
    Feet   Top Poles
    Feet   Top Poles
10 Pin Cross-Arms Complete
10 Pin Alley Cross-Arms Complete
10 Pin Alley Cross-Arms Complete
10 Pin Terminal Cross-Arms Complete
6 Pin Cross-Arms Complete ..
23-inch Braces
28-inch Braces
$\frac{5}{8}$x4 inches Car Bolts
$\frac{5}{8}$x . inches Mach Bolts
$\frac{5}{8}$x. inches Mach Bolts
$\frac{5}{8}$x , inches Mach Bolts
No. 2 Side Braces .
No 3 Side Braces
No 4 Side Braces . ..
Pair Trans Glass.
Pony Glass
Miles 080 Copper Wire, Bare
Miles No 12 Steel Wire, Bare
Miles 080 Copper Wire, Insulated
Miles No 12 Steel Wire, Insulated
080 Joints
080 Half Joints ,
No 12 Joints .
Lbs 080 Tie Wire
Lbs No 12 Tie Wire
No 18 Twisted Pair Bridle Wire
Test Clamps No 8
Feet No 4 Steel Wire
Feet $\frac{5}{8}$ Pr Strand
Feet $\frac{1}{2}$ Pr Strand
No 3 Miller Anchors
5-inch Stombaugh Anchors .
6-inch Stombaugh Anchors
$\frac{5}{8}$-inch x 8-foot Guy Rods
Anchor Lugs ..
Pole Strand Protector Strips
Pole Steps
3 Bolt Guy Clamps ....
Thimbles .
4-inch Lag Screws .
Lbs Shingle Nails . .
Line Fuses .
Misc Material .

      Total Material .

Labor, including Board and Teaming
Carfare
Freight
General Supervision
Labor Removing Old Material .

      Grand Total

. . , Estimator

FORM 48.

190 ..

Estimated Material to be Removed at

.

Items

		Estimated Original Cost.
Pr	Gauge Cable	
Pr	Gauge Cable	
Pr	Gauge Cable	
Pr	Gauge Cable	
Pr	Gauge Cable	
Pr	Gauge Cable	
Strand		
6 Pin Cross-Arms Complete		
10 Pin Cross-Arms Complete		
Feet	Top Poles	
Feet	Top Poles	
Feet	Top Poles	
Feet	Top Poles	
Miles	Wire . .	
Miles	Wire . .	
Misc Material		

Total Material   .   .   .   . .

Estimated Original Labor.

LINE GANG
Labor, Board and Teaming
Carfare   .   .
Freight
General Supervision   .   .   .
SPLICERS
Labor, Board and Teaming
Carfare   .
Freight
General Supervision

Grand Total   .

.... Estimator.

FORM 49.

.. . . 190 ..

Estimate for Toll Line Construction . .. .

. . . .

Items	Cost
. Feet .... Top Poles . .	
, .. Feet Top Poles	
.. Feet . Top Poles	
. .. Feet Top Poles .	
. .. Feet . . Top Poles	
. . . Feet Top Poles	
. . 10 Pin Cross-Arms Complete	
. . 1¼x7¾ Pins	
23-inch Braces ,	
. 28-inch Braces	
. ⅝x4 inches Car Bolts	
... ⅝x ... inches Mach Bolts	
⅝x . inches Mach Bolts	
⅝x inches Mach Bolts	
4-inch Lag Screws	
. Lbs Shingle Nails	
Miles 104 Copper Wire	
.. Miles 080 Copper Wire	
Miles No 12 Steel Wire	
104 Joints	
. 104 Half Joints	
. 080 Joints	
080 Half Joints	
.... No 12 Joints	
.. Lbs 104 Tie Wire	
Lbs 080 Tie Wire	
... Lbs No 12 Tie Wire	
... A T & T Glass	
Trans Glass Pieces	
.. 1¼x9 Trans Pieces	
. 3 Bolt Guy Clamps	
.... ⅝x8 Guy Rods	
Anchor Lugs	
Pole Strand Protector Strips	
Pole Steps	
No 5 Wix Test Connectors	
No 6 Wix Test Connectors	
Misc Material	

Total Material

Labor, Board and Teaming
Carfare
Freight
General Supervision
Labor Removing Old Material

Grand Total

... . Estimator

FORM 50.

. . .   .190 ..

Estimate for Cable at.. ....

. .. .

Items.				Cost
.. Feet ... Pr. .... Gauge Cable			.	
.. Feet . Pr .... Gauge Catle.				
Feet Pr .... Gauge Cable				
. Feet Pr .. Gauge Cable			.	
Feet Pr Gauge Cable			.	. .
. ... Feet Pr Gauge Cable			.	
.. Pr. . Gauge Marlin Hangers				
. Pr Gauge Marlin Hangers			.	.	
.... Pr Gauge Marlin Hangers	. . ..
Feet ⅝ Pr Strand . .				
Feet ½ Pr Strand . . .			.	.
A T & T Guy Clamps			.. .	. ..
A T. & T. Mess Supports.			..	.
⅝x8 Guy Rods				
25 Pr Unprotected Boxes				.
25 Pr Protected Boxes .			.	..
. . Pr Boxes				
. . Feet No 18 Twisted Pair Bridle Wire				
. . 080 Joints				
Thimbles .				
. Feet Leather Cleating .				
. ⅝x . Mach Bolts .				
. ⅝x . Mach. Bolts.. . . ,				
. ⅝x Mach Bolts .				
. T No 2 Cable Arms				
. . 1¼x9 Trans. Pins				
. 23″ Braces . . .				.
.. 28″ Braces .				
½x4″ Lag Screws				
. ⅝x Car Bolts .				
. ⅝x Car Bolts .				.
Pair Trans Glass . .				.
Saddle Balconies				
No 2 Side Braces .				
No 3 Side Braces				
No 4 Side Braces				.
. Feet No 6 Copper Ground Wire				
Ground Rods				
Pencil Fuses .. .				
Line Fuses ..				
Lbs Marlin				.
Test Clamps No 8				
Feet No 4 Steel Wire				.
Lbs Soapstone				.
Vault Cable Supports				
Pot Head Saddles				
20 Pr Blocks . .				
. . Pot Head Discs .				.
Balls Lacing Wire				
Anchor Lugs .				
Pole Strand Protector Strips				.
. 3 Bolt Guy Clamps				...
. 4½″x . Lead Sleeves . .	.. ..	.
. 4″ x Lead Sleeves	... . ..	..	.
3½″x Lead Sleeves	.. . ..	
. .. 3″ x. Lead Sleeves	. . .. .	
. . . 2½″x Lead Sleeves	. .. . ..	
.. . 2″ x . Lead Sleeves .	. ... .	
. 1½″x . Lead Sleeves	.	
,..... 1″ x.... Lead Sleeves,,,,,,,,,,,,,,,, , , .. ,......... , ... ,.,		

Lbs ½x½ Solder
Lbs Triangular Solder
Lbs Par Wax
Lbs Beeswax
Rolls Muslin
Boxes Tubes
Candles
Pasters
Rolls Tape
Misc Material

Total Material

LINE GANG
Labor, Board and Teaming
Carfare
Freight
General Supervision
Labor Removing Old Material

SPLICERS
Labor, Board and Teaming
Carfare
Freight
General Supervision

Grand Total

Estimator

190

FORM 51

Estimate for Conduit at

Items   Cost

Duct Feet 2 Duct Conduit
Duct Feet 3 Duct Conduit
Duct Feet 4 Duct Conduit
Duct Feet 6 Duct Conduit
5/16-inch Dowel Pins
3-inch Sewer Til
4-inch Sewer Tile
6-inch Sewer Tile
3-inch St Louis Curves
4-inch St Louis Curves
3-inch Tile Curves
Yards Burlap 6 inches Wide
Line Feet 2x8 Creosoted Plank
Line Feet 2x10 Creosoted Plank
Line Feet 2x12 Creosoted Plank
Feet Common Lumber
Bbls Cement
Yards No   Stone
Yards No   Stone
Yards No   Stone
Sewer brick
Yards Sand
6-inch Sewer Grates
"P" Traps
Vault Frames and Covers
Vault Small Frames and Covers
3 inch Iron Pipe in 3-feet Lengths
3 inch Iron Pipe in 12-feet Lengths
2½ inch Iron Pipe in 12-feet Lengths
2¼ inch Iron Pipe in 12-feet Lengths
2 inch Iron Pipe in 12-feet Lengths
1½ inch Iron Pipe in 12-feet Lengths
1¼ inch Iron Pipe in 12-feet Lengths
   to   Reducers
   to   Reducers
   to   Reducers
   to   Reducers
Pipe Hooks
Conduit Plugs
Ft Creosote Pump Log
Misc Material

Total Material
Labor, Board and Teaming
Carfare
Freight
General Supervision
Repairing
Labor Removing Old Material

Grand Total

Estimator

Form 52

Estimate No . . . . .

... . TELEPHONE COMPANY

Estimate for . . . . . Work

. . 190

... .

General Manager

Dear S.r I request that authority be given for the . construction

work within described at an expenditure not to exceed $

Yours respectfully

Estimate Approved

. .

Engineer Superintendent

190

To the Executive Committee

Gentlemen I recommend that the sum of $ be appropriated for

.

Yours respectfully,

Approved

President General Manager

190

General Manager

Dear S r At a meeting of the Board of Directors, held this day, it was voted that

your above recommendation No be approved and the . ... and

expense amounting to $ be authorized

Yours respectfully,

.. ..

Secretary

Form 52 Continued

Estimate No

     ....   **TELEPHONE COMPANY**
           Superintendent   190 .

Dear Sir   *The following estimate covers the proposed work of

..

Por recapitulation see page No 4   Respectfully submitted for consideration
                 ..   Superintendent of Construction

| PLANT DISPLACEMENT | | | | MATERIAL | PLANT RENEWED OR ADDED | | | | Cost in Excess of Estimate | Cost Below Estimate |
| Quantity | | Value† | | | Quantity | | Cost | | | |
Preparation of Estimate	Completion of Work	Preparation of Estimate	Completion of Work	Description	Estimated	Actual	Estimated	Actual		
.	.		.	Ft Poles	.					
				Ft ''						
		.	..	Ft '' .						
				Ft ''						
		.	.	Pin Arms Complete						
.				Pin '' ''						
				Pin . '' .						
				Mi No Copper Wire .						
..				Mi No ...	..					
			.	Mi No Steel Wire						
				Mi No						
				Mscellaneous Material						
				Ft Pr Ga Aerial Cable						
		.		Ft Pr Ga ''						
.				Ft Pr Ga ' ..						
			.	Pr Cable Boxes						
				Pr '' .				.		
			.	Miscellaneous Material .						
				Ft Conduit		.	.			
				Ft Lateral		.	...			
				Vault Covers and Frames						
		..		Mscellaneous Material					.	
				Ft Pr Ga U G Cable			.			
				Ft Pr ''			.			
				Ft Pr '' .	.					
			.	Ft Pr ''						
			.	Pr Cable Boxes						
				Pr ''					.	
....				Miscellaneous Material						
.	.	.	.	Labor, Board and Teaming						
.		:		Car Fare						
			...	Freight						
	.	.		Paving			.			
	.			Right of Way	.					
	.		..	General Supervision .						
.				Total approximate value plant displaced‡						
				Credit actually received for 'old'' material						
				Total estimated cost proposed work						
..	.		.	Total actual cost						

*In case of reconstruction, give present condition of line, including material to be taken down—also other information pertaining to the subject

†Transfer to be made to Maintenance Account
   From Aerial of   .. $ (Divided, Material, $ ..   Labor, $ ... . .)
   Cable (U G) of $.   .   {   ''   '' $ '' $ ... . . }
   Conduit (U G) of $.   ''   '' $

‡Estimated original cost

NOTE   This estimate should be accompanied by a diagram or map indicating the location and nature of the work to be done

Form 52 Continued

Superintendent

The work described in the foregoing estimate was completed on   190 ,
material was used and expense incurred as shown in itemized statement on opposite page
For recapitulation of measurements, etc , see page 4

190   .. ...   .

                                                          Supt of Construction.

General Manager

The above report on work finished by the Construction Department is respectfully
submitted

190

                                                          Superintendent

Auditor

Noted and respectfully forwarded for your attention and files.

190

                                                          General Manager,

I certify that the record of   construction herein contained has been entered upon
the books and maps of this office The work has been done properly, and the character and
quantity of material used in completion of work is as stated

190

                                                          Engineer

I certify that there has been reported to me on this ESTIMATE, as per Pay-Rolls and

Vouchers on file, an EXPENDITURE of   . . $

And a CREDIT of $. ,
which has been distributed as follows   .

ACCOUNTS	DR	ACCOUNTS		CR
$			$	. .
$			$.	......
$			$	.....
$			$	. .

Plant displaced by this work has been covered by the following entry

ACCOUNTS	DR	ACCOUNTS		CR.
$	.		$	. ..
$			$	.
$			$	.... .
$			$	.

REMARKS   ...

..   . .

....   190   .   . .. .
                                                          Auditor

Form 52 Continued

Estimate No

RECAPITULATION OF MEASUREMENTS, ETC
POLE LINE

	Construction		Reconstruction	
	Estimated	Actual	Estimated	Actual
No Miles				
Average size of poles				
Av No pin arms per hole				
Miles No wire				
Miles No wire				
Miles No wire				
Miles No wire				
Cost	Estimated, $		Actual, $	

AERIAL CABLE

	No Feet	No of Conductors	Size of Conductors (B & S Ga)
Estimated			
Actually erected		.	
Estimated			. .
Actually erected			
Estimated			
Actually erected			.
Estimated			
Actually erected	.		
Cost	Estimated $	Actual $	

CONDUIT

	Estimated	Actually Installed
Style of conduit	.	
No of feet of trench		
No of duct feet	.	
No of Manholes		.
Cost	Estimated $	Actual, $

UNDERGROUND CABLE

	No of Feet	No of Conductors	Size of Conductors (B & S Ga)
Estimated	...		
Actually pulled in			
Estimated	.		
Actually pulled in			
Estimated			. .
Actually pulled in			....
Estimated			
Actually pulled in		....	
Estimated			
Actually pulled in.			
Estimated			
Actually pulled in		..	
Estimated			
Actually pulled in		.	
Estimated			
Actually pulled in			
Cost	Estimated $	Actual, $	

Form 53

CONSTRUCTION COST DEPARTMENT

For month of

Expense Report of

Date	Commutation Rides between Main Office and	Rate per Ride	Amount	Cash Car Fare	Board				Day Rate	Livery	Incidentals	Total (not including Salary)	Salary	Total Expense
					B	D	S	L						
1														
2														
3														
4														
5														
6														
7														
8														
9														
10														
11														
12														
13														
14														
15														
16														
17														
18														
19														
20														
21														
22														
23														
24														
25														
26														
27														
28														
29														
30														
31														
Totals														

APPENDIX A.

COST OF MATERIALS AND LABOR IN CONSTRUCTING TELEPHONE LINE.

By J. C. Slippy.

The following data on the cost of the different classes of telephone construction work have been compiled from the actual records of a large company, covering a period of five years. While the figures may seem unreasonably high when compared with figures usually presented, it should be remembered that they include all the expenses in connection with the construction work, so that the average costs given should hold for the entire plant construction. The percentages given as cost of freight, supervision, teaming, travel and board have in all cases been derived from the actual expenditures for these items.

MESSENGER AND CABLE CONSTRUCTION.

The average wages paid for messenger strand work, aerial and underground cable work, and terminal and cable-box work were as follows

Foreman, strand and cable work, per 9 hrs . . .$3 00
Linemen, strand and cable work, per 9 hrs... .. .. 2 70
Groundmèn, strand and cable work, per 9 hrs.... ... . 1.75
Teams, strand and cable work, per 9 hrs.... ... . 3.50
Cable splicers, cable splicing, per 8 hrs 3.75
Cable helpers, cable splicing, per 8 hrs 2 50

Messenger Construction.—The examples of messenger construction given below each represent 1,000 ft of 16,500-lb. strand in place, including cost of suspending cable but not the cost of cable

190

Example I.—For 400-pair, 22-gage and 200-pair, 19-pair cable

Materials

1,100 ft. messenger strand @ $.0229		$ 25.19
10 messenger clamps @ $.0578		.578
10 14 in crossarm bolts @ $.0456		.456
20 square washers @ $ 0086		172
8 3-bolt clamps @ $ 107		856
850 19 in marlin clips @ $7 93 per M		6.740
5% freight, incidentals, etc		1 70

Labor:

1,100 ft messenger placed @ $ 005		$ 5 50
10 messenger clamps placed @ $ 07		70
850 19 in marlin clips placed @ $ 0075		6 375
1,000 ft. cable hung @ $ 015		15 00
1 bond placed @ $1 25		1 25
Testing		2 09
Splicing		3 36
Supervision, 10%, teaming, 12%, travel and board, 12% = 42%		14 395
Cost of 1,000 feet		84 362
General expense 10%		8 436

Total cost of 1,000. feet		92 798
Cost of one mile		489 98
Cost of one foot		0 0928

Example II—For 200-pair, 22-gage, and 100 and 150-pair, 19-gage cable

Materials·

1,100 ft messenger strand @ $ 0229		$ 25.190
10 messenger clamps @ $ 0578		.578
10 14 in crossarm bolts @ $0 456		456
20 square washers @ $ 0086		172
8 3-bolt guy clamps @ $ 107		856
850 16 in marlin clips @ $7 14 per M		6 069
5% freight, incidentals, etc		1.666

Labor

1,100 ft messenger placed @ $ 005		5.50
10 messenger clamps placed @ $ 07		70
850 16 in marlin clips placed @ $.0075		6 375
1,000 ft cable hung @ $ 015		15 00
1 bond placed @ $1 25		1 25
Testing		2 09
Splicing		3 36
Supervision, 10%, teaming, 12%, travel and board, 20% = 42%		14 395
Cost of 1,000 feet		83 657
General expense 10%		8 366

Total cost of 1,000 feet		$ 92 023
Total cost of one mile		485 76
Total cost of one foot		0 09201

Example III.—For 100-pair, 22-pair, and 50 and 25-pair, 19-gage cable

Material

1,100 ft messenger strand @ $0 0229		$ 25 190
10 14 in crossarm bolts @ $0 0456		456
10 messenger clamps @ $0 0578		578
20 square washers @ $0 0086		172
8 3-bolt guy clamps @ $0 107		856
550 14 in. marlin clips @ $6 67 per M		3 668
5% freight, incidentals, etc		1.546

Labor

1,100 ft. messenger placed @ $0 005		5 50
10 messenger clamps placed @ $0 07		70
550 14 in marlin hangers placed @ $0 0075		4.125
1,000 ft cable hung @ $0 015		15 00
1 bond placed @ $1 25		1 25
Testing		1 39
Splicing		2 29
Supervision, 10%, teaming, 12% travel and board, 20% = 42%		12 707
Cost of 1,000 feet		75 428
General expense 10%		7.543

Total cost of 1,000 feet		$ 82 971
Total cost of one mile		438 082
Total cost of one foot		0 08297

Example IV —For 25 and 50-pair, 22-gage cable
  Materials
1,100 ft messenger strand @ $0 0229 .. ..$ 25 190
   10 messenger clamps @ $0 0578 578
   10 14 in crossarm bolts @ $0 0456 456
   20 square washers @ $0 0086 172
    8 3-bolt guy clamps @ $0 107 856
  550 11 in. marlin clips @ $5 93 per M 3 261
     5% freight, incidentals, etc 1 526
  Labor
1,100 ft messenger strand placed @ $0 005 .. $ 5 50
   10 messenger clamps placed @ $0 07 . 70
  550 11 in marlin clips placed @ $0 0075 4 125
2,000 ft cable hung @ $0 015 . 15 00
    1 bond placed @ $1 25 1 25
     Testing 1 06
     Splicing 1 48
     Supervision, 10%, teaming, 12%, travel and board, 20% = 42% 12 228
     Cost of 1,000 feet 73 382
     General expense 10% . 7 338
                                                                   ─────────
     Total cost of 1,000 feet $ 80 720
     Total cost of one mile 426 096
     Total cost of one foot . . 0 08072

Aerial Cable Construction.—The following figures for aerial cable construction give for each size cable the cost of original construction and the junk value of materials, and by subtracting the second from the first the total and yearly depreciation for the assumed period of life. The selling price as junk allowed is $0 056 per pound.

Example I —No 22 B & S gage cable.
  First Cost

Size	Price F O B	Cost Per Ft for Mess Wire and Erec	Total First Cost Per Foot	Per Mile
25-pr	$0 1`34	$0 0807	$0 1941	$1,025 00
50-pr	1722	0807	2529	1,335 00
100-pr	28665	0830	3696	1,951 00
200-pr	5544	0920	6464	3,413 00
300 pr	7413	0928	8341	4 404 00
400-pr	92715	0928	1 0199	5,886 00

  Junk Value

Size	Weight Per Ft Lbs	Junk Value at $0 056 Per Lb	Deduct for Taking Down	Net Junk Value
25-pr	$0 9o	$0 0532	$0 025	$0 0282
50-pr	1 40	0784	025	0534
100-pr	2 20	1232	025	0982
200-pr ...	4 15	2324	025	2074
300-pr . .	5 15	2884	025	2634
400-pr	6 25	3500	025	3250

  Depreciation

	25-pr	50-pr	100-pr	200-pr	300-pr	400-pr
First cost	$0 1941	$0 2529	$0 3696	$0 6464	$0 8341	$1 0199
Net junk value	0282	0534	0982	2074	2634	325
	─────	─────	─────	─────	─────	─────
Depreciation	$0 1659	$0 1995	$0 2714	$0 4390	$0 5707	$0 6949
*Dep per year . .	0138	0166	0226	0365	0475	.0579

*Based upon a life of 12 years

Example II—No 19 B & S gage cable·
  First Cost

Size	Price F O B	Cost Per Ft for Mess Wire and Erec	Total First Cost. Per Foot	Per Mile
25-pr	$0 16645	$0 08297	$0 2394	$1,264 00
50-pr	26775	08297	3507	1,852 00
100-pr	5208	09202	6128	3,236 00
150-pr	672	09202	764	4,034 00
200-pr	83685	0928	9297	4,909 00
300-pr	1 1456	0928	1 2384	6,539 00

  Junk Value

Size	Weight Per Ft Lbs	Junk Value at $0 056 Per Lb	Deduct for Taking Down	Net Junk Value
25-pr	1 30	$0 0728	$0 025	$0 0478
50-pr	2 10	1176	025	0926
100-pr	3 40	1904	025	1654
150-pr	4 30	2408	025	2158
200-pr	5 75	3220	025	2970
300-pr	6 90	3864	025	3614

  Depreciation

	25-pr	50-pr	100-pr	150-pr	200-pr	300-pr
First cost	$0 2394	$0 3507	$0 6128	$0 7640	$0 9297	$1 2384
Net junk value	0478	.0926	1654	.2158	2970	3614
Depreciation	$0 1916	$0 2581	$0 4474	$0 5482	$0 6327	$0 8770
*Dep. per year	.0159	0215	0372	0456	0527	073

  *Based upon a life of 12 years

Example III—No 16 B & S gage cable
  First Cost

Size	Price F O B	Cost Per Ft for Mess Wire and Erec	Total First Cost Per Foot	Per Mile
25-pr	$0 32025	$0 09202	$0 41227	$2,177 00
50-pr	54705	0928	63985	3,378 00

  Junk Value

Size	Weight Per Ft Lbs	Junk Value at $0 056 Per Lb	Deduct for Taking Down	Net Junk Value
25-pr	2 1	$0 1176	$0 025	$0 0926
50-pr	4 1	2296	025	2046

  Depreciation

	25-pr	50-pr
First cost	$0 41227	$0 63985
Net junk value	0926	2046
Depreciation	$0 31967	$0 43525
*Depreciation per year	0266	.03625

  *Based upon a life of 12 years

Example IV.—13/16 B & S gage composite cable:
  First Cost

Size	Price F O B	Cost Per Ft for Mess.Wire and Erec	Total First Cost. Per Foot	Per Mile,
25-pr	$0 312	$0 0920	$0 404	$2,133 00
50-pr.	590	0928	6828	3,605 00

  Junk Value

Size	Per Ft Lbs	Junk Value at $0 056 Per Lb.	Deduct for Taking Down	Net Junk Value
25-pr	3 0	$0 168	$0 025	$0 143
50-pr ..	4 8	2688	025	2438

  Depreciation

	25-pr	50-pr
First cost	$0 404	$0 6828
Net junk value	143	2438
Depreciation	$0 261	$0 4390
*Depreciation per year	0213	0365

  *Based upon a life of 12 years

Underground Cable Construction.—The figures for underground cable construction are similar in character and purpose to those for aerial cable construction.

Example I —No 22 B & S gage cable

First Cost

Size	Price F O B	Cost Per Foot for Installation	Total First Cost. Per Foot	Per Mile
100-pr	$0 28665	$0 0339	$0 3205	$1,693 00
200-pr	5544	0406	5950	3,142 00
300-pr	7413	04839	78969	4,170.00
400-pr	92715	05699	.98414	5,195 00
600-pr	1 244	07103	1 31503	6,943.00

Junk Value

Size	Weight Per Ft Lbs	Junk Value at $0 056 Per Lb	Deduct for Removal	Net Junk Value
100-pr	2 2	$0 1232	$0 03	$0 0932
200-pr	4 1b	2324	03	2024
300-pr	5 15	2884	03	.2584
400-pr	6 25	350	03	3200
600-pr	8 50	4760	03	4460

Depreciation

	100-pr	200-pr	300-pr	400-pr	600-pr
First cost	$0.32055	$0 5950	$0 78969	$0 98414	$1 315
Net junk value	09320	2024	25840	32000	446
Depreciation	$0 22735	$0 3926	$0 53129	$0 66414	$0 869
*Depreciation per year	01136	0196	02656	0332	04345

*Based upon a life of 20 years

Example II —Underground Cable, No. 19 B & S gage cable

First Cost

Size	Price F O B	Cost Per Foot for Installation	Total First Cost Per Foot	Per Mile
100-pr	$0 5208	$0 03408	$0 55488	$2,930 00
150-pr	672	03642	70842	3,740 00
200-pr	83685	04147	87832	4,638 00
300-pr	1 1455	04986	1 19536	6,312 00

Junk Value

Size	Weight Per Ft Lbs	Junk Value at $0 056 Per Lb	Deduct for Removal	Net Junk Value
100-pr	3 4	$0 1904	$0 03	$0 1604
150-pr	4 2	2408	03	2108
200-pr	5 75	3220	03	2920
300-pr	6 9	3864	03	3564

Depreciation

	100-pr.	150-pr	200-pr	300-pr
First cost	$0 55484	$0 70842	$0 87832	$1 19536
Net junk value	1604	2108	2920	35640
Depreciation	$0 39444	$0 49762	$0 5893	$0 83896
*Depreciation per year	.01972	02438	029816	041946

*Based upon a life of 20 years

Example III.—No 16 B & S. gage cable

First Cost:

Size	Price F O B	Cost Per Foot for Installation	Total First Cost Per Foot	Per Mile
25-pr	$0 32025	$0 033	$0 35325	$1,865 00
50-pr	54705	03408	58113	3,068 00
100-pr	8358	04147	87727	4,632 00
150-pr	1 14765	04896	1.19661	6,318 00

Junk Value

Size	Weight Per Ft Lbs	Junk Value at $0 056 Per Lb	Deduct for Removal	Net Junk Value
25-pr	2 1	$0 1176	$0 03	$0 076
50-pr	4 1	2296	03	.1996
100-pr	6 1	3416	03	3116
150-pr	7 6	4256	.03	3956

Depreciation

	25-pr	50-pr	100-pr	150-pr
First cost	$0 35325	$0 58113	$0 87727	$1.19661
Net junk value	0876	1996	3116	3956
Depreciation	$0 26565	$0 38153	$0 56567	$0 801
*Depreciation per year	01328	019076	02828	.04005

*Based upon a life of 20 years.

Example IV —Composite 13/16 B & S gage cable
First Cost

Size	Price F O B	Cost Per Foot for Installation	Total First Cost Per Foot	Per Mile
25-pr	$0 312	$0 03642	$0 34842	$1,840 00
50-pr	590	04147	63147	3,334 00
125-pr.	1 162	04986	1 21186	6,399 00

Junk Value

Size	Weight Per Ft Lbs	Junk Value at $0 056 Per Lb	Deduct for Removal	Net Junk Value
25-pr	3 0	$0 168	$0 03	$0 138
50-pr	4 8	2688	03	2388
125-pr	7 6	4256	03	3956

Depreciation

	25-pr	50-pr	125-pr
First cost	$0 34842	$0 63147	$1 21186
Net junk value	138	2388	3956
Depreciation	$0 2104	$0 39267	$0 81626
*Depreciation per year.	01052	01963	040813

*Based upon a life of 20 years

Cable Splicing Underground.

—The following eleven examples of the cost of underground cable splicing comprise both ordinary and high capacity cables and give costs of both labor and materials.

Example I.—25 pair, 22 gage cable
Materials

1½ lbs wiping metal @ $ 21	$ 315
¼ lb paraffine @ $ 0636	032
50 paper sleeves @ $ 02 per pr	01
1 1½x16 in lead sleeve	22
10% freight, incidentals, etc	058
	$ 635

Labor

Splicing	$ 1 05
Testing	70
10% supervision, etc	175
	$ 1 925
Cost of splice	$ 2 560
General expense, 10%	256
Total cost of splice	$ 2 816
Average cost per foot of cable, based upon splice every 325 ft	$ 00866
Average cost per pair	$ 1126

Example II.—50 pair, 22 gage cable
Materials

2 lbs wiping metal @ $ 21	$ 42
¾ lbs paraffine @ $ 0636	048
100 paper sleeves @ $ 02 per 100	02
1 2x16 in lead sleeve	352
10% freight, incidentals, etc	084
	$ 924

Labor

Splicing	$ 1 48
Testing	1 06
10% Supervision, etc	254
	$ 2 794
Cost of splice	$ 3 718
General expense, 10%	372
Total cost of splice	$ 4 09
Average cost per foot of cable, based upon splice every 325 ft	$ 01258
Average cost per pair	$ 0819

Example III—100 pair, 22-gage cable

Materials

3 lbs wiping metal @ $ 21	$	63
1 lb paraffine @ $ 0636		064
200 paper sleeves @ $ 02 per 100		04
1 2½x16 in lead sleeve		432
10% freight, incidentals etc		116
	$ 1 2826	

Labor

Splicing	$ 2 29	
Testing	1 39	
10% supervision, etc	363	
	$ 4 048	
Cost of splice	5 331	
General expense, 10%	533	
Total cost of splice	**$ 5 864**	
Average cost per foot of cable, based upon splice every 325 ft	$	018
Average cost per pair	$	0586

Example IV.—200-pair 22-gage cable

Materials

1½ lbs wiping metal @ $ 21	$	735
1½ lbs paraffine @ $ 0636		0954
400 paper sleeves @ $ 02 per 100		08
1 3x18 in lead sleeve		465
10% freight, incidentals, etc		1375
	$ 1 5129	

Labor

Splicing	$ 3 36	
Testing	2 09	
10% supervision, etc	55	
	$ 6 00	
Cost of splice	**$ 7 513**	
General expense, 10%	751	
Total cost of splice	**$ 8 264**	
Average cost per foot of cable, based upon splice every 325 ft	$	0254
Average cost per pair	$	04132

Example V—300-pair, 22-gage cable

Materials

1½ lbs wiping metal @ $ 21	$	735
1½ lbs paraffine @ $ 0636		0954
600 paper sleeves @ $ 02 per 100		12
1 3½x22 in lead sleeve		72
10% freight, incidentals etc		167
	$ 1 837	

Labor

Splicing	$ 4 70	
Testing	2 75	
10% supervision	75	
	$ 8 20	
Cost of splice	**$10 04**	
General expense, 10%	1 00	
Total cost of splice	**$11 04**	
Average cost per foot of cable, based upon splice every 325 ft	$	0339b
Average cost per pair	$	0368

Example VI —400-pair, 22-gage
Materials

4 lbs wiping metal @ $ 21	$	84
2 lbs paraffine @ $ 0636		127
300 paper sleeves @ $ 02 per 100		16
1 4x22 in lead sleeve	1 02	
10% freight, incidentals, etc		215
	$ 2 363	

Labor

Splicing	$ 6 05	
Testing	3 47	
10% supervision, etc		952
	$10 472	
Cost of splice	$12 834	
General expense, 10%	1 283	
	$14 117	
Total cost of splice		
Average cost per foot of cable based upon splice every 325 ft	$	04343
Average cost per pair	$	03529

Example VII —600-pair, 22-gage cable
Materials

4½ lbs wiping metal @ $ 21	$	945
2½ lbs paraffine @ $ 0636		159
1,200 paper sleeves @ $ 02 per 100		24
1 4½x22 in lead sleeve	1 125	
10% freight, incidentals, etc		2469
	$ 2 716	

Labor.

Splicing	$ 8.50	
Testing	4 85	
10% supervision, etc	1 34	
	$14 69	
Cost of splice	$17 406	
General expense, 10%	1 741	
	$19 147	
Total cost of splice		
Average cost per foot of cable, based upon splice every 325 ft	$	0589
Average cost per pair	$	0319

Example VIII —100-pair, 19-gage, High Capacity cable
Materials

3 lbs wiping metal @ $ 21	$	63
1 lb paraffine @ $ 0636		064
200 paper sleeves @ $ 02 per 100		04
1 3x16 in lead sleeve	485	
10% freight incidentals, etc		1219
	$ 1 341	

Labor

Splicing	$ 2 29	
Testing	1 39	
10% supervision etc	368	
	$ 4 048	
Cost of splice	$ 5 389	
General expense, 10%	539	
	$ 5 928	
Total cost of splice		
Average cost per foot of cable, based upon splice every 325 ft	$	01824
Average cost per pair	$	05928

Example IX.—150-pair, 19-gage, High Capacity cable

Materials

3 lbs wiping metal @ $ 21	$	63
1 lb paraffine @ $ 0636		064
300 paper sleeves @ $ 02 per 100		06
1 3x16 in. lead sleeve		485
10% freight, incidentals, etc		124
	$ 1 363

Labor.

Splicing	$	2 75
Testing		1 60
10% supervision, etc		44
	$ 4 79
Cost of splice	.$ 6 15
General expense, 10%		615
	$ 6 763
Total cost of splice	$ 6 763
Average cost per foot of cable, based upon splice of every 325 ft	$	0208
Average cost per pair	$	0451

Example X—200-pair, 19-gage, High Capacity cable

Materials

3½ lbs wiping metal @ $ 21	$	735
1½ lbs paraffine @ $ 0636		0954
400 paper sleeves @ $ 02 per 100		08
1 3½x18 in lead sleeve		72
10% freight, incidentals, etc		163
	$ 1 793

Labor

Splicing	$	3 36
Testing		2 09
10% supervision, etc		55
	$ 6 00
Cost of splice	$ 7 793
General expense, 10%		779
	$ 8 572
Total cost of splice	$ 8 572
Average cost per foot of cable, based upon splice of every 325 ft	$	02637
Average cost per pair	$	04286

Example XI—300-pair, 19 gage, High Capacity cable

Materials

4 lbs wiping metal @ $ 21	$	84
2 lbs paraffine @ $ 0636		127
1 4x22 in lead sleeve	1	02
600 paper sleeves @ $ 02 per 100		12
10% freight, incidentals, etc		211
	$ 2 318

Labor

Splicing	$	4 70
Testing		2 75
10% supervision, etc		75
	$ 8 20
Cost of splice	$10 518
General expense, 10%		1 052
	$11 57
Total cost of splice	$11 57
Average cost per foot of cable, based upon splice of every 325 ft	$	0356
Average cost per pair	$	0385

Terminals.—Four examples of cost oɪ terminals, including both materials and labor, are given·

Example I —Cost of 10-pair Terminal in Place
Materials

1 14 A. terminal with 7 ft D C cable	$ 3 03
2 lbs. wiping metal @ $ 21	42
¾ lbs paraffine @ $ 0636	0477
1 2x20 in lead sleeve	3525
10% freight, incidentals, etc	385

Labor

1 14 A terminal placed	$ 50
1 10-pair tap from 50-pair cable	2 16
1 10-pair tap tested	36
10% supervision, etc	302

Total	$ 7 557
General expense, 10%	756
Total cost	$ 8 313
Average cost per pair	$ 8313

Example II —Cost of 11-pair Terminal in Place
Materials

1 14-B Terminal with 7 ft D C cable	$ 3 12
2 lbs wiping metal @ $ 21	42
¾ lbs paraffine @ $ 0636	0477
1 2x20 in lead sleeve	3ᵗ2ᵗ
10% freight, incidentals, etc .	394

Labor·

1 14-B Terminal, placed	$ 50
1 11-pair tap from 50-pair cable	2 16
1 11-pair tap tested	36
10% supervision, etc	302

Total	$ 7 656
General expense 10%	766
Total cost	$ 8 422
Average cost per pair	$ 765

Example III —Cost of 16-pair Terminal in Place
Materials·

1 14-C Terminal with 7 ft D C Cable	$ 3 788
2 lbs wiping metal @ $ 21	42
¾ lbs paraffine @ $ 0636	0477
1 2x20 in lead sleeve	3525
10% freight, incidentals, etc	4608

Labor

1 14-C Terminal placed	$ 60
1 15-pair tap from 50-pair cable	2 23
1 15-pair tested	50
10% supervision, etc	335

Total	$ 8 754
General expense, 10%	$ 87ɔ
Total cost	$ 9 62ɔ
Average cost per pair	$ 642

Example IV —Cost of 26-pair Terminal in Place
Materials

1 14-D Terminal with 7 ft D C cable	$ 5 526
2 lbs. wiping metal @ $ 21	42
¾ lbs paraffine @ $ 0636	0477
1 2¼x20 in lead sleeve	4325
10% freight, incidentals, etc	6426

Labor

1 14-D Terminal placed	$ 75
1 25-pair tap from 50-pair cable	3 62
1 25-pair tap tested	70
10% supervision, etc	497

Total	$12 536
General expense, 10%	1 254
Total cost	$13 79
Average cost peɪ pair	$ 552

Cable Boxes.—Five examples of cost of cable boxes are given including both materials and labor costs

Example I.—Cost of 25-pair Cable Box in Place
Materials

1	25-pair cable box unequipped	$ 4 175
2	10-pair 7-A fuse plates, plain @ $2 33	4 66
1	5-pair 7-A fuse plate, plain @ $1 061	1 061
50	7-A fuses @ $6 30 per 100	3 15
2	lbs insulating compound @ $ 075	15
150	ft No 20 pothead wire @ $ 01198	1 797
1½	lbs wiping metal @ $ 21	315
1	2x20 in lead sleeve	3525
1	pole seat	2 00
2	½x4½ in lag screws @ $ 0093	0186
	10% freight, incidentals, etc	1 763

Labor

1	25-pair cable box, placed	$ 1 00
50	wires soldered on terminals @ $ 01	50
50	wires numbered on terminals @ $ 03	1 50
1	25-pair pothead made	3 20
1	25-pair cable tested	70
1	pole seat placed	75
	10% supervision, etc	765

Total	$27 86
General expense, 10%	$ 2 76
Total cost	$30 62
Average cost per pair	$ 1 224
For copper back No 7-A fuse plate with lightning arrestors add	$ 4 037

Example II.—Cost of 50-pair Cable Box in Place
Materials

1	50-pair cable box unequipped	$ 5 04
4	10-pair 7-A fuse plates, plain, @ $2 33	9 32
2	5-pair 7-A fuse plates, plain, @ $1 061	2 122
100	7-A fuses, @ $6 30 per 100	6 30
3	lbs insulating compound, @ $ 075	225
300	ft No 20 pothead wire, @ $ 01198	3 594
2	lbs wiping metal, @ $ 21	42
1	2½x20 in lead sleeve	4325
1	pole seat	2 00
2	½x4½ in lag screws, @ $ 0093	0186
	10% freight, incidentals, etc	2 947

Labor

1	50-pair cable box placed	$ 1 00
100	wires soldered on terminals @ $ 01	1 00
100	wires numbered on terminals @ $ 03	3 00
1	50-pair pothead made	4 87
1	50-pair cable tested	1 06
1	pole seat placed	75
	10% supervision, etc.	1 166

Total	$45 245
General expense, 10%	4 524
Total cost	$49 769
Average cost per pair	$ 995
For copper back No 7-A fuse plate with lightning arrestors, add	$ 7 41

Example III—Cost of 100-pair Cable Box in Place

Materials

1 100-pair cable box, unequipped		$ 5 98
8 10-pair 7-A fuse plates, plain, @$2 33		18 64
4 5-pair 7-A fuse plates, plain, @ $1 061		4 244
200 7-A fuses, @ $6 30 per 100		12 60
4 lbs insulating compound @ $ 075		30
600 ft No 20 pothead wire, @ $ 01198		7 188
3 lbs wiping metal, @ $ 21		63
1 3½x24 in lead sleeve	.	72
1 pole seat		2 00
2 ¼x4½ in lag screws, @ $ 0093		0186
10% freight, incidentals, etc	. .	5 23

Labor·

1 100-pair cable box placed		$ 1 50
200 wires soldered on terminals @ $ 01		2 00
200 wires numbered on terminals @ $ 03		6 00
1 100-pair pothead made	.	8 00
1 100-pair cable tested	. .	1 39
1 pole seat placed	.	73
10% supervision, etc		1 964

Total .. .		$79 154
General expense, 10% . .		7 915

Total cost .		$87 069
Average cost per pair		$ 8707
For copper back No 7-A fuse plates with lightning arrestors add		$16 50

Example IV—Cost of 150-pair Cable Box in Place

Materials

1 150-pair cable box unequipped		$ 7 22
15 10-pair 7-A fuse plates, plain, @ $2 33		34 95
300 7-A fuses @ $6 30 per 100		18 90
5 lbs insulating compound @ $ 075		375
900 ft of No 20 potnead wire @ $ 01198		10 782
4 lbs wiping metal @ $ 21		84
1 4x21 in lead sleeve		1 02
1 pole seat		2 00
2 ½x4½ in lag screws @ $ 0093		0186
10% freight, incidentals, etc		7 61

Labor

1 150-pair cable box placed		$ 1 50
300 wires soldered on terminals @ $ 01		3 00
300 wires numbered on terminals @ $ 03	.	9 00
1 150-pair pothead made		9 00
1 150-pair cable tested		1 60
1 pole seat placed	. .	75
10% supervision, etc .. .		2 485

Total		$111 05
General expense, 10%		11 10

Total cost		$122 15
Average cost per pair		$ 814
For copper back No 7-A fuse plates with lightning arrestors, add	. . $ 23 51

Example V —Cost of 200-pair Cable Box in Place
Materials

1 200-pair cable box unequipped		$ 10 665
20 10-pair 7-A fuse plates, plain, @$2 33		46 60
400 7-A fuses @ $6 30 per 100		25 20
6 lbs insulating compound @ $ 075		45
1,200 ft No 20 pothead wire @ $ 01198		14 376
1 4x24 in lead sleeve		1 02
5 lbs wiping metal @ $ 21		1 05
1 pole seat		2 00
2 ¼x4½ in lag screws @ $ 0093		0186
10% freight, incidentals, etc		10 1388
Labor		
1 200-pair cable box placed		$ 1 75
1 pole seat placed		.75
400 wires soldered to terminals @ $ 01		4.00
400 wires numbered to terminals @ $ 03		12 00
1 200-pair pothead made		10 25
1 200-pair cable tested		2 09
10% supervision, etc		3 084
Total		**$145 441**
General expense, 10%		14 54
Total cost		$159 98
Average cost per pair		$ 7999
For copper back, No 7-A fuse plates with lightning arrestors, add		$ 31 35

Pole Line Construction.

The organization of the gang and the wages paid per pole line construction were as follows:

Item.	Per 9-hr. day
1 foreman, at $3.	$ 3.00
3 linemen, at $2 75	8 25
2 groundmen, at $1.75	3.50
1 team, at $3.50	3 50
Total	$18.25

In the costs following the items of "hauling" and "teaming" will be noted. The hauling of poles covers the expense of removing them from freight station to pole yard, and the item of teaming covers the expense of transporting them from the yard to the work. The item of 7½ per cent for travel, board and incidentals covers the expense of the entire force while employed in travel from one exchange to another. Men were not allowed expenses when located in town.

The divisions of pole line construction are pole erection and wire stringing. Pole erection is subdivided into Exchange Poles, Toll Line Poles, Farmer Line Poles, Guy Poles, Anchors, Cross Arms, etc

Exchange Poles, Class A.—Class A pole line is designed to carry an ultimate load of 6 cables and 60 toll and trunk wires on cross arms Spans in straight sections are approximately 100 ft in length

Example I.—Cost of One Mile 45-ft Chestnut Pole Line

Materials.		Per Pole	Per Mile
52 45-ft. 7½ in. top poles, including freight	.	$ 7 58	$394 16
1,040 iron steps @ $ 02367	.	473	24 62
260 wood steps @ $ 009081	.	045	2 36
Carbolineum Avenarius	.	06	3 12
Spikes, 5-20, 5-60	.	035	1 82
Paint, 1 qt for 10 ft . @ $ 17	.	68	35 36
200 ft 6-M guy wire @ $ 0086	.		1.72
8 guy clamps @ $ 0958	.		77
4 anchor logs @ $1 50	.		6 00
4 anchor rods @ $ 225	.		90
10% freight, incidentals, etc	.	887	47 08

Labor			
Unloading	.	$ 40	$20 80
Shaving	.	65	33 80
Cutting one gain	.	10	5 20
Cutting roof	.	10	5 20
Boring holes on ground	.	02	1 04
Driving iron steps @ $ 0125	.	25	13 00
Placing wood steps @ $ 015	.	075	3 90
Placing carbolineum	.	27	14 04
Digging holes	.	60	31 20
Raising poles	.	1 10	57,20
Tamping	.	32	16 64
Banking poles	.	05	2 60
Hauling poles	.	40	20 80
Painting poles @ $ 0125 per foot	.	50	26 00
4 anchor holes dug, earth, @ $3 00	.		12 00
4 anchor holes tamped, earth, @ $1 50	.		6 00
4 guys placed @ $1 00	.		4 00
Supervision, 7½%	} = 30%	1 451	82 03
Teaming, 15%			
Travel and board, 7½%			

Total	.	$16 046	$873 36
General expense, 10%	.	1 605	87 34
Grand total ..		$17 651	$960 70

Example II—Cost of One Mile, 40-ft Chestnut Pole Line

Materials		Per Pole	Per Mile
52 40-ft 7½ in top poles, including freight	.	$ 6 58	$342 16
832 iron steps @ $ 02367		379	19 69
260 wood steps @ $ 009081		045	2 36
Carbolineum Avenarius		060	3 12
Spikes, 5-20, 5-60	.	035	1 82
Paint, 1 qt for 10 ft . @ $ 17		595	30 94
200 ft 6-M guy wire @ $ 0086			1 72
8 guy clamps @ $ 0958			77
4 anchor logs @ $1 50			6 00
4 anchor rods @ $ 225			90
10% freight, incidentals, etc		769	40 95

Labor			
Unloading	.	$ 35	18 20
Shaving		55	28 60
Cutting one gain		10	5 20
Cutting roof	. .	10	5 20
Boring holes on ground	.	02	1 04
Driving iron steps @ $ 0125 . .		20	10 40
Placing wood steps @ $ 015		075	3 90
Placing carbolineum	. . . .	27	·14 04
Digging holes	.	60	31 20
Raising poles	.	63	32 76
Tamping		22	11 44
Banking poles		05	2 60
Hauling poles	.	30	15 60
Painting poles @ $ 0125 per ft		438	22 75
4 anchor holes dug, earth, @ $3 00	.		12 00
4 anchor holes tamped, earth, @ $1 50			6 00
4 guys placed @ $1 00			4 00
Supervision, 7½% ..	} = 30%	1 171	67 48
Teaming, 15%			
Travel, board and incidentals, 7½%			

Total	.	$ 13 54	$742 84
General expense, 10%		1 35	74 28
Grand total	.	.$ 14 89	$817 12

Example III —Cost of One Mile, 35-ft Chestnut Pole Line

Materials

		Per Pole	Per Mile
52	35 ft 7½ in top poles, including freight	$ 5 07	$283 64
676	iron steps @ $ 02367	308	16 00
260	wood steps @ $ 009081	045	2 36
	Carbolineum Avenarius	060	3 12
	Spikes, 5-20, 5-60	035	1 82
	Paint, 1 qt for 10 ft . @ $ 17	51	26 52
200	ft 6-M guy wire @ $ 0086		1 72
8	guy clamps @ $ 0958	.	77
4	anchor logs @ $1 50		6 00
4	anchor rods @ $ 225		90
	10% freight, incidentals, etc	603	32 29

Labor

		Per Pole	Per Mile
	Unloading	$ 30	$ 15 60
	Shaving	50	26 00
	Cutting one gain	10	5 20
	Cutting roof	10	5 20
	Boring holes on ground	02	1 04
	Driving iron steps @ $ 0125	163	8 45
	Placing wood steps @ $ 015	075	3 90
	Placing carbolineum	27	14 04
	Digging holes	60	31 20
	Raising poles	47	24 44
	Tamping	18	9 36
	Banking poles	05	2 60
	Hauling poles	25	13 00
	Painting poles @ $ 0125 per ft	375	19 50
4	anchor holes dug earth @ $3 00		12 00
4	anchor holes tamped, earth, @ $1 50		6 00
4	guys placed @ $1 00	.	4 00
	Supervision 7½%		
	Teaming 15% } = 30%	1 04	60 46
	Travel, board and incidentals, 7½%		
	Total	$ 11 12	$617 13
	General expense, 10%	1 11	61 71
	Grand total	$ 12 23	$678 84

Example IV.—Cost of One Mile 30-ft Chestnut Pole Line

Materials

		Per Pole	Per Mile
52	30-ft 7½ in top poles, including freight	$ 3 65	$189 80
468	iron steps @ $ 02367	213	11 08
260	wood steps @ $ 009081	045	2 36
	Carbolineum Avenarius	060	3 12
	Spikes, 5-20, 5-60	035	1 82
	Paint, 1 qt for 10 ft @ $ 17	425	22 10
200	ft 6-M guy wire @ $ 0086		1 72
8	guy clamps @ $ 0958		77
4	anchor logs @ $1 50		6 00
4	anchor rods @ $ 225		90
	10% freight, incidentals, etc	443	23 97

Labor

		Per Pole	Per Mile
	Unloading	25	13 00
	Shaving	35	18 20
	Cutting one gain	10	5 20
	Cutting roof	10	5 20
	Boring holes on ground	02	1 04
	Driving iron steps @ $ 0125	113	5 85
	Placing wood steps @ $ 015	075	3 90
	Placing carbolineum	27	14 04
	Digging holes	60	31 20
	Raising poles	35	18 20
	Tamping	15	7 80
	Banking poles	05	2 60
	Hauling poles	20	10 40
	Painting poles @ $ 0125 per ft	313	16 25
4	anchor holes dug, earth @ $3 00		12 00
4	anchor holes tamped, earth @ $1 50		6 00
4	guys placed @ $1 00		4 00
	Supervision, 7½%		
	Teaming 15% } = 30%	882	52 46
	Travel, board and incidentals, 7½%		
	Total	$ 8 694	$490 98
	General expense, 10%	869	49 10
	Grand total	$ 9 563	$540 08

Exchange Poles, Class B.—Class B pole line is designed to carry an ultimate load of 4 cables and 40 bare toll and trunk wires on cross arms, or an ultimate of 6 cables, if no bare wire is employed. Spans in straight sections are approximately 110 ft in length. Four examples of cost are given, one each for 25-ft., 30-ft., 35-ft. and 40-ft. poles. It will be noted that the costs are for chestnut poles, painted and "preserved" by Carbolineum Avenarius, and include all materials for poles in place ready for wire stringing. Traveling expenses, board of men and incidental expenses are also included

Example I—Cost of One Mile, 40-ft Chestnut Pole Line

	Per Pole	Per Mile
Materials		
48 40-ft 7 in top poles, including freight	$ 6 58	$315 84
768 iron steps @ $ 02367	379	18 18
240 wood steps @ $ 009081	045	2 16
Carbolineum Avenarius	057	2 74
Spikes, 5-20, 5-60	035	1 83
Paint, 1 qt for 10 feet @ $ 17	595	28 56
200 ft 6-M guy wire @ $ 0086		1 72
8 guy clamps @ $ 0958		77
4 anchor rods @ $ 225		90
4 anchor logs @ $1 50		6 00
10% freight, incidentals, etc	769	37 86
Labor		
Unloading	35	16 80
Shaving	55	26 40
Cutting one gain	10	4 80
Cutting roofs	10	4 80
Boring holes on ground	02	96
Driving iron steps @ $ 0125	20	9 60
Placing wood steps @ $ 015	075	3 60
Placing carbolineum	27	12 96
Digging holes	60	28 80
Raising poles	63	30 24
Tamping	22	10 56
Banking poles	05	2 40
Hauling poles	30	14 40
Painting poles @ $ 0125 per ft	438	21 00
4 anchor holes dug, earth @ $3 00		12 00
4 anchor holes tamped, earth, @ $1 50		6 00
4 guys placed @ $1 00		4 00
Supervision, 7½%.		
Teaming, 15% = 30%	1 171	62 80
Travel, board and incidentals, 7½%		
Total	$ 13 54	$688 53
General expense, 10%	1 35	68 85
Grand total	$ 14 89	$757 38

Example II.—Cost of One Mile, 35-ft Chestnut Pole Line

Materials	Per Pole	Per Mile
48 35-ft 7 in top poles including freight	$ 5 07	$243 36
624 iron steps @ $ 02367	308	14 77
240 wood steps @ $ 009081	045	2 16
Carbolineum Avenarius	057	2 74
Spikes, 5-20, 5-60	035	1 68
Paint, 1 qt for 10-ft @ $ 17	51	24 48
200 ft 6-M guy wire @ $ 0086		1 72
4 guy clamps @ $ 0958		77
4 anchor logs @ $1 50		6 00
4 anchor rods @ $ 225		90
10% freight, incidentals, etc	603	29 86

Labor	Per Pole	Per Mile
Unloading	30	14 40
Shaving	50	24 00
Cutting one gain	10	4 80
Cutting roof	10	4 80
Boring holes on ground	02	96
Driving iron steps @ $ 0125	163	7 80
Placing wood steps @ $ 015	075	3 60
Placing carbolineum	27	12 96
Digging holes	60	28 80
Raising poles	47	22 56
Tamping	18	8 64
Banking	05	2 40
Hauling poles	25	12 00
Painting poles @ $ 0125 per foot	375	18 00
4 anchor holes dug, earth @ $3 00		12 00
4 anchor holes tamped, earth @ $1 50		6 00
4 guys placed @ $1 00		4 00
Supervision, 7½%		
Teaming, 15% } = 30%	1 04	56 32
Travel, board and incidentals, 7½%		
Total	$ 11 12	$572 48
General expense, 10%	1 11	57 25
Grand total	$ 12 23	$629 73

Example III.—Cost of One Mile, 30-ft Chestnut Pole Line

Materials	Per Pole	Per Mile
48 30-ft 7 in poles, including freight	$ 3 65	$175 20
432 iron steps @ $ 02367	213	10 22
240 wood steps @ $ 009081	045	2 16
Carbolineum Avenarius	.057	2 74
Spikes, 5-20, 5-60	035	1 68
Paint, 1 qt for 10 ft @ $ 17	425	20 40
200 ft 6-M guy wire @ $ 0086		1 72
8 guy clamps @ $ 0958		77
4 anchor logs @ $1 50		6 00
4 anchor rods @ $ 225		90
10% freight, incidentals, etc	443	22 18

Labor	Per Pole	Per Mile
Unloading	25	12 00
Shaving	35	16 80
Cutting one gain	10	4 80
Cutting roof	.10	4 80
Boring holes on ground	02	96
Driving iron steps @ $ 0125	113	5 40
Placing wood steps @ $ 015	075	3 60
Placing carbolineum	27	12 96
Digging holes	60	28 80
Raising poles	35	16 80
Tamping	15	7 20
Banking	05	2 40
Hauling poles	20	9 60
Painting poles @ $ 0125	313	15 00
4 anchor holes dug earth @ $3 00		12 00
4 anchor holes tamped, earth @ $1 50		6 00
4 guys placed @ $1 00		4.00
Supervision, 7½%		
Teaming, 15% } = 30%	882	48 94
Travel, board and incidentals, 7½%		
Total	$ 8 691	$456 03
General expense 10%	869	45 60
Grand total	$ 9 560	$501 63

Example IV.—Cost of One Mile 25-ft Chestnut Pole Line
Materials

	Per Pole	Per Mile
48 25-ft 7 in top poles, including freight	$ 2 53	$121 44
288 iron steps @ $ 02367	142	6 82
240 wood steps @ $ 009081	045	2 16
Carbolineum Avenarius	057	2 74
Spikes, 5-20, 5-60	035	1 68
Paint, 1 qt for 10 ft @ $ 17	34	16 32
200 ft 6-M guy wire @ $ 0086		1 72
8 guy clamps @ $ 009081		77
4 anchor logs @ $ 75		3 00
4 anchor rods @ $ 225		90
10% freight, incidentals, etc	315	15 00
Labor		
Unloading	20	9 60
Shaving	30	14 40
Cutting one gain	10	4 80
Cutting roof	10	4 80
Boring holes on ground	02	96
Driving iron pole steps @ $ 0125	075	3 60
Placing wood steps @ $ 015	075	3 60
Placing carbolineum	27	12 96
Digging holes	60	28 80
Raising poles	28	13 44
Tamping	15	7 20
Banking poles	05	2 40
Hauling poles	20	9 60
Painting poles @ $ 0125 per ft	25	12 00
4 anchor holes dug, earth @ $1 50		6.00
4 anchor holes tamped, earth, @ $1 00		4 00
4 guys placed @ $1 00		4 00
Supervision, 7½%		
Teaming, 15% = 30%	801	42 65
Travel, board and incidentals, 7½%		
Total	$ 6 935	$358 12
General expense, 10%	694	35 81
Grand total	$ 7 639	$393 93

Exchange Poles, Class C.—Class C pole line is designed to carry an ultimate load of 2 cables, with no bare wires on the poles; or an ultimate of 20 bare wires on cross arms, and no cables on the poles; or an ultimate of 10 pairs of outside distributing wire, with no bare wires or cables. Spans in straight sections are approximately 120 ft. in length. Five examples of cost are given, one each for 25-ft., 30-ft., 35-ft., 40-ft., and 45-ft. poles, painted, "preserved" and erected with all equipment ready for stringing wire. The costs also include all incidental items such as traveling expenses, board of workmen, freight and haulage expenses, etc.

Example I—Cost of One Mile, 45-ft Chestnut Pole Line

Materials.

	Per Pole	Per Mile.
44 45-ft 6 in top poles, including freight	$ 7 08	$311 52
880 iron steps @ $ 02367	473	20 83
220 wood steps @ $ 009081	045	2 00
Carbolineum Avenarius	06	2 64
Spikes, 5-20, 5-60	035	1 54
Paint, 1 qt for 10 ft @ $ 17	68	29 92
200 ft 6-M guy wire @ $ 0086		1 72
8 guy clamps @ $ 0958		77
4 anchor logs @ $ 75		3 00
4 anchor rods @ $ 225		90
10% freight, incidentals, etc	837	37 48

Labor

Unloading		40	17 60
Shaving		65	28 60
Cutting one gain		10	4 40
Cutting roof		10	4 40
Boring holes on ground		02	88
Driving iron steps @ $ 0125		25	11 00
Placing wood steps @ $ 015		075	3 30
Placing carbolineum		27	11 88
Digging holes		60	26 40
Raising poles		1 10	48 40
Tamping		32	14 08
Banking poles		05	2 20
Hauling poles		40	17 60
Painting poles @ $ 0125 per ft		50	22 00
4 anchor holes dug, earth, @ $1 50			6 00
4 anchor holes tamped, earth, @ $1 00			4 00
4 guys placed @ $1 00			4 00
Supervision, 7½%	} = 30%		
Teaming, 15%		1 451	68 02
Travel, board and incidentals, 7½%			
Total		$ 15 50	$707 08
General expense, 10%		1 55	70 71
Grand total		$ 17 05	$777 79

Example II—Cost of One Mile 40-ft Chestnut Pole Line

Materials

	Per Pole	Per Mile
44 40-ft 6 in poles, including freight	$ 5 93	$260 92
704 iron steps @ $ 02367	379	16 16
220 wood steps @ $ 009081	045	2 00
Carbolineum Avenarius	057	2 51
Spikes, 5-20, 5-60	035	1 54
Paint, 1 qt for 10-ft @ $ 17	595	26 18
200 ft 6-M guy wire @ $ 0086		1 72
8 guy clamps @ $ 0958		77
4 anchor logs @ $ 75		3 00
4 anchor rods @ $ 225		90
10% freight, incidentals, etc	704	31 57

Labor

Unloading		35	15 40
Shaving		55	24 20
Cutting roof		10	4 40
Cutting one gain		10	4 40
Boring holes on ground		02	88
Driving iron steps @ $ 0125		20	8 80
Placing wood steps @ $ 015		075	3 30
Placing carbolineum		27	11 88
Digging holes		60	26 40
Raising poles		63	27 72
Tamping		22	9 68
Banking poles		05	2 20
Hauling poles		30	13 20
Painting poles @ $ 0125 per ft		438	19 25
4 anchor holes dug, earth, @ $1 50			6 00
4 anchor holes tamped, earth, @ $1 00			4 00
4 guys placed @ $1 00			4 00
Supervision, 7½%	} = 30%		
Teaming, 15%		1 17	55 71
Travel, board and incidentals, 7½%			
Total		$ 12 82	$588 69
General expense, 10%		1 28	58 87
Grand total		$ 14 10	$647 56

Example III.—Cost of One Mile, 35-ft Chestnut Pole Line
Materials

	Per Pole	Per Mile
44 35 ft 6 in top poles, including freight	$ 4 32	$190 08
572 iron steps @ $ 02367	308	13 54
220 wood steps @ $ 009081	045	2 00
Carbolineum Avenarius	057	2 51
Spikes, 5-20, 5-60	035	1 54
Paint, 1 qt for 10 ft @ $ 17	51	22 44
200 ft 6-M guy wire @ $ 0086		1 72
8 guy clamps @ $ 0958		77
4 anchor logs @ $ 75		3 00
4 anchor rods @ $ 225		90
10% freight incidentals, etc	528	23 92

Labor.

Unloading ..				30	13 20
Shaving ..				50	22 00
Cutting one gain .				10	4 40
Cutting roof				10	4 40
Boring holes on ground				02	88
Driving iron steps @ $ 0125				162	7 15
Placing wood steps @ $ 015				075	3 30
Placing carbolineum				27	11 88
Digging holes ..				60	26 40
Raising poles .				47	20 68
Tamping . .				18	7 92
Banking poles ..				05	2 20
Hauling poles				25	11 00
Painting poles @ $ 0125 per ft				375	16 50
4 anchor holes dug, earth, @ $1 50					6 00
4 anchor holes tamped, earth, @ $1 00					4 00
4 guys placed @ $1 00					4 00
Supervision, 7½%	{				
Teaming 15%	=	30%	1 036		49 77
Travel board and incidentals 7½%	{				
Total				$ 10 29	$478 92
General expense 10%				1 03	47 89
Grand total .				$ 11 32	$526 81

Example IV —Cost of One Mile 30-ft Chestnut Pole Line
Materials.

	Per Pole	Per Mile
44 30-ft 6 in top poles including freight	$ 3 15	$138 60
396 iron steps @ $ 02367	213	9 37
220 wood steps @ $ 009081	045	2 00
Carbolineum Avenarius	057	2 51
Spikes, 5-20, 5-60	035	1 54
Paint, 1 qt for 10 ft @ $ 17	425	18 70
200 ft 6-M guy wire @ $ 0086		1 72
8 guy clamps @ $ 0958		77
4 anchor logs @ $ 75		3 00
4 anchor rods @ $ 225 .		90
10% freight, incidentals, etc	393	17 91

Labor·

Unloading				25	11 00
Shaving				35	15 40
Cutting one gain				10	4 40
Cutting roof . .				10	4 40
Boring holes on ground.				02	88
Driving iron steps @ $ 0125				113	4 95
Placing wood steps @ $ 015				075	3 30
Placing carbolineum . . .				27	11 88
Digging holes ...				60	26 40
Raising poles				35	15 40
Tamping .				15	6 60
Banking poles				05	2 20
Painting poles @ $ 0125 per ft				313	13 75
Hauling poles				20	8 80
4 anchor holes dug earth @ $1 50					6 00
4 anchor holes tamped, earth @ $1 00					4 00
4 guys placed @ $1 00					4 00
Supervision 7½%	{				
Teaming, 15%	=	30%	882		43 01
Travel, board and incidentals, 7½%	{				
Total				$ 8 14	$383 39
General expense, 10%				81	38 34
Grand total				$ 8 95	$421 73

Example V.—Cost of One Mile, 25 ft Chestnut Pole Line
Materials

		Per Pole	Per Mile.
44	25-ft 6 in top poles, including freight	$ 2 03	$ 89 32
264	iron steps @ $ 02367	.142	6 25
220	wood steps @ $ 009081	.045	2 00
	Carbolineum Avenarius	.057	2.51
	Spikes, 5-20, 5-60	035	1 54
	Paint, 1 qt for 10 feet @ $ 17	34	14 96
200	feet 6-M guy wire @ $ 0086	...	1 72
8	guy clamps @ $ 0958	..	77
4	anchor logs @ $ 75	....	3 00
4	anchor rods @ $ 225		.90
	10% freight, incidentals, etc	265	12 30
	Labor.		
	Unloading	20	8 80
	Shaving	30	13 20
	Cutting one gain. ..	10	4 40
	Cutting roof .	10	4 40
	Boring holes on ground	02	88
	Driving iron steps @ $ 0125	075	3 30
	Placing wood steps @ $ 015 .	075	3 30
	Placing carbolineum	27	11 88
	Digging holes	60	26 40
	Raising poles	28	12 32
	Banking poles	05	2 20
	Tamping	15	6 60
	Hauling poles .	.20	8 80
	Painting poles @ $ 0125 per ft	.25	11 00
4	anchor holes dug, earth @ $1 50	...	6 00
4	anchor holes tamped, earth, @ $1 00	....	4 00
4	guys placed @ $1 00	...	4 00
	Supervision, 7½%		
	Teaming, 15% = 30%	.801	39 44
	Travel, board and incidentals, 7½%		
	Total	$ 6 385	$306 19
	General expense 10%	639	30 62
	Grand total	$ 7 024	$336 81

Toll Line Poles, Class D.—Class D pole line is designed to
carry 30 or more bare wires on cross arms   Spans on straight
sections are approximately 130 ft. in length

Example 1—Cost of One Mile, 40 ft Chestnut Pole Line
Materials

		Per Pole	Per Mile.
40	40-ft 7-in top poles including freight	$ 6 58	$263 20
	Carbolineum Avenarius	057	2 28
200	ft 6-M guy wire @ $ 0086		1 72
8	guy clamps @ $ 0958		77
4	anchor logs @ $ 75 .		3 00
4	anchor rods @ $ 225		90
	10% freight, incidentals, etc	664	27.19
	Labor.		
	Unloading	.35	14 00
	Shaving . . .	.55	22 00
	Cutting one gain .	.10	4 00
	Cutting roof . . .	.10	4 00
	Boring holes on ground	02	.80
	Placing carbolineum	.27	10 80
	Digging holes . .	.60	24 00
	Raising poles	.63	25 20
	Tamping	22	8 80
	Banking poles . .	.05	2 00
	Hauling poles	.30	12 00
4	anchor holes dug, earth, @ $1 50	...	6 00
4	anchor holes tamped, earth @ $1 00	..	4 00
4	guys placed @ $1 00	...	4 00
	Supervision, 7½%		
	Teaming, 15% = 30%	957	42 48
	Travel, board and incidentals, 7½%		
	Total	$ 11 448	$483 14
	General expense, 10%	1 145	48 31
	Grand total	$ 12 59	$531 45

Example II.—Cost of One Mile, 35-ft Chestnut Pole Line

Materials

	Per Pole	Per Mile
40 35-ft 7-in top poles, including freight	$ 5 07	$202 80
Carbolineum Avenarius	057	2 28
200 ft 6-M guy wire @ $ 0086		1 72
8 guy clamps @ $ 0958		77
4 anchor logs @ $ 75		3 00
4 anchor rods @ $ 225		90
10% freight, incidentals, etc	513	21 15

Labor.

			Per Pole	Per Mile
Unloading			30	12 00
Shaving			50	20 00
Cutting one gain			10	4 00
Cutting roof			10	4 00
Boring holes on ground			02	80
Placing carbolineum			27	10 80
Digging holes			60	24 00
Raising poles			47	18 80
Tamping ..			18	7 20
Banking poles			05	2 00
Hauling poles			25	10 00
4 anchor holes dug, earth, @ $1 50				6 00
4 anchor holes tamped, earth, @ $1 00 .				4 00
4 guys placed @ $1 00 .				4 00
Supervision, 7½%	} = 30%	852		38 28
Teaming, 15%				
Travel, board and incidentals, 7½%				
Total			$ 9 332	$398 50
General expense			933	39 85
Grand total			$ 10 27	$438 35

Example III.—Cost of One Mile, 30-ft Chestnut Pole Line

Materials

	Per Pole	Per Mile
40 30-ft 7-in top poles including freight	$ 3 65	$146 00
Carbolineum Avenarius	057	2 28
200 ft 6-M guy wire @ $ 0086 .		1 72
8 guy clamps @ $ 0958		77
4 anchor logs @ $ 75		3 00
4 anchor rods @ $ 225		90
10% freight, incidentals, etc .	371	15 47

Labor

			Per Pole	Per Mile
Unloading			25	10 00
Shaving			35	14 00
Cutting one gain			10	4 00
Cutting roof			10	4 00
Boring holes on ground			02	80
Placing carbolineum			27	10 80
Digging holes			60	24 00
Raising poles			35	14 00
Tamping			15	6 00
Banking poles			05	2 00
Hauling poles			20	8 00
4 anchor holes dug, earth, @ $1 50				6 00
4 anchor holes tamped, earth, @ $1 00				4 00
4 guys placed @ $1 00				4 00
Supervision, 7½%	} = 30%	732		33 43
Teaming 15%				
Travel, board and incidentals, 7½%				
Total			$ 7 25	$315 22
General expense, 10%			73	31 52
Grand total . .			$ 7 98	$346 74

Toll Line Poles, Class E.—Class E pole line is designed to carry an ultimate load of 20 bare wires on cross arms Spans on straight sections are approximately 130 ft in length.

Example I —Cost of One Mile, 45-ft Chestnut Pole Line

Materials

		Per Pole	Per Mile
40	45-ft 6-in top poles, including freight	$ 7 08	$283 20
	Carbolineum Avenarius	06	2 40
200 ft	6-M guy wire @ $ 0086		1 72
8	guy clamps @ $ 0958	.	77
4	anchor logs @ $ 75	.	3 00
4	anchor rods @ $ 225		90
	10% freight, incidentals, etc	714	29 20

Labor

Unloading .		40	16 00
Shaving		65	26 00
Cutting one gain		10	4 00
Cutting roof		10	4 00
Boring holes on ground		02	80
Placing carbolineum		27	10 80
Digging holes		60	24 00
Raising poles		1 10	44 00
Tamping		32	12 80
Banking poles		05	2 00
Hauling poles		40	16 00
4 anchor holes dug, earth. @ $1 50			6 00
4 anchor holes tamped, earth, @ $1 00			4 00
4 guys placed @ $1 00			4 00
Supervision 7½%			
Teaming, 15%	= 30%	1 203	52 32
Travel, board and incidentals, 7½%			

Total		$ 13 067	$547 91
General expense, 10%		1 307	54 79
Grand total		$ 14 37	$602 70

Example II —Cost of One Mile, 40-ft Chestnut Pole Line

Materials

		Per Pole	Per Mile
40	40-ft 6-in top poles, including freight	$ 5 93	$237 20
	Carbolineum Avenarius	057	2 28
200 ft	6-M guy wire @ $ 0086		1 72
8	guy clamps @ $ 0958		77
4	anchor logs @ $ 75		3 00
4	anchor rods @ $ 225		90
	10% freight, incidentals, etc	599	24 59

Labor

Unloading		35	14 00
Shaving		55	22 00
Cutting one gain		10	4 00
Cutting roof		10	4 00
Boring holes on ground		02	80
Placing carbolineum		27	10 80
Digging holes		60	24 00
Raising poles		63	25 20
Tamping		22	8 80
Banking poles		05	2 00
Hauling poles		30	12 00
4 anchor holes dug, earth @ $1 50			6 00
4 anchor holes tamped, earth, @ $1 00			4 00
4 guys placed @ $1 00			4 00
Supervision 7½%			
Teaming 15%	= 40%	957	42 48
Travel, board and incidentals 7½%			

Total		$ 10 733	$454 54
General expense, 10%		1 073	45 45
Grand total		$ 11 81	$499 99

Example III.—Cost of One Mile, 35-ft Chestnut Pole Line
Materials:

	Per Pole	Per Mile
40 35-ft 6-in top poles, including freight	$ 4 32	$172 80
Carbolineum Avenarius	057	2 28
200 ft 6-M guy wire @ $ 0086		1 72
8 guy clamps @ $ 0958		77
4 anchor logs @ $ 75		3 00
4 anchor rods @ $ 225		90
10% freight, incidentals, etc	438	18 15

Labor

	Per Pole	Per Mile
Unloading	30	12 00
Shaving	50	20 00
Cutting one gain	10	4 00
Cutting roof	10	4 00
Boring holes on ground	02	80
Placing carbolineum	27	10 80
Digging holes	60	24 00
Raising poles	47	18 80
Tamping	18	7 20
Banking poles	05	2 00
Hauling poles	25	10 00
4 anchor holes dug, earth, @ $1 50	.	6 00
4 anchor holes tamped, earth, @ $1 00		4 00
4 guys placed @ $1 00		4 00
Supervision, 7½%		
Teaming, 15% } = 30%	852	38 28
Travel, board and incidentals, 7½%		

	Per Pole	Per Mile
Cost	$ 8 507	$365 50
General expense, 10%	851	36 55
Total cost	$ 9 36	$402 05

Example IV—Cost of One Mile, 20-ft Chestnut Pole Line
Materials

	Per Pole	Per Mile
40 20-ft 6-in top poles, including freight	$ 3 15	$126 00
Carbolineum Avenarius	057	2 28
200 ft 6-M guy wire @ $ 0086		1 72
8 guy clamps @ $ 0958		77
4 anchor logs @ $ 75	.	3 00
4 anchor rods @ $ 225		90
10% freight, incidentals etc	321	13 47

Labor

	Per Pole	Per Mile
Unloading	25	10 00
Shaving	35	14 00
Cutting one gain	10	4 00
Cutting roof	10	4 00
Boring holes on ground	02	80
Placing carbolineum	27	10 80
Digging holes	60	24 00
Raising poles	35	14 00
Tamping	15	6 00
Banking poles	05	2 00
Hauling poles	20	8 00
4 anchor holes dug, earth, @ $1 50		6 00
4 anchor holes tamped, earth, @ $1 00		4 00
4 guys placed @ $1 00		4 00
Supervision, 7½%		
Teaming 15% } = 30%	732	33 48
Travel, board and incidentals, 7½%		

	Per Pole	Per Mile
Cost	$ 6 70	$293 22
General expense, 10%	67	29 32
Total cost	$ 7 37	$322 54

Example V —Cost of One Mile, 25-ft Chestnut Pole Line

Materials

	Per Pole	Per Mile
40 25-ft 6-in top poles, including freight	$ 2 03	$ 81 20
Carbolineum Avenarius	057	2 23
200 ft. 4-M guy wire @ $ 0086		1 72
8 guy clamps @ $ 0958		77
4 anchor rods @ $ 225		90
4 anchor logs @ $ 75		3 00
10% freight, incidentals, etc	209	8 99

Labor.

			Per Pole	Per Mile
Unloading			20	8 00
Shaving			30	12 00
Cutting one gain			10	4 00
Cutting roof			10	4 00
Boring holes on ground			02	80
Placing carbolineum			27	10 80
Digging holes			60	24 00
Raising poles			28	11 20
Tamping			15	6 00
Banking poles			05	2 00
Hauling poles			20	8 00
4 anchor holes dug, earth @ $1 50				6 00
4 anchor holes tamped, earth, @ $1 00				4 00
4 guys placed @ $1 00				4 00
Supervision, 7½%	}	= 30%	681	31 44
Teaming, 15%				
Travel, board and incidentals, 7½%				

	Per Pole	Per Mile
Total	$ 5 247	$235 10
General expense, 10%	525	23 51
Grand total	$ 5 77	$258 61

Farmer Line Poles.

—This line is designed to carry either 4 bare wires on brackets, or an ultimate of 10 wires on a cross arm. Spans on straight sections are approximately 160 ft. in length.

POLES.

Example I —Cost of One Mile Farmer's Line with Four Brackets

Materials

	Per Pole	Per Mile
33 25-ft 5-in top poles, including freight	$ 1 20	$ 39 60
4 oak brackets @ $ 0163	042	2 40
Spikes, 4-40, 4-60	028	92
200 ft No 6 steel wire for guys		56
4 5-ft 1X guy stubs @ $ 60		2 40
8 ½x4-in lag screws @ $ 0078		06
10% freight, incidentals, etc	127	4 59

Labor

			Per Pole	Per Mile
Digging holes, 4 ft ...			60	19 80
Raising poles			28	9 24
Tamping			15	4 95
Banking			05	1 65
Hauling and unloading			20	6 60
4 brackets placed @ $ 01			04	1 32
4 guy holes dug, earth, @ $ 40 (4 ft)				1 60
4 guy holes tamped, earth, 4-ft @ $ 15				60
4 guys placed @ $1 00				4 00
Supervision, 7½%	}	= 30%	396	14 94
Teaming, 15%				
Travel, board and incidentals, 7½%				

	Per Pole	Per Mile
Total	$ 3 113	$115 23
General expense 10%	311	11 52
Grand total	$ 3 42	$126 75

Example II.—Cost of One Mile Farmer's Line With One Cross
Arm

Materials

	Per Pole	Per Mile
33 25-ft 5-in top poles, including freight	$ 1 20	$ 39 60
200 ft No 8 guy wire		56
4 ft 1-x guy stubs @ $ 60		2 40
8 ½x4-in lag screws @ $ 0078		06
10% freight, incidentals, etc	12	4 26

Labor

			Per Pole	Per Mile
Digging holes, earth, 4-ft			60	19 80
Raising poles			28	9 24
Tamping			15	4 95
Banking			05	1 65
Hauling and unloading			20	6 60
4 guy holes dug earth, 4-ft @ $ 40				1 60
4 guy holes tamped, earth, 4-ft @ $ 15				60
4 guys placed @ $1 00				4 00
Supervision, 7½%				
Teaming, 15%	} = 30%		384	14 53
Travel, board and incidentals, 7½%				
Cost of 1 crossarm	.		1 32	43 56
Total			$ 4 30	$153 41
General expense, 10%	.		43	15 34
Grand total	,		$ 4 73	$148 75

Guy Poles.—The data include the cost of structural iron,
cast iron pipe and wooden guy poles

Example I —16-Ft Structural Iron Pole in Place

Materials

1 16-ft guy pole (891 lbs , @ $ 029)	$ 25,839
1 10-ft anchor log	1 50
1 set fittings	5 50
3 cu yds concrete for base in place	18 00
10% freight, incidentals, etc	5 084
	$ 55 923

Labor

Placing fittings		$ 1 00
Digging 10-ft hole, earth		3 00
Raising pole	.	2 00
Tamping		1 50
Supervision, 7½%	} = 30%	
Teaming 15%		2 25
Travel and board, 7½%		
		$ 9 75
Cost of pole		$ 65 67
General expense, 10%		6 57
Grand total		$ 72 24

Example II —18-Ft Structural Iron Pole in Place

Materials

1 18-ft guy pole (1,003 lbs , @ $ 029)	$ 29 087
1 10-ft anchor log	1 50
1 set fittings	5 50
3 cu yds concrete for base in place @ $6 00	18 00
10% freight, incidentals, etc	5 409
	$ 59 495

Labor

Placing fittings		$ 1 00
Digging 10-ft hole, earth		3 00
Raising pole		2 00
Tamping		1 50
Supervision, 7½%	} = 30%	
Teaming, 15%		2 25
Travel and board 7½%		
		$ 9 75
Cost of pole	..	$ 69 246
General expense, 10%	,	6 925
Grand total	,	$ 76 171

Example III.—20-Ft Structural Iron Pole in Place
Materials

1 20-ft. guy pole (1,114 lbs , @ $ 029)	$ 32 306
1 10-ft anchor log	1 50
1 set fittings	5 50
3 cu yds concrete for base in place @ $6 00	18 00
10% freight, incidentals, etc	5 73
	$ 62 03

Labor

Placing fittings		$ 1 00
Digging 10-ft hole, earth		3 00
Raising pole		2 00
Tamping		1 50
Supervision, 7½%		
Teaming, 15%	} = 30%	2 25
Travel and board, 7½%		
		$ 9 75

Cost of pole	$ 72 786
General expense, 10%	7 270
Grand total	$ 80 065

Example IV —20-Ft Iron Pipe Guy Poles in Place

1 20-ft pole @ $ 75 per ft	$ 15 00
¼ cu yd concrete for base in place @ $6 00	1 50
10% freight, incidentals etc	1 65
	$ 18 15

Labor

Hole dug, earth		$ 1 00
Pole raised		2 00
Pole tamped		50
Pole banked		05
Supervision, 7½%		
Teaming, 15%	} = 30%	1 07
Travel and board, 7½%		
		$ 4 62

Cost of pole	$ 22 77
General expense, 10%	2 28
Grand total	$ 25 05

Example V.—Cost of 18-Ft Iron Pipe Guy Pole in Place $ 23 23

Example VI —Cost of 16-Ft Iron Pipe Guy Pole in Place $ 21 42

Example VII —Cost of 25-Ft Wood Guy Pole in Place
Materials

1 25-ft Chestnut 7-in top pole including freight	$ 2 53
Carbolineum Avenarius	057
10% freight, incidentals, etc	258
	$ 2 846

Labor

Unloading		$ 20
Shaving		30
Placing carbolineum		27
Digging hole		60
Raising pole		28
Tamping		15
Banking		05
Supervision, 7½%		
Teaming, 15%	} = 30%	555
Travel and board 7½%		
		$ 2 41

Cost of pole	$ 5 25
General expense, 10%	53
Total	$ 5 78

Example VIII —Cost of 20 ft wood guy pole in place $ 5 177

Wood Anchor Logs.—The cost of materials and labor for wood anchor logs in place was as follows

Example I —Wood anchor logs
Materials

1 5-ft anchor log, including freight		$	.75
1 ⅝-in x 7-ft rod			.225
10% freight, incidentals, etc			098
		$	1 073

Labor

1 5-ft anchor hole dug, earth		$	1 50
1 5-ft anchor hole tamped			1 00
Supervision, 7½%			
Teaming, 15% . } = 30%			.75
Travel and board, 7½%			
		$	3 25

Cost of log		$	4 32½
General expense, 10%	. .		43
Total		$	4 75½

For rock excavation add $3 58

Example II —10-Ft Chestnut Log in Place
Materials

1 10-ft anchor log including freight		$	1 50
1 1⅜ in x 7-ft anchor rod			225
10% freight and incidentals			173
		$	1 898

Labor

1 10-ft anchor hole dug, earth		$	3 00
1 10-ft anchor hole tamped, earth			1 50
Supervision 7½%			
Teaming, 15% } = 30% .			1 35
Travel and board, 7½%			
		$	5 85

Cost of log	⟨	$	7 74½
General expense, 10% .			774
Total		$	8 52½

For rock excavation add $7 1½

Cross Arms —Cost of 1, 10-ft, 10 pin cross arm in place
Materials

		Per Pole	
1 10-ft, 10-pin cross arm @ $ 665		$	665
10 Standard locust pins @ $ 0105			105
10 6-d Nails @ $ 00015			002
1 pair 28-in cross arm braces @ $ 08			080
2 ⅜x4-in carriage bolts @ $ 0061			012
1 Fetter drive screw @ $ 0093			009
1 14-in cross arm bolt @ $ 037			037
2 Square washers @ $ 0068			014
10% freight, incidentals, etc			0924
		$	1 016

Labor

1 cross arm distributed @ $ 03		$	03
10 pins placed @ $ 0025			025
1 pair cross arm braces placed @ $ 03			03
1 10-pin cross arm placed @ $ 15 .			15
Supervision, 7½% .			
Teaming, 15% } = 30%			0705
Travel and board, 7½% .			
		$	305

Cost of one arm	.	$	1 321
General expense, 10%			132
Total		$	1 454

Wire Stringing.—The following example shows the method of arriving at the cost of wire stringing

Cost of One Pair No 14 N B S Gage, H D Copper, on One Mile Class "A" Pole Line

Materials	
204 lbs No 14 copper @ $ 235	$ 47 94
104 lbs glass @ $ 01885 .	1 96
Tie wire, line joints, e c .	30
5% freight, etc	2 51
	$ 52 71

Labor		
*2 wires strung one mile @ $5 81 . .	$ 11 62	
104 glass placed @ $ 01	1 04	
Supervision, 7½%	} = 15%	1 90
Travel and board, 7½%		
		$ 14 56
Cost of one pair		$ 67 27
General expense, 10% .		6 727
Total .		$ 74 00

*Team hire included in cost of stringing

As the number of poles per mile varies with the class of line and the cost of stringing with the number of wires, the above is given, simply to show the different items considered in arriving at the costs given in Tables I to V

Table I—Cost of One Mile H D Copper on Class "A" Pole Line

	Cost of No 14 N B S	Cost of No 12 N B S	Cost of Cross Arms	Total Cost No 14	Total Cost No 12
1 pr	$ 74 00	$102 308	$ 75 40	$149 40	$177 708
2 pr	132 422	202 498	75 40	207 822	277 898
3 pr	194 907	300 021	75 40	270 307	375 421
4 pr	258 128	398 280	75 40	333 528	473 680
5 pr	317 715	492 905	75 40	393 115	568 305
6 pr	390 780	601 008	150 50	541 580	751 808
7 pr	448 665	693 931	150 80	599 460	844 731
8 pr	506 136	786 440	150 80	656 936	937 24
9 pr	560 502	875 844	150 80	711 302	1026 644
10 pr	617 950	968 330	150 80	768 75	1119 13

Table II—Cost of One Mile H D Copper on Class "B" Pole Line

	Cost of No. 14 N B S	Cost of No 12 N B S	Cost of Cross Arms	Total Cost No 14	Total Cost No 12
1 pr	$ 67 017	$102 058	$ 69 60	$136 617	$171 658
2 pr	131 918	202 000	69 60	201 518	271 600
3 pr	194 151	299 274	69 60	263 751	368 874
4 pr	257 12	397 284	69 60	326 72	466 884
5 pr	316 455	491 660	69 60	386 055	561 260
6 pr	389 268	599 514	139 20	528 468	738 714
7 pr	446 878	692 165	139 20	586 078	831 365
8 pr	505 270	785 598	139 20	644 470	924 798
9 pr	558 234	873 603	139 20	697 434	1012 803
10 pr	615 430	965 840	139 20	754 63	1105 040

Table III—Cost of One Mile H D Copper Class "C" Pole Line

	Cost of No 14 N B S	Cost of No 12 N B S	Cost of Cross Arms	Total Cost No 14	Total Cost No 12
1 pr	$ 66 700	$101 808	$ 63 80	$130 500	$165 608
2 pr	131 554	201 730	63 80	195 454	265 530
3 pr	193 410	298 524	63 80	257 210	362 324
4 pr.	256 132	396 284	63 80	319 932	460 084
5 pr	316 220	490 410	63 80	379 02	554 21
6 pr	387 786	598 014	127 60	515 386	725 614
7 pr	445 172	690 438	127 60	572 772	818 038
8 pr	502 144	782 448	127 60	629 744	910 048
9 pr	555 011	871 353	127 60	683 611	998 953
10 pr	612 950	963 340	127 60	740 55	1090 940

Table IV.—Cost of One Mile H D Copper on Class "D" or "E" Pole Line

		Cost of No 14 N B S	Cost of No 12 N B S	Cost of Cross Arms	Total Cost. No 14	No 12
1 pr		$ 66 52	$101 559	$ 58 00	$124 520	$159 559
2 pr		130 925	201 002	58 00	188 925	259 002
3 pr	.	192 681	297 777	58 00	250 681	355 777
4 pr		255 134	395 288	58 00	313 134	453 288
5 pr		313 972	489 165	58 00	371 972	547 165
6 pr	..	336 289	596 520	116 00	502 289	712 52
7 pr	..	443 425	688 695	116 00	559 425	804 695
8 pr.		500 148	780 456	116 00	616 148	896 456
9 pr		553 765	869 112	116 00	669 765	985 112
10 pr	.	610 465	960 85	116 00	726 465	1076.85

Table V —Cost of One Mile No 12 B W G Steel Wire on Class "D" or "E" Pole Line

		Cost of No 12 B W G Wire	Cost of Cross Arm	Total Cost.
1 pr	. . . . .	$ 25 318	$ 58 00	$ 83 318
2 pr		48 520	58 00	106 520
3 pr	.. . . .	69 054	58 00	127 054
4 pr	.	90 324	58 00	148 324
5 pr	.	107 960	58 00	165 960
6 pr	... ...	139 074	116 00	255 074
7 pr	..	154 508	116 00	270 508
8 Lr		170 528	116 00	286 528
9 pr		182 943	116 00	298 943
10 pr	. .	198 440	116 00	314 440

The cost of one mile No. 12 B. W. G steel wire on farmer's line with one cross arm (33 poles to the mile) figures as follows:

	Cost of No 12 B W G Wire
. 1 pr . . .	$ 24 874
2 pr	47 632
3 pr .	67 722
4 pr	88 548
5 pr	105 740

The cost of one mile No. 12 B W G. steel wire on farmer's line with brackets figures as follows

	Cost of Wire
1 pr	$24 874
2 pr	47 632

The cost of No. 14 N B S. weatherproof wire on Class A pole line was as follows:

Materials
364 lbs No 14 N B S, W P @ $ 23½ .... $ 85 54
104 glass @ $ 01885 .... 1 96
Tie wires, etc .... .50
5% freight, etc 4 40

.... $ 92 40

Labor:
2 wires strung one mile @ $7 83 .... $ 15 66
104 glass placed @ $ 01 .... 1 04
Supervision, 7½%
Teaming, 5½% } = 15%. 2 51
Travel, board, etc , 2½%

.... $ 19 21

Total $111 61
General expense, 10% 11 16

Cost of one mile $122 77
Cost of one foot 0203

The cost of No 14 B & S twist on Class A pole line was as follows·

Materials

5,280 ft twist @ $ 0187	$ 97 75
52 brackets @ $ 0367	1 908
52 knobs @ $ 01606	835
104 lag screws @ $ 0078	811
52 bolt @ $ 0069	359
Tie wire, etc	1 00
5% freight	5 132
	$107 775

Labor

One mile twist strung @ $7 83		$ 7 83
52 brackets placed @ $ 02		1 04
Supervision, 7½%.		
Teaming, 5%........	} = 15%	1 33
Travel, board, etc., 2½%.		
		$ 10 20

Cost	$117 975
General expense, 10%	11 797
Cost of one mile	$129 772
Cost of one foot	$ 0245

The average cost of one subscriber's drop, using No. 14 B & S twisted pair, was as follows.

Materials

200 ft No 14 B & S twisted pair @ $ 0187	$ 3 74
5 house knobs @ $ 01388	07
Portion of distributing bracket and knob expense	06
5% freight and incidentals	194
	$ 4 064

Labor

200 ft No 14 twist strung including the placing of all supports, etc		$ 2 00
Supervision, 7½%		
Teaming, 5%	} = 15%	30
Travel, board, etc , 2½%		
		$ 2 30

Cost of one drop	$ 6 364
General expense, 10%	636
Cost	$ 7 00

UNDERGROUND CONDUIT CONSTRUCTION.

The costs on underground conduit construction are derived from the contract prices paid for this work. In explanation it may be said that in the city in which this work was done "politics" made it impossible to do the work in any other way then by contract with certain contractors. The specifications and contract prices on which the figures given here are based are as follows:

General Specifications.—The specifications were as follows:

(1) *Multiple Duct Conduit with Concrete Protection at Top, Bottom and Sides.*—The foundation for this conduit shall be not less than 4 ins. thick After the foundation has been allowed to set, a layer of cement mortar shall be placed upon it and the conduit laid on this cement, breaking joints The joints shall be made by wrapping a strip of muslin 6 ins wide and long enough to make 1½ turns around the ends of the pieces to be jointed. This muslin wrapper shall be dipped into a thin mixture of cement mortar, and after being placed on the ducts, shall be covered with ½-in. cement mortar on top and sides. After the requisite number of ducts are laid and the joints well formed, 3 ins. of concrete shall be well tamped in place on each side and 4 ins on top

(2) *Multiple Duct with Concrete Base and Plank Protection at the Top*—The foundations for this conduit shall be the same as in Case No. 1. After the foundation has been allowed to set, a layer of cement shall be placed upon it and the conduit laid on this cement, breaking joints. The joints shall be made by wrapping a strip of muslin 6 ins. wide around the ends of the pieces to be jointed. This strip of muslin shall be dipped into a thin mixture of cement mortar just before being placed A cement collar shall be formed over this muslin wrapper. After these cement collars have set, fine dirt shall be well tamped in place on the sides, great care being taken not to break the collars

After about 1 in. of fine dirt is placed on top of the conduit, a 1½-in creosoted plank or planks shall be placed on top so that the planking shall extend about 1 in beyond the conduits on each side.

(3) *Multiple Duct Conduit with Plank Protection at Top and Bottom.*—The foundation for this conduit consists simply of 1½-in. creosoted planking. This planking shall be placed on the bottom of the trench on an even solid surface The joints shall be sealed by wrapping a strip of canvas soaked in a mixture of hot tar and pitch and shall be 6 ins wide and long enough to make 1½ turns around the pieces to be jointed. The trench shall be filled with fine earth and tamped to the level of the top of the ducts, and 1½ in creo-

soted plank or planks shall be placed on the top of the conduit.

Concrete.—Concrete for manholes shall be composed of 2 parts cement, 5 parts sand and 10 parts of washed gravel or crushed limestone. This concrete shall be mixed on a wooden or iron mixing board or in a mixer, but in no case shall it be mixed on the ground or street This concrete shall first be made by mixing the sand and cement dry and then adding the broken stone after the sand and cement are well mixed; then enough water shall be added to bring the mixture to such a consistency that when tapped with the back of a shovel the water shall appear on the surface. The cement used shall be the Atlas brand of Portland cement or its approved equivalent. Sand shall be good, sharp sand, free from loam, dirt, or other foreign matter. The crushed limestone shall be of such size that all of it shall pass through a ring $1\frac{1}{2}$ ins in diameter in every direction, and none of it shall pass through a ring $\frac{3}{4}$-in. in diameter If gravel is used for concrete it shall be well screened and washed and of the same dimensions as specified for crushed stone Concrete for duct foundation shall be composed of 1 part Atlas Portland cement or its approved equivalent, 2 parts fine, sharp sand, and 5 parts of crushed limestone or gravel This limestone or gravel shall be of such a size that all of it shall pass through a ring $\frac{3}{4}$-in. in diameter and none of it shall pass through a ring $\frac{1}{4}$-in in diameter This concrete shall be mixed the same as specified above for concrete for manholes

Cement Mortar.—Shall be made of 2 parts Atlas Portland cement and 5 parts good, sharp sand, free from loam, mica or other foreign matter.

Brick Manholes —All brick shall be first class, hard-burned sewer brick, and shall be wet just before being laid. The brick masonry shall be laid in cement mortar. The bricks shall be laid in a full bed of mortar upon all sides Every third course of brick shall be a course of headers No bats are to be used in the construction of manholes.

Contract Prices.—The contract prices are as follows.

City Work—

Earth trench excavation down to 8 ft	$ 1 89 cu yd
Earth manhole excavation	1 89 cu yd
Earth trench excavation, 8 ft to 12 ft	2 00 cu. yd
Rock manhole excavation	2 75 cu yd
Rock trench excavation	2 75 cu yd
Earth trench excavation	1 35 cu yd
Earth manhole excavation	1 62 cu yd
Rock trench excavation	2 00 cu yd
Common brick in place in M H walls	30 00 per M.
Concrete in concrete manhole	7 00 cu yd
Concrete in manhole bottoms	4 50 cu yd
Old rails and beams in place	1 85 C lbs.
Beams, angles and rails in place	2 20 C lbs
Miscellaneous concrete	5 00 cu yd
Large castings, weighing 1,100 to 1,150 lbs in place	25 00 ea
Taking up and replacing asphalt pavement	2 25 sq yd
Taking up and replacing asphalt pavement, concrete base	3 00 sq yd
Taking up and replacing block stone pavement	50 sq yd
Taking up and replacing block stone pavement, concrete base	2 50 sq. yd.
Taking up and replacing block stone pavement, tarred	85 sq yd
Taking up and replacing cobblestone pavement	.35 sq yd
Taking up and replacing brick street pavement, old	40 sq yd
Taking up and replacing brick street pavement, new	1 25 sq yd.
Taking up and replacing flagstone pavement	45 sq yd
Taking up and replacing old granolithic pavement	1 85 sq yd
Sand	06 bu.
Gravel	05 bu
Cement	625 sack
Labor	175 hr
Foreman	35 hr
Team	50 hr
Cart	275 hr

Conduit Costs.—The cost of McRoy conduit in place for three classes of construction is given in Table VI.

Manholes.—On an average, manholes are 325 ft apart, so that to the cost of every 325 ft. of conduit laid it will be necessary to add the cost of one manhole, of the class used as given below

Concrete Manhole, Two Way.—Prices for material in place:

10 yds earth excavation at $1 89	$ 18 90
5 7 yds concrete at $7 00	39 90
400 lbs iron beams at $1 85 per cwt	7 40
1 large casting	21 50
1 connection to sewer	20 00
100 brick for top at $30 00 per M	3 00
2 cable pulls at $0 50	1 00
30 hanger sockets at $0 05	1 50
24 conduit plugs at $0 05	1 20
10 per cent incidentals, etc	11 44
Total	.$125 84

Note—48 sq ft paving additional

Concrete Manhole, Three Way.—Prices for material in place.

11 yds earth excavation at $1 89	$ 20 79
6 yds concrete at $7 00	42 00
400 lbs iron beams at $1 85 cwt	7 40
1 large casting	21 50
1 connection to sewer	20 00
100 brick for top at $30 00 per M	3 00
2 cable pulls at $0 50	1 00
30 hanger sockets at $0 05	1 50
24 conduit plugs at $0 05	1 20
10 per cent incidentals, etc	11 84
Total	$130.23

Note—48 sq ft paving additional

Brick Manhole, Two Way, 9-in Wall.—Prices for material in place:

11 yds. earth excavation at $1 89 .	$ 20 79
5 yds concrete bottom at $4 50	2 25
1700 brick at $30 00 per M .	51 00
400 lbs iron beams at $1 85 per cwt	7 40
1 large casting .	21 50
1 connection to sewer .	20 00
2 cable pulls at $0 50 .	1 00
30 hanger sockets at $0 05	1 50
24 conduit plugs at $0 05	1 20
10 per cent incidentals, etc	12 66
Total	$139 30

Note—48 sq ft of paving additional

Brick Manhole, Three Way, 13-in. Wall —Prices for material in place:

13 yds earth excavation at $1 89	$ 24 57
6 yds. concrete in bottom at $4 50	2 70
2550 brick at $30 00 per M .	76 50
400 lbs iron beams at $1 85 per cwt	7 40
1 large casting .	21 50
1 connection to sewer . .	20 00
2 cable pulls at $0 50	1 00
30 hanger sockets at $0 05	1 50
24 conduit plugs at $0 05	1 20
10 per cent incidentals etc	15 63
Total ..	$172 00

Note—48 sq. ft. paving additional

Table VI.—Showing Cost per Lineal Foot of McRoy Conduit in Place, No Manholes

Number of ducts	2	4	6	8	10	12	14	16	18	20	22	24	28	30	32	36	
Case I.																	
Cobblestone paving	$1 23	$1 60	83	$2 15	$2 43	$2 61	$2 92	$3 13	$3 34	$3 53	$3 78	$3 93	$4 48	$4 75	$5 00	$5 55	
Brick paving	1 26	1 62	1 85	2 17	2 46	2 63	2 94	3 16	3 36	3 56	3 80	3 96	4 51	4 77	5 02	5 58	
Plain blockstone paving	1 31	1 67	1 90	2 22	2 51	2 68	2 99	3 20	3 41	3 61	3 85	4 00	4 56	4 83	5 07	5 62	
Flagstone paving	1 34	1 71	1 94	2 26	2 54	2 72	3 04	3 23	3 44	3 64	4 01	4 04	4 59	4 96	5 10	5 65	
Blockstone with tar	1 48	1 84	2 07	2 39	2 68	2 85	3 17	3 36	3 57	3 77	4 01	4 17	4 72	4 99	5 23	5 78	
Granolithic with tar	1 97	2 34	2 57	2 89	3 18	3 35	3 67	3 86	4 07	4 27	4 51	4 67	5 22	5 49	5 73	6 28	
Plain asphalt with tar	2 17	2 54	2 77	3 09	3 38	3 55	3 87	4 06	4 27	4 47	4 71	4 87	5 42	5 69	5 93	6 48	
Blockstone with concrete base	2 29	2 66	2 89	3 21	3 50	3 67	3 99	4 18	4 39	4 59	4 83	4 99	5 54	5 81	6 05	6 60	
Asphalt with concrete base	2 53	2 90	3 13	3 45	3 74	3 91	4 33	4 42	4 63	4 83	5 07	5 25	5 78	6 05	6 29	6 84	Ave
Average cost for all pavements	1 73	2 10	2 33	2 65	2 94	3 11	3 43	3 62	3 83	4 03	4 27	4 43	4 98	5 25	5 49	6 04	3 75
Average cost per duct foot	87	.53	39	33	29	26	25	23	21	20	19	18	18	.175	17	167	288
Case II.																	
Cobblestone paving	1 21	1 55	1 75	2 09	2 33	2 60	2 79	2 98	3 26	3 50	3 81	4 05	4 60	4 88	5 12	5 49	
Brick paving	1 23	1 57	1 77	2 12	2 36	2 62	2 81	3 01	3 28	3 53	3 83	4 08	4 63	4 90	5 14	5 52	
Plain blockstone paving	1 28	1 62	1 82	2 17	2 41	2 67	2 86	3 06	3 33	3 58	3 88	4 13	4 68	4 95	5 19	5 56	
Flagstone paving	1 31	1 66	1 85	2 20	2 44	2 71	2 89	3 09	3 36	3 61	3 92	4 16	4 71	4 98	5 23	5 60	
Blockstone with tar	1 45	1 79	1 99	2 34	2 58	2 84	3 03	3 23	3 50	3 75	4 06	4 30	4 85	5 12	5 36	5 74	
Granolithic with tar	1 94	2 28	2 48	2 83	3 07	3 33	3 52	3 72	3 99	4 24	4 54	4 79	5 34	5 61	5 85	6 23	
Plain asphalt with tar	2 14	2 48	2 68	3 03	3 27	3 53	3 72	3 92	4 19	4 44	4 74	4 99	5 54	5 81	6 05	6 43	
Blockstone with concrete base	2 26	2 60	2 80	3 15	3 39	3 65	3 84	4 04	4 31	4 56	4 86	5 11	5 66	5 93	6 17	6 55	
Asphalt with concrete base	2 50	2 84	3 04	3 39	3 63	3 89	4 08	4 28	4 55	4 80	5 10	5 35	5 90	6 17	6 41	6 79	
Case III																	
Cobblestone paving	1 22	1 41	1 56	1 84	2 04	2 17	2 36	2 49									
Brick paving	1 25	1 44	1 59	1 87	2 07	2 20	2 39	2 52									
Plain blockstone paving	1 30	1 52	1 64	1 92	2 12	2 28	2 44	2 57									
Flagstone paving	1 33	1 55	1 67	1 95	2 15	2 28	2 47	2 60									
Blockstone with tar	1 47	1 66	1 81	2 09	2 29	2 42	2 61	2 74									
Granolithic with tar	1 96	2 15	2 30	2 58	2 78	2 91	3 10	3 23									
Plain asphalt with tar	2 17	2 34	2 49	2 77	2 97	3 10	3 29	3 42									
Blockstone with concrete base	2 28	2 46	2 61	2 89	3 09	3 28	3 41	3 54									
Asphalt with concrete base	2 52	2 71	2 85	3 13	3 33	3 46	3 65	3 78									

Note.—Case I—Concrete protection all around ducts. Case II—Concrete bottom and plank on top. Case III—Plank on bottom and creosoted plank on top.

APPENDIX B.

MISCELLANEOUS COST DATA ON POLE LINE AND

UNDERGROUND CONDUIT CONSTRUCTION.

The following cost data on pole line and underground conduit construction have been compiled by the editors of ENGINEERING-CONTRACTING from articles published in that journal and from other sources as named in the text.

Cost of Two Short Telephone Lines.—The two lines were respectively 10 miles long and 14 miles long; their cost per mile was as follows:

10-Mile Line.

Labor	Per Mile
1.7 days foreman at $4	$ 6.80
1 7 days sub-foreman at $3	5 10
4 days climbers at $2.50	10 00
10 5 days groundmen at $2 25	23.63
17 9 days total at $3.10	$ 55.53

Materials	
28 poles at $1 50	$ 42.00
28 cross-arms at 15 cts	4 20
28 steel pins at 4 cts	1.12
28 glass insulators at 4 cts	1 12
56 lag screws and washers at 1½ cts	0 84
305 lbs No 9 galv wire at 4 2 cts	12 81
Total materials	$ 62 09
Total labor and material	$117.62

More than 90 per cent of the poles were 25 ft. long, the rest were 30 to 40 ft in length

14-Mile Line.

Labor: Per Mile
2.2 days foreman at $3.50 . . . . $ 7.70
2.2 days sub-foreman at $3 . . . . 6.60
5.3 days climber at $2 75 . . . . 14.58
11.4 days groundman at $2 25 . . . . 25.64

21.5 days total at $2 54 . . . .$ 54.52
Materials:
32 poles at $1.50 . . . .$ 48.00
32 brackets at 1½ cts 0.48
380 lbs. No. 8 galv. wire at 4 2 cts. 15.96
10 lbs. No. 9 galv wire at 4 2 cts. 0.42
1½ lbs. fence staples at 2½ cts. 0.04
32 insulators at 4 cts. 1.28

Total materials . . . .$ 66 18
Total labor and materials $120 70
2 telephones at $12 50 . . . .$ 25 00
200 ft. office wire 1.40

Labor Cost of High Power Transmission Line.—The line was pole line and its total length was 9,500 ft along a public road. The poles and cross-arms were delivered at one end of the line by railroad, so the average haul on material was about one mile. The poles were from 30 to 33 ft long, measuring from 5 to 9 ins. at the top and from 12 to 18 ins. at the butt.

The wages paid for a 10-hr. day on the work were as follows: Foreman, $3 00; laborers, $1.50; linemen, $2.50; team 2 horses and driver, $4 50

Hauling.—The poles were hauled on a two-horse wagon, one man assisting the driver in loading and unloading them. Naturally a large per cent of the cost of hauling was in taking the poles from the cars and unloading them from the wagon. The poles were of chestnut, fairly light, and 8 to 10 poles could be hauled at a trip The cost of hauling the poles was:

Team $22 50
Laborers 7 50

Total $30 00

Digging Holes.—In digging the holes for the poles, one man worked on a hole. He used a digging bar, a shovel with extra long handle and a spoon with same length handle. The holes were dug 5 ft. deep and were 30 ins. in diameter at the top and about 18 ins. at the bottom, making an average diameter of 2 ft. From each hole was excavated 0.58 cu. yd. The material was a red sandy clay, and the holes were all dry. There were 74 holes dug. The cost was:

Foreman	$17 25
Laborers	55.50
Total	.$72.75

The cost per hole was as follows·

Foreman	$0.23
Men	0 75
Total	$0 98

The cost per cu yd. was as follows:

Foreman	$0.40
Men	1.30
Total	$1.70

It will be noticed that one man dug 2 holes per day

Raising Poles.—The pole raising was done by hand   A deadman and a jenny were used, these being manipulated by two men. The foreman or a lineman held a metal slide in the hole for the butt of the pole to slide against, keeping it from gouging into the side of the hole   The rest of the crew used pikes to lift the top of the pole, and place it in the hole. The crew consisted of the foreman, one lineman and about 7 men

The method of operation was as follows: The pole was rolled to the hole by means of bars and cant hooks   The slide meantime was placed in the hole   Then the crew lifted the small end onto the jenny which held it until the deadman was put in place. With the pole resting on the deadman, the pikes were brought into play, and as the pole was lifted the deadman was moved up under the pole until the final lift came that sent the pole into the hole. Then it was turned and lined

up, the lineman assisting the foreman in this work, after which
the refilling of the hole was done

A record of this work was kept in detail on a number of
poles, from which it was found that the average time consumed in the work was as follows

Getting ready to set pole, 3 minutes, raising pole, 6 minutes; lining pole, 2 minutes, filling and tamping earth in hole,
1 man shoveling and 3 tamping, 10 minutes, several men
standing by the pikes to steady the pikes; moving to next
hole, 4 minutes, total time, 25 minutes

When everything is working well this average can be maintained, but a little time is occasionally lost due to unforseen
obstacles that prevent this speed   The cost of raising the
poles was:

Foreman	..$10.50
Laborers	.. 37 50
Lineman	.. 8 75
Total	..$56.75

This, for the 74 poles, gives a cost per pole of the following

Foreman	$0.14
Laborers	. 0.50
Lineman	.. 0 12
Total	..$0 76

Cross-Arms.—Before raising the poles, and while the laborers were digging the holes, the linemen were at work dapping
the poles to receive the cross-arms. The cross-arms used
were 8-pin arms, two being placed on each pole At all times
in the line, double cross-arms were used, that is, a cross-arm
was put on each side of the poles. This was the case for
nine poles. For future needs the poles were dapped in 3
places. This made 240 daps necessary. The poles, as stated,
were chestnut The cost of dapping the poles was $22.62,
making a cost per dap of 9.8 cts.

One lineman placed the cross-arms, the team hauling them
along as needed, and the driver acting as the lineman's
"ground hog." The sketch, Fig. 88, shows how these arms

were placed, and braced with two pieces of galvanized iron.
In all, 166 cross-arms were used   The cost of this work was.

Hauling with team... .. ..$21.37
Lineman ...., ... 6.25
                                                  ———
    Total $27 62

The high cost of this was due to the fact that the team was
charged to this work for the entire time of placing the cross-
arms, as it waited at each pole while the arms were being put
in place. The cost per cross-arm was 17 cts.

One lineman and a helper placed the insulators. The cost
of this was:

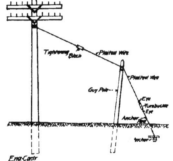

Fig 88 —Method of Guying Transmission Line Pole

Lineman $3 75
Helper 2 25
                                                    ———
    Total   .   .   . $6 00

Only six insulators were put on a cross-arm, thus making
12 to a pole, except at the turns, as the line was to carry 12
wires. In all 996 insulators were used, hence the cost per
unit was 0 6 cts

Guy Poles.—In building lines with a number of wires on
them, it is necessary to guy all poles where there are turns in
the line, and on long straight lines some of the poles must also
be guyed   The sketch, Fig 88, shows the method used in
guying this line, and is one frequently used   The guy pole

holes were dug of about the same dimensions as the holes
for the line poles   The cost was·

Foreman $1 50
Laborers 6 75
                                                              ———
    Total $8.25
The cost per hole was·
Foreman $0.17
Laborers 0.75
                                                              ———
    Total $0.92
The raising of the poles cost.
Foreman $3 00
Laborers 9 00
                                                              ———
    Total $12.00

This makes a cost per pole of $1 33   This is large, owing
to the fact that the men lost considerable time moving from
pole to pole and carrying their tools, also to the fact that each
pole had to be cut and trimmed, as these guy poles were
made from rejected line poles

The method of placing the guy wires to the poles was as
follows: The wire was fastened to each of the two poles, and
then brought to the tightening block as shown in the sketch
With blocks and tackle fastened to the two poles, the poles
were brought to a snug bearing and the wires were made fast
around the tightening block, shown in the sketch. The wires
go around the block in grooves made for the purpose at right
angles to each other. While the linemen and their helpers are
doing this work, the laborers are digging the anchor hole and
placing the anchor rod   To this is fastened a turn buckle, and
a wire is run from the guy pole to the turn buckle   The blocks
and tackle are then fastened to a handy tree or stump, or if
necessary to the anchor rod and the guy pole is pulled back,
tightening the guy wire between the two poles, while the turn
buckle is screwed up, thus making all the guy wires taut. At
times, instead of making an anchor as shown, the anchor wire
can be fastened to a convenient tree   Both kinds of anchors
were used in this case   The cost of this work was

Foreman	...			...	.	.$1.50
Linemen	.			. .	.	. 3 75
Laborers	..	....	.	....		... 3 75
Total	...	....				$9.00

This made a cost of $1.00 per pole, making a total cost per guy pole of $3 25.

About one-half of this line ran through the edge of woods or by shade trees. A few trees had to be cut down and a number trimmed ; some tall bushes were also cut down. The foreman looked after this work part of one day when all his force was at work upon it, but for the most part linemen were in charge of several laborers doing this work The cost of it was as follows

Foreman	..		.	.	.	.$ 2.25
Lineman			,	.	.	18 12
Men	.		.		.	13 13
Total		.	..	. .	.	... $33 50

Stringing the Wires—As previously stated, 12 wires were strung on the poles. The wires were light weight. The team hauled the wire, and one horse was used in helping to string it, the other horse standing idle In line work, a team is nearly always necessary, yet there are times that it may stand idle for hours, thus increasing the cost of that item to which it is charged When there is nothing else for the wagon to do it is used to carry the tools along the line as the men work In stringing the wire the horse pulled a rope fastened to two strands of wire at one time, thus running out two wires, and making six trips of the horse to string out the 12 wires For this work 3 linemen were used, but in fastening the wires to the insulators only 2 linemen were used, and the wires were pulled tight by the helpers with blocks and tackle The cost was

Foreman	.		.		.	.$ 18.00
Linemen				..	..	37.50
Laborers	....			. ...	.	27.00
Team		.	.		.	36.00
Total	.	.	.	....	.	$118.50

In all 21 6 miles of wire were strung and this made a cost of $5 50 per mile of wire

Changing Poles—At the ends of the line, where connections were made with the old line of poles, some poles had to be changed to make them suitable for the new service. There were 3 of these at one end and 1 at the other The work consisted in taking down the old poles and putting in their place poles from 40 to 45 ft long Cross-arms had to be put on the new poles, and the wires changed over to the new poles It took a half day for the crew to do each pole, thus spending 2 days on the 4 poles The cost of this was

Foreman	$ 6 00
Lineman	2 50
Laborers	39 00
Team	9 00
Total	$56 50

This gave a cost per pole of $14.12 In line work the foreman is always a lineman, and in doing odd jobs this frequently keeps the cost down, as he will often do work that a lineman is called upon to do As the lineman is the higher priced man he should be allowed to do only such work as the helper is not able to do

Total Cost—The total cost of the entire work was as follows

Hauling	$ 30.00
Digging holes	72.75
Raising poles	56.75
Dapping cross-arms	22.62
Placing cross-arms and insulators	33.62
Guy poles	29.25
Trimming trees and bushes	33 50
Stringing and fastening wires	118 50
Changing old poles	56.50
Total	$453 49

There being 1 6 miles of line built, the cost per mile for each item was:

Hauling	$ 18.75
Digging holes	45.47
Raising poles	35.47
Dapping cross-arms	14 14
Placing cross-arms and insulators .	21 01
Guy poles	18.28
Trimming trees and bushes.	20.94
Stringing and fastening wires	74 06
Changing old poles.....	35 31

Total $283 43

For the 74 new poles erected this makes a cost per pole for the completed line of $6.13.

Cost of 28-Mile Telegraph Line.—The line was 28 miles long with 32 poles to the mile and was built in British Columbia The wire was single No. 8 B. B galvanized iron wire. The itemized cost per mile was as follows:

Labor:	Cost.
1 day foreman at $3.50... . ...$ 3 50	
1 day sub-foreman at $3 .. . . 3.00	
2.7 days climber at $2.50.... .. . . 6 75	
2.5 days framer at $2 25.. .. . . .. 5.62	
0.7 day blacksmith at $2 25 . . . 1.58	
4 6 days groundman at $2 . .. .. 9 20	

12 5 days total at $2.40. . . . . ..$29 65

Materials:	
32 25-ft poles at $1.25. . .	$40.00
32 wood brackets at 1¼ cts	0 40
32 glass insulators at 4 cts	1 28
5 lbs nails at 2½ cts	0 12
½ lb staples at 3 cts.	0 02
380 lbs. No 8 B B galv wire at 5 cts .	19 00
2 lbs. tie wire at 3 cts . . . ·.	0 06

Total materials $60 88

Total labor and materials $90.53

Cost of Excavating Trolley Pole Holes by Machine.—The machine consisted of an ordinary flat car, at one end of which was stationed a hoisting engine with a small boiler under cover. About the center of the car was placed an outrigger that projected over the side, containing a vertical shaft about 3 ins. in diameter, which slid through a bevel gear This shaft had on the bottom an ordinary screw bit 2 ft. in diameter similar to that used on small hand augers for boring post holes. Another bevel gear on a horizontal shaft meshed with the one mentioned above and was driven by the hoisting engine by sprocket wheel. A wire rope running through the hoisting engine was connected with the top of the vertical shaft and enabled the operator to raise and lower it at will. It required five men to operate the machine—an engineer at $2 50, a fireman at $2 00, a foreman at $2 50, and two laborers at $1 75. The number of holes bored depended a great deal on the character of the soil, but through this section (Ohio) would average 50 a day On the other end of the car was placed a mast and boom with which the poles were raised and set in the holes. This work could be done by the same number of men and they would dig the holes and place about 30 poles per day. One axle of the car was connected to the hoisting engine with a sprocket chain for the purpose of moving the car by its own power A speed of seven or eight miles per hour could be attained. It is stated that the machine would have been more efficient had there been a stronger engine connected with it. At the wages given above the labor cost per hole for boring was 21 cts The labor cost of digging holes and setting 30 poles per day was 35 cts. per pole.

Method and Cost of Digging 600 Trolley Pole Holes.—The overhead construction was of two kinds, span wire which needs a pole on each side of the track, and single poles with a bracket to hold the trolley wire. This divided the work into two groups, and the span wire construction was further divided into double and single track work The class of material in which the holes were dug, as well as the size of the butt of the pole, made additional division of the work. The cost of the work will be given under five groups.

A 10-hr. day was worked and the foreman was paid $3.00 per day and the laborers $1 50 The work was done during the months of February to July. The gang of men worked at

digging the holes, raising the poles, and other overhead work
during this period of time, but the cost of each item of work
was kept separate In digging the holes, the tools that the
men used were   A digging bar, see Fig. 89a ; a round point
shovel, see Fig 89b, and a spoon, see Fig. 89c. The length
of the handles on these was 8 ft   The holes were spaced as
follows: For span construction on tangents, the poles were
110 ft. apart On 12° curves or less they were from 80 to 110
ft. apart, while on curves of 150 ft. radius or less they were
spaced from 40 to 50 ft apart.

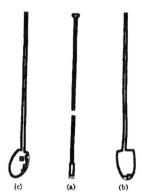

(c)   (a)   (b)

Fig 89 —Tools foi Digging Trolley Pole Holes.

Group I In this lot 82 holes were dug. It was for span
construction of 4,775 ft of double track   The poles were from
12 to 15 ins. in diameter at the butt, so the holes were dug
about 2 ft. in diameter. The depth of the hole was governed
by the specifications, which called for all holes to be 6 ft. deep,
this depth to be in the natural ground   Hence where there
was an embankment, the hole had to be as much deeper than
6 ft , as the height of the embankment was above the natural
ground at the place where the pole was to be planted

This is an instance of where conditions surrounding work
may change, yet specifications are not changed to suit the new
conditions. When these specifications were first drawn, all

the poles on suburban lines of the company in question, were
not placed equi-distant from the center line of the track   In
cuts they were so spaced, but, wherever embankments occurred, longer poles were used, as the poles were placed outside of the toe of the slope of the embankment. This pre-
vented having the poles in line, which made the line of poles
appear unsightly, and it also added to the length of the span
wire. For these and other reasons, the arrangement of poles
was changed and they were set equi-distant from the center
line on the embankment as well as in the cut. Under these
circumstances where the embankments had settled and were

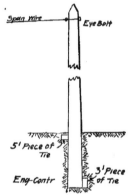

Fig 90 —Method of Ground Bracing Pole

made of good material, there was no need of making the holes
more than 6 ft., but as the specifications called for a greater
depth, the holes were so dug. They varied from 6 to 12 ft
deep. In this group 40 pole holes were dug 6 ft. deep, the
rest being from 9 to 12 ft , 30 holes being of the last named
depth.   The roadbed on this section was all embankment,
made of cinders and slag from a steel plant. In digging the
30 deepest holes the cinders and slag kept running into the
holes, causing about three to four times as much material to be
excavated as would otherwise have been taken from the hole
It was estimated that this doubled the yardage excavated from
the 82 holes.

In order to brace the poles under ground, an 8 ft. second-hand sawed tie was cut into two pieces, one 3 ft. long and the other 5 ft. long, and placed as shown in the cut, Fig 90. The short piece was put in the bottom of the hole and the large pieces at the top. This also increased the amount of material that was taken from the holes. This extra material averaged 4 cu. ft for each hole, and the contractor was paid extra for this work When holes were dug of a greater depth than the length of the shovel handle, a foot or more of earth was dug out of the surface of the ground at the side of the hole, and the workman stood in this depression, thus allowing him readily to reach with his shovel and spoon to the bottom of• the hole

The cost of digging the 82 holes was ·

Foreman ... . ‹	.$ 27.90
Laborers	95.25
Total	$123.15

The cost per hole was as follows ·

Foreman	$ .34
Laborers	1 16
Total , ...	$1.50

This high cost was due to the cinders as previously ex-plained The cost per cubic yard was

Foreman	$ .13
Laborers	.47
Total	.$ .60

The cost per lineal foot of double track for the hole digging was:

Foreman	$0 006
Men	. 0 020
Total	$0.026

Group II All of these holes, 88 in number, were 6 ft. deep. The poles were a little heavier than those in Group I, so the holes were 2½ ft. in diameter Each hole had 28 cu ft of

earth in it, thus making 91 cu. yds for all the holes This
was the first work done, and the men were not accustomed to
handling their long handled shovels.

The cost of digging the holes was:

Foreman ...   . $ 23.10
Laborers 83.10
_____
Total $106.20

This gave a cost per hole of the following ·

Foreman $0.27
Laborers 0 94
_____
Total $1.21

The cost per cubic yard was as follows:

Foreman .   . . ..' $0.25
Laborers 0.91
_____
Total $1.16

As there was 4,590 lin ft. of double track, the cost of digging holes per lineal foot was

Foreman $0.005
Laborers 0.018
_____
Total $0.023

Group III. This was span wire construction for single
track work, there being 17,160 lin. ft. of track. In all 320 pole
holes were dug. The holes averaged 3½ ft. in diameter, and
were from 6 ft. to 12 ft. deep. About 20 per cent. were deeper
than 6 ft., 10 per cent. being 8 or 9 ft deep, and 10 per cent
from 10 to 12 ft. deep. From the holes 510 cu. yds. of earth
were excavated, being 1 6 cu. yds as an average from each
hole. This large size hole was needed because the poles were
extremely large in diameter and heavy—much larger than
there were needed. This, too, was owing to the specifications,
which stated the smallest size in diameter that would be
accepted, but failed to state the largest dimensions that would
be taken Some of the poles furnished by the timber contractor were 3 ft. or more in diameter at the butt. This not

only added to the cost of digging the hole, but also to the
setting of the poles, and other details of the work   Special
eye bolts had to be made for a large number of the poles, and
some longer cross-arms had to be obtained to carry the feed
wires.

Ten of the 6-ft holes were dug in quicksand. These gave
some trouble, and additional expense   An expedient used in
digging these holes was to take a barrel and after knocking
the two heads out of it, to put it in the hole   Then all the
excavation was done from within the barrel, sinking it as the
hole was dug   Thus the sides of the hole were sheathed, and
by means of a hand pump the water was kept out, while the
digging was going on. If the quicksand occurs for a greater
depth than the height of one barrel, a second barrel should be
used on top of the first   This second one should be a little
larger than the first, so it will go down around the lower one.
The pole must be set in such holes as soon as they are dug

The total cost of digging the 320 holes was as follows:

Foreman	.\$ 77.80
Laborers	. 349 35
Total	.\$427.15

This gave the following cost per hole

Foreman	\$0.24
Laborers	1 09
Total	.\$1.33

The cost per cubic yard for the 510 cu yds. was.

Foreman	.. ....\$0 13
Laborers	0.68
Total	\$0 81

The cost per lineal foot of single track for the hole digging
was as follows:

Foreman	. ... \$0.005
Laborers	0.020
Total	\$0.025

Group IV. This was for 2,188 lin. ft of single track, a branch of the other line. The curves were sharper, hence the poles on the curves were closer than on the main line. The poles were all less than 20 ins. in diameter, so the holes were made 2 ft. in diameter. There were 64 poles, and only a few of the holes were deeper than 6 ft. About 19 cu. ft. were excavated from each hole, no underground braces being used This made 45 cu. yds. excavated from the 64 holes. The cost of digging the holes was:

Foreman	$ 9.00
Laborers	40.50
Total	$49 50

The cost per hole was as follows

Foreman	$0.14
Laborers	0.65
Total	$0.79

The following was the cost per cubic yard.

Foreman	$0 20
Laborers	0 90
Total	$1 10

The cost per lineal foot of single track for the digging was as follows

Foreman	$0.004
Laborers	0.018
Total	$0 022

Group V. This was side pole construction for single track, using a bracket made of pipe, on the pole There were 5,700 lin ft. of this construction, the poles being spaced about 80 ft. apart. Only a few of the holes were deeper than 6 ft., but as the poles were large ones the holes were 3½ ft in diameter. The bracing blocks were used for these poles An average of 36 cu ft was excavated from each hole, and, as there were 69 holes, 92 cu yds were excavated

The cost of digging the holes was ·

Foreman	..$12 00
Laborers	54 00
Total	$66 00

This gives a cost per hole of:

Foreman	.$0.18
Laborers	0 78
Total	$0 96

The cost per cubic yard was as follows.

Foreman	$0.13
Laborers ...	0.59
Total	..$0.72

The cost per lineal foot of single track was

Foreman	.$0 002
Laborers . ... ;.	0 010
Total	$0 012

A comparison of the cost of each group is shown in the following table, also the average cost for the entire job

	Total cost	Cost per hole	Cost per cu. yd	Cost per lin ft Double track	Single track.	No. poles.
Group I	$123 15	$1.50	$0.60	$0 026	.	82
Group II ..	106.10	1 21	1 16	0 023	. .	88
Group III .	427 15	1 33	0 81	..	$0.025	320
Group IV	49 50	0 79	1 10	.	0.022	64
Group V ..	66 00	0 96	0.72	. ..	0.012	69
Average	.....	1.24	0 82	0 0245	0.0235*	

*Bracket construction (Group V) left out of this average.

It will be noticed that the cost per hole varied directly with the size of the hole. Adding to the diameter and the depth increased the cost. The cost per cubic yard was high when the hole was small and low when the hole was large. The cost per lineal foot for span wire construction varied but little. Naturally the single track was about the same as double track

*Electrical Conduit Construction at Memphis, Tenn.— Underground conduits for electric wires are coming into such general use in our larger cities that information concerning the engineering of conduit work and the cost of installing conduits must needs be useful to owners and managers of electric lighting and other companies who may be called upon to remove poles from the streets in certain portions of their cities or towns and place the wires underground.

The preliminary engineering work includes the planning of the conduit system, with the street location of ducts and manholes; deciding on style and number of ducts to be used and methods of laying, locating manholes and service boxes, preparing the drawings, estimating the cost of the work, and getting matters in such shape that bids may be asked or the work carried out by day labor under the supervision and general direction of the company's engineer As the writer recently put in about 250,000 ft of duct at Memphis, Tenn., first planning the system, then making the estimates, and finally having all the work done by the day, this article will deal with work done in this way.

The city of Memphis had already a district $1\frac{1}{2}$ x $\frac{3}{4}$ miles served by underground conduits. The plant of the Memphis Consolidated Gas & Electric Co. is situated $\frac{3}{4}$-mile east of the eastern limit of this underground district, and it was decided to install a duct system to connect the plant with that district, so that the business portion of the city would have electric light and power by a complete underground system from the generating plant to the customers' premises. For this purpose there were required when the work began, 12 ducts for 2,300-volt alternating current feeders, 4 ducts for 500-volt direct current feeders, 2 ducts for three-phase alternating current feeders and 3 ducts on each run for distribution purposes, making 21 ducts if all were run on one street, or 24 ducts if runs were made on two streets

*Reprinted from an article by F A Proutt in Engineering News, April 14, 1904

The plant is situated on Beale St , some distance east from the south end of the old underground district   If all ducts were run down Beale St., it would have been necessary, on reaching the underground district at Hernando St , to run a number of cables to the north end of the district and put in enough extra ducts for future business.   In time the question of distributing the cables from Beale and Hernando Sts to their various terminals would have been a serious one, consequently it was decided to make two runs from the plant, the plant then being at one point of a triangle. as shown in Fig. 91 ; and then branching one of the feeders so that three sets of feeders are connected with the underground district about equally distant apart   This method requires 24 ducts for present requirements.

Fig 91 —Map of Underground Conduit System

As the city is growing very rapidly it was estimated that at some future time the load would be double that at present, but if it increased more than this it would be better to put in a duct line on another street   It was, therefore, decided to put 27 ducts on Beale St to De Soto St and branch at this point, continuing 18 on Beale St. to Hernando St , and running 18 to Monroe St   The two 18-duct runs make 36 in place of 27, but the object of putting 18 in each case in place of 12 and 15 was that the cost was very little more, and it gave a choice of taking 18 cables on either run, which might be a great consideration at some future time should heavy business develop in some particular locality   On the Adams St run it was decided to put 18 ducts, making a total of 45 ducts from the plant with present requirements of 24   Deciding on how many extra ducts to put in is a matter of personal

opinion and must be determined largely by the amount of
money that the electric company cares to spend.

After deciding on the number of ducts and the streets on
which they shall be run, comes the location of manholes and
service boxes. As a general rule manholes should be placed
at all street intersections and the engineer should, with two or
three assistants, walk over the proposed duct route. One of
these assistants should carry a bucket of black asphalt paint
and the other two a tape line. Beginning at one end of the
line, a manhole should be located and a spot painted on an

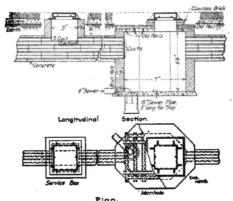

Fig. 92.—Standard Manhole and Service Box.

adjacent wall or fence to mark its center. For convenience in
distinguishing manholes from service boxes, a cross for the
former and a circle for the latter answer very well.

The men with tape line then start from the first manhole
mark, and the engineer should have a city map of some kind.
On this he locates the manholes, then the service boxes between the manholes, and marks the distances, so that when a
section of street has been gone over a rough map has been
made showing locations of manholes and service boxes and
distances between them. When construction begins the paint
marks give a ready means of finding locations.

Manholes should not be over 500 ft. apart, unless in exceptional cases; but may be 500 ft. without giving trouble in pulling the cables, provided, of course, that the run between manholes is reasonably straight. The service boxes should be located entirely with reference to building along the route and should be, as a rule, located so that the center of the box is on a line between two lots on one side of the street or the other. In other words, all boxes should be so located that the laterals from them may be run to the greatest number of buildings with the shortest laterals possible. Some boxes may be only 80 ft. apart and some may be 220 ft., but they will average about 150 ft. As already stated, the ducts were put in for running feeders to the old underground district, but in all underground work the distribution system along the route should be taken care of while the work is being done and this is the purpose of the service box. A manhole and service box are shown in Fig. 92. The service boxes, as shown, are 3 ft. square, and deep enough to take in only the three upper ducts of the conduit.

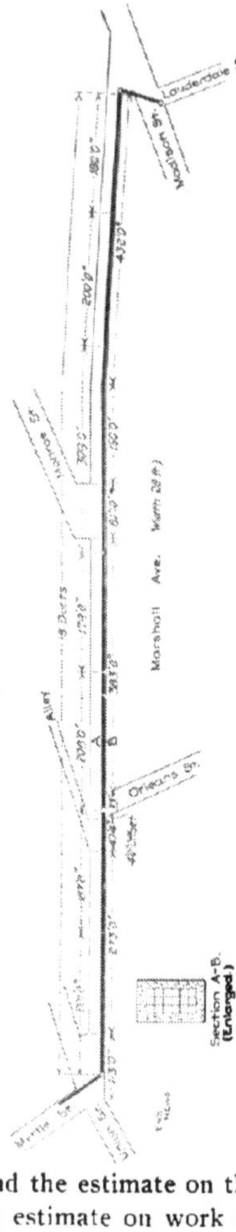

After deciding on the streets to be used, the number of ducts, and locations of manholes and service boxes as far as it is possible to locate the two latter from the surface of the street (for usually street paving covers a number of obstacles to conduit work), street maps may be got out, as shown in Fig. 93 (original scale 50 ft. to 1 in.) and the estimate on the cost of the work made up. Making an estimate on work of

Fig. 93.—Example of Street Map of Conduit System.

this kind is somewhat difficult, for the engineer does not know what he may find under the paving, or what kind of weather will prevail. These two features are very important factors in the cost of the work.

It is a good plan for the company's engineeer to take the City Engineer into his confidence, as either he or some of his employes know much about locations of fire cisterns, water and gas pipes, sewers, etc. In putting in the work mentioned in this article, we found that submitting all our plans to the City Engineer before beginning any work, benefited us, not only in the good feeling this created, but in the fund of information to be obtained from him and his assistants, and in the very timely suggestions he often had to offer for overcoming obstacles that might be encountered in carrying on this work. If you find out from the City Engineer which of his assistants has been longest connected with the sewer department, this individual can usually tell you not only how to drain the manholes but practically where all the pipes in the street are located.

The very first thing to be decided, however, in making up the estimate, is the style of duct to be used. There are several kinds on the market; wood, cement, paper, vitrified clay, etc. While all are no doubt good, we believe that the vitrified clay is the best. We also think that multi-duct section is better than single-duct section, and in our work used 6-duct section and 3-duct section only. We adopted the practice of entirely surrounding the conduit with concrete. As this is only a protection against picks of workmen in making other excavations, and also to prevent dirt from washing in at the joints, a really good concrete is not necessary, still it should not be too poor. We used Portland cement concrete, with crushed rock (washed gravel may be used with good results), making the mixture 1 part cement, 4 of sand and 8 of crushed rock. In any ordinary ground this makes a thoroughly satisfactory mixture. The thickness of concrete should be 3 ins all around the conduit. In the above mixture, the finished volume of concrete will be practically the same as the volume of stone, the sand and cement simply filling the interstices between the stones, and as Portland cement has practically

4 cu. ft to the barrel, the cost of concrete may be **readily** estimated.

The next thing will be the amount of dirt to be handled, which can be easily estimated. The price of handling will depend largely on the disposition to be made of the dirt, and the relative amount of backfilling as compared with total excavations   In laying multiple-duct conduits it is better to make a narrow ceep ditch and put the sections one on top of the other, than to have a shallow wide ditch. The time of laying will be much less in the former case, less dirt will have to be moved, less pavement will be torn up, and less concrete used. The top of the concrete should not be less than 30 ins. below surface of paving   This gives room for water and gas services, and puts a good cushion of earth above the ducts, so that there is no chance of very heavy vehicles crushing the duct material

In an 18-duct run made up of multiple ducts of six sections each, each section would measure about 9 x 13 ins , and laying three sections one above the other would require a ditch as follows   3 ins for lower concrete, 3 ins. for upper concrete, 27 ins for ducts, 30 ins for earth and paving above ducts, or a total depth of 5¼ ft. The width will be 13 ins for duct and 3 ins. on each side for concrete, making 19 ins. From this the amount of earth to be excavated can be estimated and also the amount to be backfilled.

In the work covered by this article, manholes are located about 500 ft. apart, and the service boxes have 3-duct openings, so that at any future time the secondary system may be changed from overhead to underground without any further duct work, except the running of lateral mains from the duct system to the premises of customers   The number of ducts provided for is approximately 75 per cent more than the number at present required, and should provide for all future requirements for an indefinite period. In fact, when the business done in the present underground district reaches the limit of the ducts provided, it would be desirable to run a third set of ducts from the plant to the business portion of the city down some other street   This is because it is undesirable to run more than 25 cables over any one route as the cost of distribution from the point where the feeders strike the main underground system would, after going a certain distance, be greater than the cost of running a new set of feeders over another street, and striking nearer the desired center of distribution As the city increases in population, of course, the amount of current used in the underground district will increase and the district will be enlarged from time to time, where pole lines have to be rebuilt, it will be a better investment to discontinue them and build an underground service.

The distances are about as follows   1. Power plant to 4th Alley and Adams St , 6,000 ft (18 ducts)   2   Power plant to Beale and De Soto Sts., 4,000 ft. (27 ducts)   3   De Soto St. and alley north of Monroe St to 4th Alley, 2,000 ft (18 ducts). 4. Beale St , from De Soto to Hernando Sts., 500 ft (18 ducts)   In all there will be about 13,150 ft of conduit, with 264,300 ft. of duct, and a summary of the cost of duct work will be as follows:

Trench and moving earth, at $1 per cu. yd (including

backfilling, tamping and hauling away surplus) ..	$ 4,550
Concreting, at $4 per cu yd . . .. .) ...	4,180
Duct material, at 6¼ cts. per duct-ft	16,519
Duct laying, ½ ct per duct-ft	1,321
40 manholes, $250 each (this allows $100 for the drain	
from manholes)	10,000
40 service boxes, $35 each . . .	1,400
Tearing out concrete in streets . ..	400
Replacing concrete	700
Repaving . . . . , .	500
City inspection of the work .	600
Engineering	2,000
Incidental expenses (lighting, watching, etc)	1,000
Tools, lumber, etc . ... •	1,000

Total $44,170	
Add 5 per cent for contingencies.	2,208

Total cost of duct work $46,378

The total estimated cost of work was $46,378, and as the work was done by the day we will next take up the method of doing it and compare the actual cost of the different ma-

terials with the estimated cost   In this way we can see the
errors made in estimating and bring out especially the fact
that in estimating work of this kind, too much care cannot be
taken in going into the special features of the work, such as
crossing streams and subways, and making connections at the
station end.   Crossing streams of water is very expensive, as
a special structure has often to be built for this work, an
example of which is described later.   In laying out a duct
system it is well to avoid as far as possible all streets having
concrete and brick or asphalt pavements, streets passing over
railway tracks or streams of water, and streets having car
tracks.   Of course some of each must be encountered, but
often parallel street or alleys will answer for main lines of
duct systems at a great saving in cost of construction

After making up the estimate on the work and having it
passed by the proper authorities, the next thing to consider is
whether the work shall be put in by contract or day work.
The cost of engineering on the work during construction will
be practically the same (as far as the company is concerned)
in either case   Cost of inspection will be more for the company if work is done by contract, as inspectors will have to
be employed to see that contractors are complying with
specifications, while if work is done by the day the foremen
take the place of the inspectors and are actually pushing the
work along   Materials and labor can, as a rule, be purchased
as cheaply by the company as by a contractor, but if a company cannot get the proper men to handle the work, it should
by all means let the work by contract, as day work would be
a losing proposition.   If such men can be had, the chances are
that the company can do the work as cheaply as a contractor
and save the contractor's profits.   As a rule, however, contract work will be the cheaper method.   In our case, the
writer had had a somewhat extensive experience in conduit
work and had several men who had been employed in this
class of work for several years, so the proper thing seemed to
be to carry out the work by the day, and this plan was pur-
sued.   All the items of cost quoted hereafter are exact, and
obtained from practical experience with the work.

In carrying on the work the first thing to have is a good
organization of labor   There should be   1, a general fore-

man; 2, a foreman of pipe layers; 3, a foreman of concrete mixing gang; 4, a foreman in charge of digging for manholes and service boxes; 5, a foreman in charge of backfilling and hauling away dirt. Also, a timekeeper; this position is a very important one, and the man filling it should be young, well educated and thoroughly reliable.

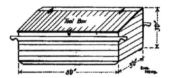

Fig. 94.—Portable Tool Box.

The foreman should not be an engineer, but rather a man who has worked a gang laying sewer, water or gas pipe, or had experience in ditching, as this man must take the lead and keep the trench opened up. We were fortunate enough to obtain a man of this kind at $18 per week. We have found that a good foreman always has a big following of laborers who will go on the work with him, provided, of course, the

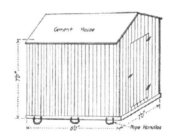

Fig. 95.—Portable Cement House.

work will last several months. This foreman was hired a month before work began, and was kept busy with one or two laborers building boxes in which to mix mortar for the brick masons, building platforms on which to dump concrete, making gages for the ditchers (which are simply pieces of lath cut to the width of the trench), making small platforms to put across the trench at people s gates, and wide bridges to put across the trench at street intersections All these must be got ready before work is begun

Then an outfit of tools must be made up. This, in our case, consisted of the following

  2 dozen wheelbarrows
  7 dozen round point shovels
  1 dozen square point shovels.
  7 dozen picks .
  30 iron tamping bars
  36 red lanterns
  2 axes.
  6 or 8 balls of cotton cord.

  25 lbs 20-penny nails.
  2 claw hammers
  3 hand saws
  1 hatchet
  1 bundle oakum
  2 "dromedary" concrete mixers
  4 or 5 crow bars
  4 chisel bars 3 ft
  6 sledge hammers
  2,000 ft common lumber, 1 x 6 ins , 14 ft.

We had four large portable tool boxes, made as shown in Fig. 94, and a small portable cement house, Fig 95 The tools also included 24 galvanized pails, and 50 ft of 2½-in. hose with a 1-in faucet in the end.

While the foreman was making up the platforms, contracts were made for stone, sand, cement, water, etc The ducts had, of course, been ordered some time previous, or in fact as soon as it was decided to put in the work The following letter was sent out to each of several manufacturers:

"We are now in the market for 45,000 ft. of 6-duct section, making 270,000 duct-ft , and 4,666 ft of 3-duct section, making 14,000 duct-ft., or 284,000 duct-ft of underground conduit material. In addition to this we will require 200 pieces of 6-duct section 6 ins. long , 200 pieces 12 ins. long, and 200 pieces 18 ins. long. These pieces are for turning curves and finishing out at manholes.

"We will require the necessary dowel pins to use in lining up the ducts. We also require that the 284,000 duct-ft of material be made up in 3-ft lengths

"Kindly quote us price as soon as possible on this material delivered f o. b cars Memphis, your company to stand all breakage that occurs in transit. The material must be thoroughly vitrified and glazed, and be entirely free of scales or projections on the inside of the ducts, and all crooked pieces will not be accepted. In other words, we want to purchase first-class material."

It will be noted that the letter calls for 284,000 duct-ft in place of 264,300 as estimated, the excess being intended to cover breakages and also for some short lateral runs that it was thought it might be advisable to put in with the balance of the work Even should some duct material be left over, it would be good stock, not suffering from exposure to weather even if carried on hand for a year or two

It will be noted also that ducts were to be delivered f o. b. Memphis, and all crooked, broken or badly glazed pieces rejected When the contract for ducts was finally placed (at 5½ cts. per duct-ft) and the material began to arrive, it was found that each car would contain from one to a dozen pieces, out of which corners would be broken. The engineer then agreed to accept all such broken pieces at half the price of a sound piece That is a 6-duct section 3 ft long would contain 18 duct-ft and be worth 99 cts , but if a corner was broken off the section, it would be accepted at 49½ cts All such damaged pieces were used in the top run of ducts in the trench and a piece of sheet zinc placed over the hole caused by the corner being broken off. Duct and zinc were all finally covered with concrete This method of accepting damaged pieces was considered satisfactory by all parties concerned

All 6-duct sections were supposed to be 3 ft. long and all 3-duct sections, 2 ft long. Owing to uneven shrinkage in the clay, however, the manufacturers are unable to make the material run exactly to length, some pieces would come 34 ins long, some 35 ins and some 36 ins. As each car arrived it was unloaded, each piece examined and gaged, and shortage noted The shipper was then notified of value of shortage and breakage and he issued a credit bill covering the amount.

These credits run all the way from $1 to $10.50 for shortage, and from 50 cts to $20 per car for breakage, so that they were well worth considering. The 3-duct sections were bought 2 ft. long in place of 3 ft , as the manufacturers claimed they could turn out much straighter material in 3-duct sections of the shorter length; as the price per duct-ft. was the same in either case, we conceded the point

The engineer should not reject crooked pieces, but rather put them in a class by themselves, as they will be found most useful in making curves where it is necessary to run the duct line over or under obstacles that may be encountered in the trench. There is, however, one class of duct that should be rejected always, and that is the section which measures 9 x 13 ins. at one end and 10 x 14 ins. at the other ⁻If accepted and hauled to the ditch to be laid, much trouble will result from attempting to make its big end coincide with the small end of a neighboring section

The specifications above quoted will be found entirely satisfactory to the purchaser, as it gives him the authority to reject unfit material and the shipper stands breakage in transit. In all such transactions the engineer should be fair minded and be willing to pay a fair price for all material that can be utilized, thus making the shipper feel that he is at least being honestly dealt with

It will be noted that the duct specifications call for a certain number of short pieces, 6, 12 and 18 ins. long. Agents selling ducts will frequently state that their ducts can be cut like cheese But as short sections can be bought at the same price per duct-ft as long sections, it pays infinitely better to buy a few short lengths than to find out from experience that cutting a vitrified clay duct is much the same as cutting a glass lamp chimney with a pair of shears. Following up the idea of buying pieces of any desired length, when all our duct laying had been completed, except evening up the ends in manholes, we ordered a lot of short sections, 1, 2 and 3 ins. long to do this So that from beginning to end we decided to let the manufacturer do all cutting for us, and we simply butted the ends together and put in the dowel pins.

In work of this kind, all material should be purchased to be delivered right on the work if possible We bought 1½-in.

crushed stone (with the dust not sifted out), delivered on the
work, at 10 cts. per 100 lbs , or from $2.50 to $3 per cu yd ,
there being a difference in the weight of different limestones
per cu. yd. Sand was bought in the same way at $1 25 per cu
yd. and "Diamond" Portland cement at $2 10 per bbl deliv-
ered.   Cast-iron tops for manholes and service boxes were
bought at $1 90 per 100 lbs., each top weighing 1,150 lbs.
Hard bricks delivered on the work cost us $7 to $7 50 per 1,000
and an arrangement was made with a firm of brick contractors
to furnish us all the masons and laborers we needed at $6 and
$2 per day, respectively. Teams were engaged at $4 per day
for two horses and driver, and $3 per day for one horse. cart
and driver   Two or three private carts belonging to colored
citizens were hired at $2 50 per day, including a driver. A
contract was made with the water company to allow the use
of all the water required on the work for $50, and then per-
mission had to be obtained from the Fire Department to
attach hose to the fire hydrants as these hydrants belong to
the city

After all arrangements of this kind had been made, the
other foremen were employed and work was begun   For a
timekeeper we engaged a young man who had worked for us
a year and then entered Purdue University to take an electrical engineering course   He was then on his vacation, the
work commencing July 6, 1903   The foreman of concrete
mixers was also a former employe, and a fellow student of the
timekeeper   The wages of these men were $2 and $2 25 per
day, respectively   The foreman who looked after manhole
and service box excavations received $2 per day, and the same
was paid to a foreman who looked after hauling dirt, while
one of our regular men at $16 50 per week saw that conduit
material was always on the ground and kept up with little
details of all kinds.

Everything being ready. a Monday morning was chosen for
the start. The general foreman lined up his men, and the
timekeeper took their names. The wagon loaded up the tool
boxes and placed them along the proposed trench line, and the
cement house was placed at a point about 300 ft. from the
starting of the trench   The sand, cement and crushed rock
men were notified to deliver material, and work was begun.

As soon as the trench was well started, a manhole excavation
was commenced, and when this was done the brick masons
began work. Duct sections were hauled out from the storage
yard (which was located on a railway siding and rented for
this purpose at $10 per month) on two-horse platform wagons,
two of them being kept busy all the time The duct was piled
along beside the trench in a continuous line, at such a distance
from it as would leave room for a wheelbarrow to pass between the trench and the ducts, with openings about 50 ft
apart in the pile of ducts to allow the wheelbarrows to pass
through.

The mixer was of the "dromedary" type, in which the concrete is mixed during transportation. It held about $\frac{5}{8}$-cu. yd
and was charged as follows. A little sand is first put in, then
$1\frac{1}{4}$ sacks of cement (which was all delivered in sacks), then
more sand, then the stone A test mixture was first made of
1 cement, 4 sand, and 8 stone After this, the sand was gaged
by a mark on the mixer, the cement by the bag, and stone
enough added to fill the mixer. The door was then closed and
the mixer driven about 150 ft. to the water plug and water
enough put in to make a good wet concrete This amount of
water was from 6 to 8 pails, depending on the amount of dust
in the stone. It was then driven to the dumping place and
dumped at these places planks being located close to the trench
and close to where ducts were being laid.

The dumping boards were platforms 6 x 12 ft , made of two
thicknesses of 1-in. pine, one thickness laid lengthwise and
one crosswise At each outside edge of the platform was a
piece of timber 2 x 4 ins , and rope handles, so that the platform could be picked up and carried along as the work moved
ahead Two platforms were placed end to end, making a
platform 24 ft. long, which gave ample room to dump material. On unpaved streets platforms are very essential for
good work. The mixers required two mules each and cost
up to $200 per mixer, f o b. Washington. They are espe-
cially suited for conduit work, saving a great deal of labor in
wheeling by barrows for long distances.

The ditchers worked close together in the trench A line
was stretched 4 ft from the curb as a rule, and the trench run

outside this line, each ditcher having a gage 19 ins long (the width of the trench) to work by.

In laying ducts, the following method was followed . First, the 3-in. concrete bottom was put in; then the boss duct man and his helper got in the ditch and laid the lower run. Two men on the bank would hand down the sections by means of a rope run through one of the holes. As soon as the first runs had been started a few lengths, the second run would begin and so with the third and fourth and fifth, taking four men for each run or layer. The pipe used had dowel pin holes on the outside or around the periphery of the duct, which is the most convenient place for them as far as the duct layers are concerned. In a 6-duct section there were six dowel holes on each end. We only used 3 pins, however, in each end, one at each side and one on top.

The joint was made as follows. A piece of cheap domestic canvas 5 ins. wide and 5 ft long was laid on the bottom of the ditch before the duct was put in position, then when the duct sections were in place there would be a piece lying directly under the joint. A boy followed each set of layers and wrapped the canvas up around the joint, overlapping the end and painting the lap with black asphaltum. This makes a first-class joint, as the canvas is only to serve the purpose of keeping the concrete out of ducts, and the cheaper this purpose can be accomplished, the better. As about 30,000 of these pieces of canvas were used on the work, a method had to be devised for cutting them. The canvas was purchased in bolts, costing 5 cts. per yd. A rough table was made with a saw-cut in it 5 ins. from one edge, and at this edge was a strip against which to push the bolt of cloth. A large butcher knife was then run through the saw-cut and cloth, cutting off a piece 5 ins. wide and the length of the bolt. This piece was wound on a reel whose circumference was 5 ft. and a cut through the cloth at the circumference made pieces 5 ft. long. This method was original, simple and thoroughly satisfactory.

In an 18-duct run the method of opening three top ducts into the service box was to put in a piece of 3-duct section at the box in place of 6-duct section. This made the lower three ducts pass through and left the upper three open.

The only skilled labor employed was for laying brick. The brick masons would lay up the walls of the manholes to the proper height, then move to the next hole. The gang excavating manholes would then return to the hole left by the brick masons and put up a temporary wood ceiling laying on it (and projecting over the walls) some pieces of old rail, they then put a box where the cover was to be and left it. The concrete men would then put on 10 ins of concrete and the hole was complete, ready for the cast-iron cover. This concrete reinforced by old rails makes a first-class top. The rails cost about $5 for each manhole, 5 x 7 ft , and the concrete about the same amount. The manholes, Fig. 92, are not square but octagonal in shape

As it is the intention to use paper insulated cables almost entirely in these ducts, and as from past experience we have found that paper insulation will not stand sharp bends like rubber covered cables, we decided to make the manholes of such shape that sharp bends could not be made in the cables. In building manholes it is well to have a standard size, but this standard cannot always be adhered to In other words, manholes must be made to suit conditions and almost any shape will do, but by all means avoid making them too small A manhole should not be less than 5 x 7 ft. inside, and every manhole should be drained We had one case where a manhole drain cost $300, but the average cost was less than $100 We would, however, have put in the drains had they cost $300 each.

In carrying on this work is is well to remember that the main point of consideration is laying ducts. Therefore let the instructions to foremen morning, noon and night be to "lay ducts." Another thing to remember on quitting at night is that next day it may be raining, therefore, prepare for the morrow Do not put conduit in 400 or 500 ft of trench and leave it with no concrete around it Every bit of pipe laid during the day should be covered with concrete before it is left at night. Following up this idea we had a number of times to work concrete men until 8 p m to get the work covered For this overtime we paid them time and a half The consequence was that we never had to pull out any work in the morning, and we lost less than $100 during the whole work on account of bad weather .

Another thing to keep in mind is that seven or eight men can excavate and build manholes, but it requires 75 or 100 men to trench and lay ducts; therefore, do not excavate for manholes faster than the masons can build them. Dig the trench straight through where the manhole is to be, lay ducts up to it on one side, then leave a space for the manhole and start laying ducts again on the other side. Always start all the duct runs even; that is, if there are four tiers of ducts, see that in starting, the ends all even up so that they will be flush with the manhole wall when it is built. But in ending the run at the next manhole opening, do not waste time trying to get the ends even, get them within 6 ins. or so and let them stand Have the masons, in building around these uneven ends, leave the hole slack so that short pieces may be

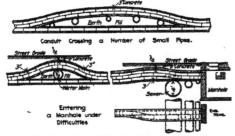

Fig 96 —Examples of Difficult Work at Obstructions.

inserted after all other work has been cleared up. Do not let masons do any duct fitting at all. A couple of men can fill in short pieces wherever needed in a few days at the windup of the work, while they would delay all the pipe layers, bank men and concrete men in trying to do so when the whole work is being carried on

It would be well to have ducts run in perfectly straight lines and without dips or pockets, but this in practice cannot be done. Perhaps the very first day the engineer will be confronted by the general foreman with the information that a 24-in. water main crosses the trench and the top of the main is only 6 ins. below the grade of the street. The engineer cannot sit down and make elaborate calculations as to the evil results of a dip in the duct line. While he is doing that, men are

standing idle. He must do the best thing that can be done
under the circumstances. If running an 18-duct section, put
12 ducts over the pipe and 6 under, and put 6 ins. of concrete
on top of the ducts in place of 3 ins. Also arrange the ducts
as shown in Fig. 96 to save concrete. If the earth is well
tamped it will not settle after the concrete has set. Again,
you may strike a lot of pipes, say 4 ft. from the surface and
right close to a proposed manhole. In our case we had the
following problem: A large brick culvert crossed the ditch
about 4 ft. from the surface, also two sewers and a water
pipe. Two rows of the ducts were carried over the pipes, etc.,
and after crossing the obstructions, put back in the regular
form of run, three in a tier. Fig. 96 shows work of this kind.

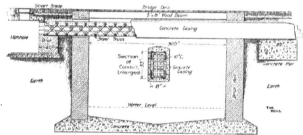

Fig. 97.—Method of Carrying Duct Over Bayou.

In another case, Fig. 97, a bayou had to be crossed under a
bridge. This bridge was an old one and liable to be pulled
down and replaced by a new one, so the duct line must be
put over the bayou in such a way that the removal of the
bridge would not interfere with the ducts. The method
adopted was as shown: Four 10-in. channels 50 ft. long were
purchased and made up into a truss with side lattice bars. A
manhole was built at one side of the bridge and a pier built
at one end of the manhole, and as part of it, the manhole
foundation being 12 ins. of concrete reinforced with old rails.
A pier of concrete 6 x 8 x 4 ft. thick was built on the other side
of the bridge and the truss rested on these two piers, entirely
independent of the bridge structure. The ducts were then
laid through the truss and ducts and truss enclosed in concrete, making practically a reinforced concrete beam. The

object of enclosing the truss in concrete was to prevent the steel from rusting.

In cases where we had about 20 sewer pipes crossing the ditch in 200 ft., the same means were employed in running the ducts as with the large water main. That is, one run of ducts was put under the sewers and covered on all sides with concrete, then earth tamped into the top of the sewer pipes, then a new concrete bottom put in 3 ins. thick and the balance of ducts put in and concrete around.

It is advisable to have a report each night of the trench-feet and duct-feet put in for the day At the end of each week, when the payroll is made up, the duct-feet laid for the week should also be made up and the price of labor per duct-foot calculated. The greatest amount of work done by us in any one day was 15,156 duct-feet in 703 ft. of trench. All our trenches were 19 ins. wide, and when 18 ducts were put in the depth was 5¼ ft , while when 27 ducts were put in, the depth was 6¼ ft The 27-ducts run was made up of 4 multiples of 6 each and one multiple of 3, making 5 sections of ducts in a tier.

Our payroll on the work for all purposes for the 18 weeks was from $36 to $1,279, and with $350 for preliminary work, putting in sewer traps, evening up ends of duct lines in manholes, etc., the total cost for all labor was $11,525. Of the amount, $1,424 was for labor on excavation, building manholes and service boxes, $2,356 for labor on sewer work, and $7,745 for trenching, mixing concrete, laying ducts, backfilling and hauling away surplus dirt. As the amount of duct laid was 251,991 duct-ft., the cost for labor was 3 07 cts. per duct-ft. The total cost of cement used was $2,196, or practically 1,046 barrels. Of this amount there was used for brickwork in manholes, 160 barrels ($336), for brickwork in service boxes, 12 barrels ($25 20), and for jointing drain pipe, 5 barrels ($10.50) This leaves $1,824 as the cost of cement used in concrete.

The total amount of sand used cost $776 54 for 635 cu yds., or an average cost of $1.22 per yd Of this sand, 74 yds were used for manhole and service-box brickwork, leaving 561 yds. for concrete work, the cost of which was $684.42. The total amount of broken stone used was 2,713,500 lbs., costing

$2,713.50, so that the total cost of all concrete work was $1,824 for cement, $684.42 for sand, and $2,713 50 for stone, making $5,221.92 for practically 1,000 cu yds. of concrete, or $5.22 per cu. yd.

Of the concrete 118 yds. were used for manhole bottoms and tops and service-box bottoms. The cost of this was $615.96, leaving $4,605.96 as the cost of concrete used around conduits, or a cost of 1 83 cts. per duct-ft The total number of bricks used for building manholes and service boxes was 118,000, which cost $871. There were 32 manholes and 48 service boxes built, manholes averaging 3,200 bricks each, and service boxes 325 bricks each. Service boxes cost complete $30 15 each, or $1,447 for 48 boxes. The average cost of manholes was $115, without sewer, and the average cost per sewer was $76 for labor and $10 for sewer pipe, making $86 The average cost of a complete manhole was thus $201. The average length of each sewer was 170 ft , 6-in. pipe being used, and the total amount paid for sewer pipe being $309 50 Only 31 sewers were run, as one manhole was built beside an old manhole and the old drain sufficed for both.

The total cost for tools of all kinds and keeping same in repair was practically $800 The cost of city inspection was $195 The cost of engineering was about $1,000. The amount paid the city for repairing streets was $1,000 The cost of various odds and ends, such as cotton cloth for covering joints, asphaltum for painting same, dowel pins for keeping ducts in alignment, unloading cars and various other incidentals was $2,230 71 The steel truss for crossing the Bayou Gayoso cost $700, and the sum of $600 was paid for new sidewalks where duct lines ran under sidewalk, making a total cost of $41,234 56 for all the work done, as shown by our books. A summary of the work as completed shows the following:

Length of Trench. Ft.	No. of Ducts.	Length of Duct. Ft.
216.2	60	12,975
3,415.0	27	92,205
7,226.5	18	137,277
324 0	24	7,776
293.0	6	1,758
11,474 7 -		251,991

The estimated amount of duct-ft. to be laid was 264,300, while the actual amount laid was only 251,991 duct-ft. The difference was a short run that was not put in, owing to the city having laid an asphalt pavement on the desired street, and it was thought advisable to leave out this small run until such time as its construction would be required.

The total amount of duct material bought, however, cost $15,564, which at 5½ cts. per ft., would represent 282,987 ft After completing the work we had in stock 28,506 duct-ft. of unbroken material or material undamaged in any way. This added to the amount put in accounts for 280,497 duct-ft. and the difference of 2,490 ft represents the loss by breakage, this loss being less than 1 per cent of the total amount purchased The loss through breakage can only be kept so low by buying the ducts to be delivered f. o. b at the place where they will be used, and arranging for payment for damaged sections, as stated earlier in this article

Summing up the total results of our experience in doing our own construction, we find as follows ·

Estimated Cost of Work.		Actual Cost of Work.	
Trenching	$ 4,550	Labor on ducts	$ 7,745
Concrete ...	4,180	Concrete for ducts...	4,606
Duct material	16,518	48 service boxes ...	1,447
Duct laying	1,321	32 manholes	3,680
40 manholes	10,000	31 manhole drains	2,666
40 service boxes	1,400	Duct material. ...	15,564
Tearing out concrete	400	Tools	800
Replacing concrete in		City inspection	195
streets	700	Repaving streets ...	1,000
Repaving	500	Steel truss over bayou	700
City inspection	600	New sidewalks..	600
Engineering .	1,000	Incidentals ..	2,231
Incidentals	1,000		
Tools, lumber, etc	1,000	Total	$41,234
Contingencies, 5%	2,208		
Total	$46,378		

In regard to the incidentals, $2,231 seems a large amount
But it cost about $7.50 to unload and inspect a car of ducts
and there were not less than 50 cars, there were used over
40,000 dowel pins at ½-ct. each, and about five barrels of
black asphaltum paint at about $30 per barrel; we also paid
$50 for city water and about $100 to plumbers for mending
broken water pipes (where in trenching the men would occasionally drive a pick through the lead service pipe). It will
be seen, therefore, that the amount would soon be made up, as
the items enumerated are only a few of the many items em-
braced in this account.

Leaving out the cost of manholes, service boxes and manhole drains, it will be noticed that the cost per duct-ft. of the
work complete was $33,441.56 divided by 251,991 duct-ft., or
13 27 cts. Had we put in the entire number of duct-feet estimated and also the number of manholes and services estimated, our total cost for ducts would have been 264,300 ×
13.27 or $35,072 for ducts, $1,206 for service boxes, and $8,040
for manholes, making a total of $44,318, plus $1,000 per engineering, which item has not yet been charged in the account.
Thus at the prices paid, had the original estimate been adhered to exactly, the cost would have been $45,318 and the
estimate $46,378.

One reason for changing the number of manholes was that
in certain locations before the street was opened, it appeared
as if two manholes would be required, one on each side of a
culvert, for instance, while on opening the street one manhole would be found sufficient, with perhaps an extra service
box.

One item not estimated at all was the steel truss over Bayou
Gayoso. This was an oversight, but (fortunately) enough
manholes were left out to more than pay for its construction.
Another item left out was the iron pipe required from the
switchboard floor at the power plant to the first manhole.
The cost of this will be about $800, but will not have to be
considered until the cables are to be installed. We have.
however, a large item of credit that has also not been considered in the foregoing figures. There is 28,506 duct-ft. of new
duct material in stock, the value of which is $1,567, and this

credit will almost balance the engineering expenses which have not yet been charged up, and also the cost of running in the station ends of iron pipe, which were not estimated on

In conclusion, I would say that throughout the entire .work we were exceedingly fortunate as to weather, labor, and material to be excavated, and these are the three items which may either make or break a contractor If all are in his favor, he will come out ahead, while if all are against him, he is almost sure in work of this kind to come out in the hole We have not enough outside data on conduit work to know whether our costs are either abnormally small or abnormally large, but we do know the figures given are absolutely correct and therefore offer them to the readers of the "Engineering News" for consideration

Cost of Electrical Conduits, Baltimore, Md.—In 1898 the electrical commission of Baltimore, Md., was organized to build a conduit system for the city, and thus compel all companies using the streets for poles to carry their wires, to take down these poles and place the wires underground Prior to this several short lines of conduit had been laid in different sections of the city by some of the telephone and electric light companies, but the real work of building conduits began in 1898

By law the electrical commission consists of the mayor, the city register and the president of the board of fire commissioners. Mr Chas E Phelps, Jr., was appointed chief engineer, and has continued in this position, designing and building a system that to date has cost nearly $2,000,000 Through the kindness of Mr Phelps, and from his reports as chief engineer, we are able to give the cost of all work done from 1898 to 1905, inclusive

All the construction work has been done by day labor, but very careful cost records have been kept and the engineering general expenses have been recorded separately from the cost of construction The organization of the department is shown by Fig 98, which is a chart that is self explanatory The materials, except those purchased in small amounts, are all bought by competitive bidding

Chief Engineer. Assistant Engineer			
Plans and Data.	Chief Draughtsmen.	Draughtsmen.	Tracers. / Assistant Linesmen.
Construction.	General Superintendent	General Foreman, Assistant Superintendent, Material Man, Foreman Teams and Storey'ds, Gang Boss Distribution	Linesmen; Foreman {Gang Bosses}
Operating and Maintenance, Cable Inspection.	Chief Cable Inspector	Assistant Chief Inspector	Foremen of Inspection. Gang Boss Rodding; Inspectors, Assistant Inspectors
District Inspection.	Chief Inspector	Inspector Overhead Lines, Inspector Underground Lines	
Paymaster and Records.	Paymaster	Assistant to Paymaster, Paymaster's Clerk	
Office and Records.	Chief Clerk.	Bookkeeper, Stenographer, File Clerk, Office Clerk	

Fig 98 —Organization Chart

The construction work commenced March 1, 1899, the five months previous to that date being consumed in preparing plans and details of the system The city conduit system, as a whole, is divided into two general parts, first, the trunk conduits, which are built for the purpose of carrying trunk lines and feeders, whether for telephone, telegraph, electric light, street railway or other service, located generally in thoroughfares, feeding different sections of the city. These trunk lines are laid out to serve these several territories by the most direct and feasible route Second, as the system was originally designed, the central or congested district of the city was laid out to be served entirely underground, with underground connections, in each separate building Extensions to this territory have been necessary Figure 99 shows the service and distributing conduits on a section of a single street.

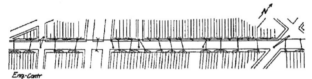

Fig 99—Service and Distribution Conduits on a Single Street

A high standard of work has been aimed at throughout the construction Vitrified terra cotta conduit has been used in all conduit lines This conduit is enveloped in concrete, which for the year 1899 and a part of 1900, was entirely of Rosendale cement For the remaining period Portland cement has been used

In 1899 the uniform thickness of this enveloping coat of concrete was 3 ins , except in a few cases where the bottom was made 4 ins Since then the thickness has been increased, the sides and top being 4 ins , while the bottom has been from 4 to 6 ins. In all soft ground the bottom concrete has been reinforced with steel rods The mixture for this work has been generally 1-3-6. The mixing has been done by hand only to a limited degree, the greater part of it being done with a dromedary mixer drawn by a horse. The concrete is dumped on the ground by the mixer alongside the trench, and shoveled into place by the men laying the conduit. No forms are needed for this concrete under ordinary circumstances.

At the very beginning of the work, the joints where the conduits knitted together were wrapped with burlap 6 ins. wide, saturated in liquid asphaltum compound. The difficulty in making air and gas tight joints has always been recognized, and while continued efforts are made to secure this, it is realized that so far as gas is concerned, the best result obtainable is to minimize its entrance into the system.

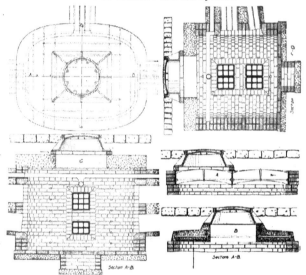

Fig. 100.—Standard Plan of Brick Manhole.

Experiments along this line carried on during the year 1899 resulted in a composition of North Carolina pitch tar, refined asphalt and wax tailings, which has proven thoroughly serviceable. The use of burlap was entirely discontinued and cheesecloth substituted, the method of applying the joint being to paint the end of the conduit pieces with the hot compound where the wrapper is to be applied; the wrappers are rolled up and saturated in the hot compound and wrapped on while hot This joint is expensive, but it is believed that the results have justified its use.

In the construction of all lines of conduit, two or three fiber pipes, depending upon the importance of the line, are laid in the layer of top concrete for the purpose of providing some ready means for arc lights or similar connections from a point of the line remote from a manhole without building an extra manhole or breaking the line of vitrified pipe.

Manholes on trunk lines are all constructed of large size A small conduit line, say of twelve ducts, would have a manhole, elliptical in plan, of a minimum of 5 x 8 ft., and of a suitable depth, depending upon the grade of the conduit, the minimum being 6 ft The size of the manholes increases with the size of the line up to a plan section of 7 x 14 ft , which

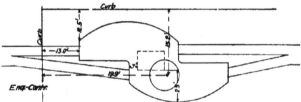

Fig 101 —Diagram of Concrete Manhole

would be suitable for the largest line built, namely à line of 81 ducts. Fig. 100 shows a standard plan of a brick manhole, with various styles of roof forms used. Similar manholes have been built of concrete

On many of the important lines of conduit where it is possible for the operation of workmen in the streets to result in damage to the manholes, it has been the practice to construct the manholes of standard form, but of larger proportionate width, building one-half of the manhole a distance in advance of the other half along the line of conduit, so that lateral connections may be made from either half of the manhole either way without the necessity of crossing cables. The diagram of such a manhole built in concrete is shown by Fig. 101. In building manholes it has been the practice to clear all obstructions so that no pipes or other obstruc-

tions pass through the manholes. Thus nothing appears in
the manholes except the cables for which they are built.

For concrete manholes for junction boxes and for distribution boxes, sectional wooden forms are made in a substantial
manner, and these forms are used over and over again. In
this manner the cost of forms has not been material.

In the central districts of the city it has been necessary to
under drain, during construction, practically all lines of con-

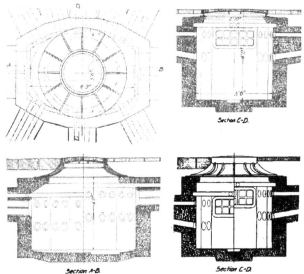

Fig. 102.—Distribution Boxes.

duit, and the presence of tide water and the poor condition
of small house drains in the street has necessitated making
special provisions. There being no system of public sewers,
and the storm water drains being on such shallow grades, it
has rarely been possible to drain manholes by gravity. All
manholes in the central district are drained by means of
ejectors, operated by water pressure from the city mains.
The practice followed has been to construct a sump in the

center of the floor in each manhole of sufficient size to contain a valve operated by a float which controls the supply of water into the ejector This is necessary to lift the water to a grade where it can flow by gravity.

The distributing system consists uniformly of a 10-duct laid 2 ducts deep and 5 ducts wide, encased in 4 ins. of Portland cement concrete, the earth covering being almost uniformly 19 ins.; the conduit line opening at intervals into

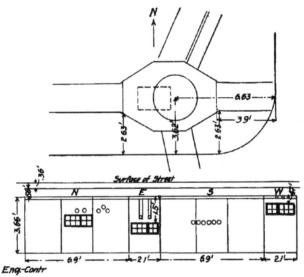

Fig 103 —Junction Boxes

service boxes which, when in sidewalks, are of terra cotta, circular in form and 36 ins. in diameter, having walls 2½ ins. thick, and a cast iron frame 5 ins in depth to allow for sidewalk paving

The main conduits, or trunk lines are laid in the streets or alleys, but many of the distributing ducts are laid under the sidewalks, and frequently on both sides of the street. The house connections are of fiber pipe, each connection consisting of two 2-in and two 3-in pipes, in some of the original work 1½-in pipes were used for service connections, but the increase in size of service cables made it unwise to continue the use of this pipe.

Distribution boxes, see Fig 102, in the street proper, are built of brick or concrete, elliptical in form. These boxes have a frame casting similar to that used on manholes, but smaller and lighter.

At the intersections of distributing lines, junction boxes are built of concrete or brick, see Fig 103 On distribution and junction boxes of all types, the frame casting is set directly on the walls, no special roof construction being required

The digging of the trenches is all done by hand The trenches for the trunk line vary in width and depth. In depth they run from 3 to 12 ft deep, being on an average of about 6 ft. In width they run from 2 ft to 4 ft. For the distributing conduits the trenches are all of the same depth, about 3 ft, and they are about 2 ft wide In the cost of excavation are included labor (both men and teams), timbering, drainage, clearing away obstructions, backfilling, in fact all the cost of excavating from tearing up the paving to turning the ditch over to the pavers In many sections of the city, trenches 5 ft. or less in depth need but little timbering.

The foregoing describes the general conditions of the work and illustrates the method and plans used A careful and well devised system of unit cost keeping is employed and from these records the following costs for 7 years of work have been compiled. In considering them the organization of forces and the cost keeping system must be explained.

The system followed in organizing the work has been to divide it into two principal parts First, the part known as "General Expenses and Monthly Payroll," and, second, "Construction Costs and Weekly Payroll" Under the latter is charged all costs and expenses which would be borne by the contractor were the work done under contract; under the former heading is charged all items of salaries and expenses which would represent the cost to the city of administering the work and doing the necessary engineering were it done under contract.

Referring to Fig 98, showing the organization chart, the expenses of organization and monthly expenses include the headings of "Plans and Data" and "Office and Records" "Construction" and "Paymaster and Records" go to make up the construction cost, with the addition of materials The items of "Operating and Maintenance," "Cable Inspection" and "District Inspection," are separate accounts that do not enter into the cost of construction

All foremen and regular employes are charged under their specific subdivisions as governed by the plan of the organization Watchmen and similar expenses in construction which cannot be readily subdivided, are charged under the general head of "Weekly Material, Tools and Labor," which is an expense account

Labor is checked out and is designated by numbers, and also by letters, indicating the particular subdivision under which it will be charged, the man himself carrying a brass check showing the number and letter Each laborer also carries a time ticket for each week, on which is punched by the timekeeper, four times each day, the hours at which time is taken In this way the man carries his own time, and any dispute with the timekeeper is avoided

All material as purchased is charged to the "Storeyard Account," under the subdivision "Weekly M T & L ," and, when used upon the work, is then charged to the particular subdivision in which used, and credit given the storeyard

A man is sent to each construction gang. termed a "lineman," whose duty it is to be the connecting link between "plans and data" and "construction," or, in other words, he reports upon printed blanks daily to the chief clerk the labor in each subdivision In addition to this, he records the dimensions, both with regard to the construction work proper, and also all foreign structures met with in the course of the work These latter data are turned in to the chief draftsman, where after being checked, they are entered in colors upon permanent plats drawn to the scale of 20 ft to 1 in

All of these reports are tabulated in the office and monthly summaries made Permanent entries of the costs under each subdivision are made at the end of each month

Up to January 1, 1906, the summary of all conduit construction was

TABLE I——WAGES PAID LABOR

Year	Rate per hour, foreman	Rate per hour gang boss	Rate per hour, pavers	Rate per hour, brick-layers	Rate per hour, rammers	Rate per hour, carts	Rate per hour, pipe layers	Rate per hour, 2-horse teams	Rate per hour, labor
1899	$0 37½	$0 31¼	$0 43¾	$0 43¾	$0 31¼	$0 31¼	$0 25		$0 20⅝
1900	37½	31¼	43¾	43¾	31¼	28⅛	25	$0 37½ 37½	20⅝
1901	37½	31¼	43¾	43¾ 43¾	31¼	28⅛	25	June 28 40⅝	20⅝
1902	37½ 37½	31¼	43¾	April 25 50	31¼	28⅛	25	40⅝ 40⅝	20⅝
1903	April 10 43¾	31¼	43¾	50 50	31¼	28⅛ 28⅛	25	August 21 45⅝	20⅝
1904	43¾	31¼	43¾	July 1 56¼	31¼	April 15 31¼	25	45⅝	20⅝
1905	43¾	31¼	43¾ April 5 50	56¼ April 5 62½	31¼ April 5 37½	31¼	25	45⅝	20⅝

The wages paid to men and teams are shown by Table I Table II shows the prices of materials for each year

In addition to materials, Table III also shows the cost of tools. In the third column from the end will be found "amount charged to depreciation, breakage, material and tools" In addition to the ordinary breakages and waste of material and tools, it has been the custom to charge off each year 20 per cent on the heavier construction equipment. Such small tools as shovels, picks, etc, the actual depreciation is charged off, because of the short life of such tools The comparatively large amounts charged off in 1904 and 1905 are accounted for by reconstruction of the conduits in the burnt district, where a much larger percentage of material was naturally lost It will be remembered that in February 1904, Baltimore suffered from a fire that destroyed a large section of the business part of the city

TABLE II.—PRICES OF MATERIALS.

Year	Brick Delivered on Line. Per 1,000 Arch	Cement. Rosendale. Per bbl	Cement. Toltec 'slag.' Per bbl	Cement. Portland. Per bbl	Terra Cotta Conduit. f.o.b. Balto. Per duct foot 4 duct	6 duct	9 duct	Fibre Conduit. f.o.b. Balto. Per duct foot 2 in.	3 in.	Fibre Bends. f.o.b. Balto. Per length 5 ft. 2 in.	5 ft. 3 in.	Lumb'r Del'v'd on line. Per 1,000 ft. 3 x 12	Sand Delivered on Line. Per ton 2,240 lbs.	Crush'd Stone Del'v'd on line. ¼-in. Per ton of 2,240 lbs.	Castings Delivered at Storeyard. Per pair 1-M & 3-M.	3-D & 4-D.	8-D & 9-D.	11-D & 12-D.
1899	$5.70	$.84	$.62	$1.38	$.066	$.0067	$.088	$.045	$.049			$13.50	$.60	$.93	$16.37	$9.50	$5.25	$12.24
1900	7.75	.81			.066	.0067	.088	.05	.05			15.00	.63	1.42	16.37		6.25	12.24
1901	6.50		.78	1.70	.066	.0067	.088	.05	.05	.45	.45	12.49	.74	1.40	16.37	8.02		
1902	6.60		.90	1.35	.066	.0067	.088	.045	.05	.45	.45	14.50	.73	1.30		8.02		
1903	7.20		1.00	2.00	.0225	.00375	.0375	.04	.0625	.45	.45	17.00	.89	11.48	10.11	14.03		
1904	7.50		1.00	1.35	.04125	.045	.0475	.05	.05	.45	.45	17.00	.67	11.60	19.11	14.03		12.24
1905	15.70		1.00	1.18								17.18	.76	1.688		10.00	5.25	

‡ Bought in open market. * Delivered on line. † F. O. B. cars. Baltimore.

TABLE III.—COST OF ALL MATERIALS USED.

Year	Store Yard Material purchased at end of each year.	Tools purchased and repairs at end of each year.	Total Store Yard material and tools.	Cost of Materials and Tools Used in Trunk Lines.* Excavation	Conduit.	Manholes.	Conduit.	Special Construction.	Tools and repairs.	Cost of Material and Tools Used in Trunk Lines.* Excavation	Concrete.	Service boxes.	Conduit.	Pole connection.	Arc light construction.	Depreciation, breakage, material, tools.	Total cost of material used in trunk lines and service and distribution.†	Inventory of material in store yard at end of each year.
1898	$282,713.15	$8,957.50	$211,200.65	$2,232.01	711.72	2,035.68	8,313.74	$10,418.66	$3,528.17	$102,213.62	$184.27	$32.91	$1,400.25		$116.00		$131,168.05	$30,032.60
1899					284.00	5,291.32	6,560.21			40,887.17								
1900	203.53	10,051.87	218,855.40		332.62	1,511.86	4,329.74	7,109.17	4,780.79	24,942.92	1,995.48	196.02	6,709.63	$360.83	$347.45	377.60	74,269.14	144,556.20
1901	182,776.80	10,929.16	191,685.96		1,050.11	3,349.93	8,506.46	413.87	1,735.68	26,160.20	1,425.15	28,249.43	123.40	433.67	120.30	84,238.95	107,447.01	
1902	121,765.80	10,977.67	132,063.47		148.12	580.79	1,578.97	1,909.86	1,466.86	24,889.90	5,430.53	214,159.20	412.26	142.22	166.99	63,184.97	72,468.80	
1903	87,228.23	11,441.95	98,749.20		604.96		9,917.93	1,297.52	2,352.95	5,847.24	253.42	51.28	6,743.20	604.02	107.09	43,077.19	55,708.01	
1904	82,683.04	15,503.78	98,186.82				5,212.30	1,948.41	2,082.50	26,046.33	6,730.68	20,467.37	1,763.10	113.03	90,285.68	34,901.14		
1905	39,141.23	16,325.61	105,466.84					12,734.77	4,303.37	3,309.53	3,050.31	6,310.34	2,021.60	74,618.88	30,849.96			

* Under this head there was an item of $445.63 for paving in 1905, and following items of General Expense, M. T. & L.: 1904, $652.41; 1905, $4,283.05.
† Under this head there was an item of $1,051.50 for paving in 1905.

The effect of this great fire on the conduit system was quite surprising, as it did but little damage   The trunk lines and the cables in them were uninjured, in spite of the intense heat and the enormous weight of debris, consisting of masonry and iron that fell on them   The piles of debris in some cases were 10 and 12 ft high   A few service box covers were broken by falling walls

Likewise the distributing system was uninjured except in a few places caused by gas explosions.   When it is remembered that only 19 ins. of earth covers these conduits and they are frequently broken by service boxes, it is a matter of surprise that the conduits were not injured   The cables in them were only injured where they entered the destroyed houses.

As gas pipes were broken throughout the entire burnt over area, there was apprehension that gas would collect in the system and explosions occur, but so well had the ventilation of the system been planned, that no serious trouble of this kind occurred, the operating department taking prompt steps to prevent the gas from collecting in the system

Nevertheless the fire caused much extra work to be done as the pole and house connections were destroyed, and not only new ones had to be made, but in rebuilding the city, many changes were necessary to meet new conditions   The cost of this work shows up in the tables under the years 1904 and 1905.

Table IV shows the details of the construction account, giving the duct feet of conduit laid, divided into terra cotta and fiber, also the number of manholes, service and junction boxes, house connections, and also special construction work, which is paid for by parties ordering it   The cost per duct foot is given.

Table V is a general summary of all the costs of work for each year, taken from ledger accounts shown in cost per duct-foot   Under "General Expense and Monthly Payroll" are given the expenses that would be known as the administration expenses of the commission having in charge the work, and engineering expenses, if the work was done by contract, while under "Construction and Weekly Payroll" are given

Total feet 1 and & D on- cted.	Net cost per duct foot.	Construction on Special Account.												Grand Total duct feet Con- structed
		Duct feet.			No of Manholes.	No. of junct boxes	No of ser- vice boxes	No of house conns	Arc light conns.	Trolley pole conns.	Fire alarm conns.	Police call conns.	Miscellane's conns.	
		Terra Cotta.	Fibre	Total										
.693 2	1804	1,958	152	2,110				26						1,604,803 20
.020 2	2323	76,101	18,253 93	94,354 93	7			10						799,375 13
440 3	2200	1,277	1,606	2,883				33						638,523 30
679 9	1807	7,689	4,295 30	11,984 30				6	...					636,654 20
441 8	2360	6,444	3,155	9,599	1			42	216					383,040 80
355 7	2150	54,589 8	25 045	79,534 80	1	21		24	406	178 72	30	11	5	22	496,991 50
040 8	1843	82,347	53,988 5	135,355 50	2	7					1				888,376 30
673 9	2009	230,605 8	106,495 73	336 901 53	12	28	141	622	250	40	11	5	32	5,647,574 43

t and Weekly Pay Roll				Termin- al pole Connec- tions.	Arc Light Connec- tions.	Total Con- struct'n expense	Total cost for each year			
les.	Conduit	Paving	Weekly M T & L							
ɔle.	Per duct foot	Per duct foot.	Per duct foot.	Per duct foot	Per duct foot.	Per duct foot.	Per duct foot	Construc- tion	General expenses	Prelim- inary expenses	Totals.
36	02	0778	008	0124			181	181	0187	0051	2048
26	0219	0825	0102	0245			.1975	1975	0279	0147	2401
63	0378	0735	0103	0283	0054	0026	2145	2145	0244	.0103	2492
06	0166	0711	0059	0208	0008	0085	1689	1589	0288	0135	3112
.90	0475	075	013	0312	0036	.0014	.2646	2646	043	0151	3227
51	0274	08	0141	0305			2328	2328	046	0117	3905
63	038	0438	009	0205			1701	.1701	0436	0082	3219
	0252	0726	009	0203	0009	0012	1926	1926	0294	0098	2318
		0794	008		..	.	1532	.1532	0187	0051	1770
70	0492	0778	0178	0203			2771	2771	0279	0147	8197
70	0372	07	0084	0138	.		224	224	0244	0103	2557
81	0312	0691	0125	0124			2011	2011	0288	.0135	2484
54	0326	075	0237	0574			2717	2717	043	0151	3298
51	0456	0692	0177	0142	0038	0019	2284	2284	046	0117	.3851
95	0632	0433	0286	02	003	0006	246	246	0436	0082	2978
	0421	0662	015	0154	0014	0006	2272	2272	0294	0098	2664

ly	Construction expense and weekly pay roll			Average total unit cost at end of year.				
kly & L.	Pole con- nections	Arc light	Grand total.					
T & L	Labor P.	Labor L.	Labor	Trunk	S. & D	Gen Exp	Prel Exp	Total
ent	Per cent	Per cent	Per cent.					
4	.	.	43	181	...	0187	0051	2048
5			45	1854	.	0215	008	2149
7	52	39	35	1896		0223	0086	2205
8	50	56	42	1869	......	0224	0094	2197
2	58	59	51	1954		0252	0099	2305
5				1964	......	0271	0101	.2335
	.		54	1926	......	0294	0098	2318
8	56	54	47					
4	..	.	46	1532	.0187	0051	177	
0			50	2564	0216	008	2860	
5	.	.	54	2307	0223	0086	2615	
5	..	..	47	2224	0232	0094	2551	
5			79	2226	0251	0099	2576	
5	51	51		2352	0270	0101	2622	
5	80	72	64	2272	0294	0098	2664	
9	60	80	54					

e 276.

th
nc
eq
th
U'
th
"1
ar
U
si
ta
tl
g

u
r

the expenses that would be the contractor's cost. It will be noticed that the general and monthly expenses are divided equally between the trunk and distribution conduits, while the construction expenses are actual figures of cost for each. Under monthly and weekly "M. T. & L." are listed all items that cannot be readily distributed. In the column headed "Preliminary Expenses" are expenses incurred in planning and designing work for the succeeding construction period Under "Organization" is listed the expense of the commission and the chief and assistant engineers. At the end of the table is given the cost per duct foot for each year, showing the cost of construction, the preliminary expenses, and the general expenses, including the engineering supervision.

Table VI indicates the percentage of labor on the total cost under each subdivision of the work. This account is kept for readily analyzing the unit costs given in Table IV

TABLE VII — NUMBER CUBIC YARDS OF EARTH EXCAVATED EACH YEAR

Year	1899	1900	1901	1902	1903	1904	1905	1906	1907
Totals	31097 74	11862 44	7155 22	6561 07	11590 45	1720 78	15476 20	9984 83	5687 18

SHOWING COST PER CUBIC YARD OF EARTH EXCAVATION FOR EACH MONTH.

Month	1899	1900	1901	1902	1903	1904	1905	1906	1907
Jan.								$2 48	$2 22
Feb								1 26	2 12
Mar								1 09	1 33
April	$1 36	$1 48	$2 12	$1 34	$1 85		$2 95	1 04	1 45
May	2 88	1 74	1 46	1 44	1 61		1 64	1 61	1 23
June	2 88	1 64	1 22	1 84	2 28		1 40	1 54	1 62
July	3 73	1 54	1 80	2 02	2 09	$32 02	1 85	1 58	
Aug	2 60	2 81	2 30	1 44	2 13	1 30	2 00	2 01	
Sept	2 41	2 50	12 48	2 11	1 73	1 53	1 25	1 41	
Oct	2 40	1 40		2 50	2 30	1 71	1 32	1 98	
Nov	2 28	4 10			1 50		1 20	1 61	
Dec	3 00	1 58	4 54		1 85		1 70		
Avg each yr	$2 61	$1 87	$1 88	$1 82	$1 94	$1 79	$1 65	$1 53	$1 69

Table VII shows the cost of earth excavation. All the material is earth, but it varies much, there being sand, loam, clay, debris of made ground, and black mud. These costs, as stated, include timbering, drainage, clearing away obstruction, backfilling and all items of digging and finishing the trench to be turned over to the pavers.

The item in July, 1904, of $32 02 per cu yd was especial emergency work, caused as a result of the fire of 1904 and bears no relation to the general work, being given to complete the record   The cost of excavation is not only given for the years of 1899 to 1905, inclusive, but also for 1906 and up to June, 1907

The average cost of the trunk lines for the entire construction period is given below per duct-foot for each item, and also the per cent that each item is of the total average cost

	Per duct foot	Per cent
Organization	$0 0088	3 8
Office	0 0048	2 1
Plans	0 0048	2 1
Month M T & L	0 0110	4 8
Preliminary Ex	0 0098	4 2
Excavation	0 0452	19 1
Concrete	0 0182	8
Manholes	0 0252	10 9
Conduit	0 0726	31 4
Paving	0 0090	3 9
Weekly M T & L	0 0203	8 8
Terminal Pole Con	0 0009	0 4
Arc Light Con	0 0012	0 5
Total	$0 2318	100 0

The average cost of the service and distribution lines itemized with percentages is also listed

Average itemized cost of service and distribution lines

	Per duct foot	Per cent
Organization	$0 0088	3 3
Office	0 0048	1 8
Plans	0 0048	1 8
Monthly M T & L	0 0110	4 1
Preliminary Ex	0 0098	3 7
Excavation	0 0583	21 4
Concrete	0 0281	10 6
Manholes	0 0421	15 8
Conduit	0 0663	24 9
Paving	0 0150	5 6
Weekly M T & L	0 0154	5 8
Terminal Pole Con	0 0014	0 5
Arc Light Con	0 0006	0 2
Total	$0 2664	100 0

It will be noticed that the cost of the conduit material runs from about 25 to 30 per cent of the total cost

Cost of Constructing Conduits in Subway Retaining Walls. —The following are cost data on the construction of tile conduit embedded in concrete side walls for subways in New York City.

Atlantic Ave., Brooklyn —The ducts were of standard 3-ft length, having an inside diameter of $3\frac{1}{4}$ ins. Multiple duct conduits were laid, being for the most part, four-hole pieces The following clauses from the specifications indicate the character of work required:

"Ends of the duct holes will be slightly bell mouthed. In case four-hole conduits are adopted there will be dowel holes left at each end, and contractor shall, when erecting same, insert iron dowels with central washer into the dowel holes in each joint, for truly centering the sections. These dowel pins shall be furnished by the contractor Wooden stoppers shall be placed in the free ends of all ducts when the work is left at night, when sections are complete, or at other times when required

"Contractor will unload all conduits and will stack, store, distribute and erect same in accordance with the drawings and specifications.

"In erecting conduits, the sections must be kept in perfect alignment throughout, and wooden mandrels, 3 ins diameter and not less than 4 ft long, shall be threaded through the holes and remain in place until the surrounding masonry has set solid. These mandrels shall have fitted to the ends a spring steel tube scraper with flue brush behind same for thoroughly cleaning out any foreign matter existing in the duct

"Butt joints of conduits shall be broken at every tier half the length of section, or as may be specially required by the engineer. Every butt joint shall be lapped around with two laps of No 6 cotton duck canvas, burlap or cheese cloth, 6 ins wide, laid 3 ins. on each abutting section, and the canvas, burlap or cheese cloth, shall be dipped in neat Portland cement grout immediately before lapping

"Every tier of conduits is to have a layer of Portland cement mortar laid on top, in which the next tier is to be bedded, even and fair In filling concrete or other masonry around conduits the same must be worked up evenly on each side so that no distortion of any kind may occur in the finished conduits "

The conduits were unloaded from boats, hauled about $1\frac{1}{2}$ miles, and piled up ready for use. The cost of unloading, hauling and piling was 08 ct. per duct-ft., and, as a duct-foot weighs about 8 lbs., this is equivalent to $1 30 per ton. Laborers received 15 cts an hour, team and driver, 45 cts

The cost of laying conduits during the year of 1903 was as follows

	Duct-ft laid.	Labor, days	Pay-roll.	Cost per duct-ft.
January	1,942	10	$ 15	0.8c
February	1,636	9	13	0.8c
April	4,512	32	55	1.2c
May	30,563	154	254	0.8c
June	37,715	205	357	0.9c
July	27,893	179	288	1.0c
August	15,293	92	142	9.9c
September	14,170	63	108	0.8c
October	10,037	43	74	0.7c
Total	143,851	787	$1,316	0.9c

From this it appears that the cost of laying was a trifle less than 1 ct. per duct-ft , and that the average wages were $1 66 per day of 10 hrs. This is the average of the common laborers delivering ducts and the skilled men laying ducts It required 150 bbls of Portland cement to lay the 143,851 duct-ft, or 1 bbl per 960 duct-ft.

During the year of 1904, there were 227,600 duct-ft laid, requiring 240 bbls. of cement, and 975 days labor. The average wages paid were $1 71 per day, and the average cost was 0 8 ct per duct-ft. for laying During the best month, 30,700 duct-ft were laid at a cost of 0 6 per duct-ft. for laying, which indicates that the workmen were not very efficient during the previous months

Rapid Transit R. R, Manhattan.—The following miscellaneous records have been secured The cost of materials for 123,483 duct-ft. was as follows

123,483 duct-ft., at 4½ cts.	$5,556
6,000 sq yds. burlap, at 4½ cts	270
275 bbls Portland cement, at $1.58	435
68 cu. yds. sand, at 50 cts ￬	34
13 sets mandrils, at $2	26
Total, 123,483 duct-ft., at 5 cts	$6,321

One barrel of cement was used for every 440 duct-ft. As an average of a large amount of work the following data were secured: 100 duct-ft required 0.22 bbl cement, 0.055 cu yd sand and 4 86 sq. yds burlap. The conduits used were 4-duct pieces in 2-ft. lengths, 9 ins. square, built up in advance of the concrete side walls which surrounded them. On one section of the subway where some 500,000 duct-ft were laid the labor cost of laying was 1½ cts. per duct-ft. On another section where 60,000 duct-ft. were laid the cost was 2½ cts per duct-ft Wages were high, bricklayers at $5.20 per day doing the work.

INDEX

283

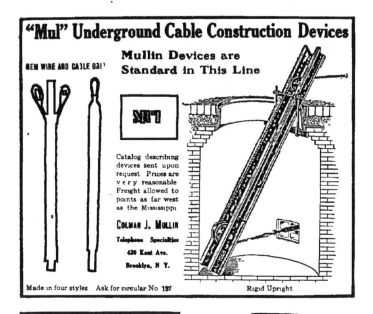

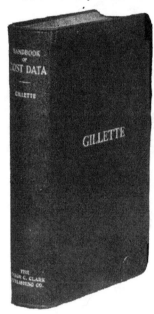